# Learning to Teach Young Children

Online resources to accompany this book are available at: http://bloomsbury.com/cw/Learning to Teach Young Children/. Please type the URL into your web browser and follow the instructions to access the Companion Website. If you experience any problems, please contact Bloomsbury at: contact@bloomsbury.com

ALSO AVAILABLE FROM BLOOMSBURY

*An Introduction to the Foundation Phase*, Amanda Thomas and Alyson Lewis
*Early Childhood Theories and Contemporary Issues*, Mine Conkbayir and Christine Pascal
*Reflective Playwork*, Jacky Kilvington and Ali Wood
*Reflective Teaching in Early Education*, Jennifer Colwell

# Learning to Teach Young Children

Theoretical Perspectives and
Implications for Practice

ANNA KIROVA
LARRY PROCHNER
CHRISTINE MASSING

BLOOMSBURY ACADEMIC
LONDON • NEW YORK • OXFORD • NEW DELHI • SYDNEY

BLOOMSBURY ACADEMIC
Bloomsbury Publishing Plc
50 Bedford Square, London, WC1B 3DP, UK
1385 Broadway, New York, NY 10018, USA

BLOOMSBURY, BLOOMSBURY ACADEMIC and the Diana logo
are trademarks of Bloomsbury Publishing Plc

First published in Great Britain 2020

Copyright © Anna Kirova, Larry Prochner and Christine Massing, 2020

Anna Kirova, Larry Prochner and Christine Massing have asserted their right under the
Copyright, Designs and Patents Act, 1988, to be identified as Authors of this work.

For legal purposes the Acknowledgements on pp. xii-xiii constitute an
extension of this copyright page.

Cover design: Adriana Brioso
Cover art: Andrew Jackson Obol

All rights reserved. No part of this publication may be reproduced or transmitted
in any form or by any means, electronic or mechanical, including photocopying,
recording, or any information storage or retrieval system, without prior
permission in writing from the publishers.

Bloomsbury Publishing Plc does not have any control over, or responsibility for,
any third-party websites referred to or in this book. All internet addresses given
in this book were correct at the time of going to press. The author and publisher
regret any inconvenience caused if addresses have changed or sites have ceased
to exist, but can accept no responsibility for any such changes.

A catalogue record for this book is available from the British Library.

A catalog record for this book is available from the Library of Congress.

ISBN: HB: 978-1-3500-3778-6
PB: 978-1-3500-3779-3
ePDF: 978-1-3500-3781-6
eBook: 978-1-3500-3780-9

Typeset by Integra Software Services Pvt. Ltd.

To find out more about our authors and books visit www.bloomsbury.com
and sign up for our newsletters.

# CONTENTS

*Figures* viii
*Preface* x
*Acknowledgements and Dedication* xii

1 **Childhood and Society** 1

   *Proposition: The way that childhood is presented plays a role in children's experiences of childhood* 1

   What are the images of childhood? 1
   How can images of childhood be used as frames for practice? 22

2 **Children Are Citizens** 25

   *Proposition: Children have rights as citizens and active members of their communities* 25

   What is the nature of children's participation in their diverse social ecologies from a rights-based perspective? 26
   How do children express citizenship rights in their cultural and national communities? 34
   What is the teacher's role in supporting children to express their rights as learners? 36

3 **Children, Communities and Cultures** 41

   *Proposition: Children's everyday life and participation in multiple communities influences their emerging social and cultural selves* 41

   How do children become members of social and cultural communities? 42
   How does children's participation in their communities influence their identity development? 52

How do teachers and parents partner in providing continuity of children's experiences across communities? 57

## 4 Experience, Learning and Development 63

*Proposition: Early experiences influence children's development and learning* 63

What is environment? 63
What is development? 67
How do children's experiences in the environment influence their learning and development? 73

## 5 Partners in Learning 81

*Proposition: Children and adults are co-constructors of knowledge and partners in learning* 81

What does it mean to learn? 81
Do children and adults learn in the same way? How do different theories view children's learning and development? 85
What does it mean for teachers to co-construct knowledge with children? 95

## 6 Meaning-making and Representing Knowledge 101

*Proposition: Children make meaning and represent knowledge in a variety of ways* 101

How do children make meaning of the world? 102
What does knowledge representation mean? 104
What is the role of language as one of the symbolic tools through which humans make meaning and construct knowledge? 110
What is the role of children's art and art making as significant ways of knowing, problem solving and creating that allow for the construction of multiple meanings? 118

## 7 Childhoods and Play 123

*Proposition: Play is an integral part of childhood* 123

What is play? 123
How is play related to development? 127
How is play related to learning, teaching and the curriculum? 140

**8  Children, Difference and Diversity** 145

*Proposition: Children have abilities, strengths and needs, as well as the right to be different* 145

How is difference defined and how are difference and diversity related? 146
Where does 'difference as deficiency' come from and how can we interrupt the practice of pathologizing children? 147
What are the markers of difference and how are they related to children's developing sense of who they are in relation to others? 150
What does it mean to honour children's right to be different? 162

**9  Teachers Are Researchers** 167

*Proposition: Early childhood educators are (also) researchers* 167

How can pedagogical documentation be a learning process? 168
How do teachers learn to document, and what does pedagogical documentation look like in classrooms? 171
How does pedagogical documentation challenge the dominant discourse? 173

**10  Children Are Collaborators in Assessment** 185

*Proposition: Children are active collaborators in and users of assessment* 185

What is assessment for? 185
How does assessment support all learners? 193

*References* 201
*Index* 239

# FIGURES

0.1 Meet Emma and Luka xiv
1.1 The free and constrained child views 5
1.2 The environmentalist view 7
1.3 The conditioned child view 9
1.4 The child and the species view 11
1.5 The agentic child view 19
2.1 Bronfenbrenner's model of development 30
2.2 Children as responsible participants through shared values 31
2.3 Children in democratic dialogue and as decision makers 37
3.1 Culture as pattern 43
3.2 Culture as boundary 49
3.3 Culture, identity and school experiences 53
4.1 Agentic materials – clay 66
4.2 Environmental factors and development 69
4.3 Role of space and materials in fixing the learner's attention 76
5.1 Children's interactions with different environments influence their development 86
5.2 Children co-construct knowledge 90
5.3 Mediating children's learning 92
5.4 Using provocations 99
6.1 Iconic or symbolic representation? 106
6.2 Children playing cultural scripts 109
6.3 Egocentric or private speech? 114
6.4 Supporting home languages in the classroom 117
7.1 Play varies across cultures 126
7.2 Do children play what they know or what they imagine? 129
7.3 Object/meaning inversion and the role of imagination 132
7.4 Imaginary situation in play is not independent of cultural context 134
7.5 Controlling children through play 139
7.6 Playful pedagogies 142
8.1 Does race have anything to do with who is 'right'? 155
8.2 Gendered role playing 158
8.3 Using technology to facilitate inclusion 161
9.1 Documentation as display 176

9.2   Observation booth: Surveying children in the name of educational research  179
9.3   A documentation dilemma (C. Thompson 2015)  180
10.1  Authentic assessment  187
10.2  Gallery teaching, Wilderspin, 1840  191
10.3  Dynamic assessment  197
10.4  Emma and Luka say goodbye  200

# PREFACE

In our experiences as teacher educators teaching foundations courses to preservice teachers and working with practicing teachers, we have realized teachers often hold strong beliefs about children, childhood, learning and teaching. However, they cannot always identify where their beliefs came from, especially in terms of the history of early childhood development and education theories. Nor are they typically aware how the established theories influencing early childhood practice found their way into present-day contexts and practices. We also noticed they rarely questioned these influential theories. Rather, they accepted them as principles or even foundational truths. We came to understand that we need to change how theories are presented and taught to preservice teachers if we are to encourage their critical thinking skills and develop their ability to evaluate the educational theories, ideologies and curricula they are being introduced to in their programme.

*Learning to Teach Young Children* is a foundations textbook that reflects our new approach to presenting theoretical perspectives, not as foundational principles for educational practice, but as propositions – 'points to be discussed or maintained in argument' (*Cambridge Dictionary*). The book is organized around ten propositions that we explore in relation to key questions that organize the arguments presented from different theoretical perspectives. Each chapter, in addition to reflecting the historical development of the main ideas, critiques the theoretical perspectives discussed. In so doing, the text encourages readers to ask 'why to' questions rather than looking for correct answers.

The discussions about the main points in each of the book's propositions are maintained at three levels. First, the text in each chapter presents different, sometimes contrasting, theoretical approaches or views on the key questions pertaining to each proposition to offer the reader many opportunities to engage in a dialogue with the text. Second, some of the key concepts defined by the different theories are discussed by our two main characters: Emma and Luka. As composite depictions of the students in our classes, Emma and Luka converse about these concepts and bring their life experiences, prior understandings, 'funds of knowledge' (Moll et al. 1992) and new learnings into these ongoing conversations. Unlike other textbooks, where the point of view of the adult learner is not made visible, we purposely included the voices and 'faces' of the preservice teachers. As learners who are encountering some of the ideas and concepts for the first time, Emma and Luka interpret them differently because of their diverse life experiences as a female and a male in different sociocultural contexts. The multimodal use of comic book conventions for these conversations allowed us to represent Emma's and Luka's thinking about events (through thought bubbles) and their discussions about their learning (through speech bubbles) from the perspectives of their own childhoods, as well as those they have gained through their experiences with young children as part of their education classes.

The third level of discussion of each proposition occurs in the process of engaging with the companion guide and website (https://www.bloomsbury.com/cw/learning-to-teach-young-children/). The companion website reviews and extends the theories, concepts and approaches described in the textbook, while the guide presents 'how to' ideas related to the propositions, along with possible implications for practice. Reflective prompts and questions allow the reader to dialogue with the content in relation to their personal experiences and beliefs. Scenarios and case studies suggest possibilities for bringing the theoretical ideas into practice.

*Learning to Teach Young Children* is thus a multilayered, multimodal text that is positioned, not as a means to acquire expert knowledge, but as an invitation to use this knowledge to generate new meanings by critically examining the content and engaging with the various educational philosophies and theoretical perspectives.

We invite you to bring your life experiences, questions and critical lens to the many possibilities this text offers.

# ACKNOWLEDGEMENTS AND DEDICATION

The work on this text began more than ten years ago when our provincial Ministry of Education asked us to develop a set of guiding principles to 'provide a framework for programming for Kindergarten' (Alberta Education 2008: 1). These guiding principles were to facilitate the implementation of a new, integrated curriculum and, in the process, assist educators working with young children, from kindergarten to grade 3.

After completing the initial tasks of reviewing the literature and identifying and drafting working descriptions of the principles, we invited the teachers in the laboratory school at our university, known as the Child Study Centre, to engage with them in a three-day retreat. The time we spent collaboratively 'unpacking' the meaning of these principles and reflecting on how they might relate to their practice allowed us to make changes they identified as necessary and meaningful. The guiding principles also became central to the early childhood courses we taught and served as a foundation for the propositions we introduce in this book. However, the propositions represent a substantial shift in our own thinking about the role of theory when learning to teach young children.

Since this text is a product of a professional collaboration among teacher educators, teachers and preservice teachers over ten years, it is impossible to name each individual who has influenced our thinking about teaching and learning in the early years. However, it is imperative to thank the dedicated teachers in the Child Study Centre at the University of Alberta, who, under the leadership of the centre's faculty director, Dr Susan Lynch, were instrumental in articulating the original set of guiding principles (2008). These teachers were, in alphabetical order, Julie Gellner, Linda Jarman, Julie Johnson, Grazyna Klimek, Lee Makovichuk, Cherilyn Maluga, Kristina Miskiw, Jacqueline Pocklington, Lesley Revell and Tera Woollard.

Of this original group of teachers, we are particularly grateful to Lee Makovichuk, who worked alongside us to develop the scenarios and the character dialogues Luka and Emma engage in throughout this book. Lee's experiences as a kindergarten teacher for over twenty years and as an early childhood teacher educator at MacEwan University were invaluable as she scripted scenarios based on real-life classroom situations with her own young students. These scenarios were brought to life by the talented illustrator Andrew Jackson Obol, whose childhood experiences in Uganda provided much-needed diversity in understanding the richness of majority-world childhoods. His ability to visualize the situations we discussed made it possible to illustrate some of the key concepts in the book that we hope will engage our readers in further discussions.

We are also grateful for the artistic and technical advice of Dr Michael Emme from the University of Victoria in terms of creating the images and embedding them within the text, and for the feedback from our colleague and long-time critical friend Dr. Darcey Dachyshyn, who has kept us grounded in the realities of newcomer and Indigenous families and children that early childhood educators and teachers work with every day.

Last but not least, this book would have not been possible without the careful, thoughtful and dedicated work of our copyeditor, Leslie Prpich, who has helped make our thoughts clearer and the flow of our three individual voices consistent.

The multilayered conversations we have had throughout the process of creating this text have allowed us to focus on the learning we hope early childhood preservice teachers will engage in as they interact with the text. We dedicate this book to them.

LUKA IS EXCITED ABOUT HIS SCHOLARSHIP! HE CAN HARDLY CONTAIN HIS SMILE AS HE IS PACKING HIS SUITCASE... FOLLOWING HIS FATHER'S FOOTSTEPS, LUKA WANTS TO MAKE A DIFFERENCE IN THE LIVES OF CHILDREN AND YOUNG PEOPLE IN HIS HOMETOWN. HE BELIEVES THAT A GOOD EDUCATION IS KEY TO THAT. THERE IS SO MUCH TO LEARN!

EMMA HAS JUST COMPLETED THE TOUR OF THE UNIVERSITY CAMPUS AND IS MOVING TO THE BIG CITY NEXT WEEK. SHE IS PROUD TO BE THE FIRST IN HER FAMILY TO BECOME A TEACHER! EMMA LIKES PLAYING WITH KIDS, READING THEM STORIES, AND MAKING CRAFTS. SHE FEELS SHE ALREADY KNOWS A LOT ABOUT YOUNG CHILDREN AND IS WONDERING WHAT ELSE SHE COULD LEARN AT UNIVERSITY.

FIGURE 0.1 *Meet Emma and Luka*

# CHAPTER ONE

# Childhood and Society

***Proposition: The way that childhood is presented plays a role in children's experiences of childhood.***

This chapter reviews historical and current images of childhood and perspectives on child development. Emphasis is given to the multiple ways of understanding childhood and of being a child. Understanding that culture and society have a significant impact on the ways in which children develop and learn influences how educators think about teaching and learning. The chapter emphasizes teaching that goes beyond child development theory as the primary knowledge base and source of curriculum and pedagogy. It is in this spirit that we ask:

1. What are the images of childhood?
2. How can images of childhood be used as frames for practice?

For additional information, reflective questions and practical implications visit: https://www.bloomsbury.com/cw/learning-to-teach-young-children/chapter-1/

## What are the images of childhood?

The field of early childhood education (ECE) is both an ideological crossroads and a space for the meeting of sometimes conflicting societal, professional and political agendas. A small number of key ideas about childhood have influenced developments in ECE over the past two centuries, ideas that have endured across time and diverse geographic, political and social contexts. Two ideas have been particularly significant drivers of policies related to ECE: (1) the notion that even very young children are capable of learning, and (2) that early experience has a significant influence on later development.

Accordingly, ECE has taken shape in the form of interventions aimed to 'affect developmental changes in children from birth to 8 years of age' (Gordon and Browne 2014: 3), focusing on activities to enhance development and impact other facets of children's lives, such as preparing children for school and assessing and adjusting their behaviour, along with such diverse aims as reducing poverty, assimilating newcomers and revitalizing culture. In short, the developmental, cultural and social space of childhood is contested territory in which stakeholders, including politicians, policymakers, educational theorists and philosophers, researchers, practitioners and parents, seek to influence early learning as a means to achieve diverse aims.

Teachers, in their work, constantly make decisions about teaching and learning. As they do so, they draw on a wide range of knowledge. An initial step in this process is deciding what counts as relevant knowledge. Is it influenced by children's prior learning experiences or interests? Or determined by the formal curriculum? Does it include knowledge about child development? In early childhood education there is a historical bias to prioritize child development knowledge as a main basis for teaching decisions. Child development knowledge includes assumptions about how children grow and learn which are often taken to be universal truths. However, the ideas are embedded in a culture and represent ideologies of child development.

A teacher's philosophy of education frames answers to the basic questions in education, helping us to achieve a broader perspective (Braun and Edwards 1972). In thinking about philosophy, we ask: Who is the child? What should be taught? Where should teaching take place? How should it occur? Who should teach? And, what is the purpose of education? Whereas a preoccupation of teacher education can be what and how to teach, this chapter centres on the question 'Who is the child?' as a way to explore notions of education, development and culture within contemporary and historical discourses of childhood. The chapter is framed around conventional images of childhood which are embedded in philosophy, science, culture and the political economy and have influenced educational policy, as well as ideas and practices of teaching and learning.

Answers to the question 'Who is the child?' are complex. A child's identity is certainly more than a learner: Children continually navigate multiple identities as daughters, brothers, workers and citizens, to name a few. Moreover, the idea that a child is a learner positions them as being in some way incomplete (Baraldi 2014), lacking in skills for school success (Biesta and Bingham 2010). Positioning refers to the practices and beliefs we hold about ourselves and that others hold about us that help construct our identities, for example, as early childhood teachers, or daughters, or citizens. Positioning children as learners in early education contexts happens in many ways: (1) through the material aspects of early childhood education in which familiar objects – LEGO, paints, paper, sand – are pedagogized, and (2) through adult–child relationships in which adults in their role as teachers become necessary for learning (Erstad et al. 2016). Pedagogized describes the way teaching and learning meanings are ascribed to materials, relationships or settings (Bernstein and Morais 2001).

Many adults remember 'playing school' as children. When ordinary objects were used as props for the play, they became 'school things' (Mitchell and Weber 1998); they were pedagogized according to children's ideas of how teaching and learning happen in a school setting. Playing school, which is a form of dramatic play, differs according to the social and cultural context, which also influences images of teachers and learners. Ann Williams (2004) describes differences between siblings playing school in Anglo and Bangladeshi British communities, with the latter focusing on teaching school literacy using practices such as providing examples and models, using direct instruction to check up on past learning, giving alternatives if the younger sibling is in difficulty and using encouraging phrases such as 'Well done!' or 'Good girl' (64). In this instance, the older siblings' image of teaching as direct instruction positions the younger sibling, as a learner, as relatively passive, with learning mainly a matter of training.

Images of the child then are always interpretations that are rooted in culture and history (Rinaldi 2006), are gendered, classed and racialized (Burman 2013), and reflect priorities of adults. And, while the image of the child as learner is a limited idea, so too is an image of the child as educator, which stems from 'a romantic, humanist narrative' (Burman 2013: 230). The popular image of the child as innocent and vulnerable contributes to surveillance and regulation in ECE programmes. Thinking about our image of the child helps us understand how the way we look at children is subjective and involves power relationships.

Cleverley and Phillips (1986) classified historical assumptions regarding Western child rearing into seven different perspectives on the idea of a child and childhood, which are outlined in this chapter: (1) the free/constrained child, (2) the environmentalist, (3) the conditioned child, (4) the child and the species, (5) the loss of innocence, (6) the ages of man view and (7) an upbringing fit for society. To these we add (8) the agentic child and (9) the child from non-Western perspectives (Reagan 2018). With reference to Western views, there is a surprising amount of overlap across theories and inconsistencies within them; many theories have serious weaknesses or have been shown to be simply wrong. Nevertheless, this particular set of theories has been highly influential in early childhood education for more than two centuries and continues to influence early childhood policy and practice. As Cleverley and Phillips described, 'it is not generally appreciated how a small number of theories – theories with sometimes controversial underpinnings – have decisively shaped the patterns of child rearing and the educational practices that have been adopted' (vii). Clearly, a single approach to education does not flow neatly from one image of childhood, and an approach may share elements of several theories. Moreover, not all theories show a commitment to a single image of the child. While the diversity of theories has contributed to the popularity of eclecticism in early childhood teaching, it is important to keep in mind that theories suggest ways of solving different problems differently.

In our daily lives we are seldom called upon to articulate our image of the child. However, our role as teachers compels us to do so (Moss and Petrie

2002). As educators in the Reggio Emilia schools in Italy have described: 'What we believe about children becomes a determining factor in defining their social and ethical identity, their rights and the educational contexts offered to them' (Rinaldi 2006: 64).

## *Conventional images*

### The free and constrained child views

The free and constrained child perspectives (Figure 1.1) derive from rival models of the child as innately good or innately evil. The model of the free child is based on the idea that children's natural innocence is corrupted by society, making it the job of teachers to protect them from dangers, whether physical, environmental, moral or spiritual. Images reflecting the idea of the free child are associated with innocence, purity, passivity and Romanticism. The model of the constrained child rests on the idea that child nature includes hereditary sin. The aim of education and child socialization is therefore to constrain a child's propensity towards sinful behaviour. An example is the eighteenth-century pietist approach to child rearing of the Rev. Francis Wayland Parker. When his fifteen-month-old son refused to let Wayland feed him, Wayland placed the 'wilful' child in his crib for twenty-four hours, occasionally offering him bread, until he finally accepted it from him (McLoughlin 1975). Breaking the child's will in this instance was seen as essential for the child's salvation, not as a means of discipline or punishment. Images of the constrained child are associated with vanity, wilfulness, weakness and lack of reason.

Both the free and constrained children were restricted by nature; early education was therefore designed with their nature in mind. Education for the constrained child followed monastic principles of passivity, surveillance and imitation (Cochelin 2000). Education for the free child used similar principles, which were manifest in pastoral power relations between the teacher and student, a Foucauldian idea in which the child learns to govern the self through techniques of 'surveillance, self-examination, obedience and self-regulation' (Hunter 1994: xxi).

An example of early education for the free child can be seen in Robert Owen's infant schools, the preschool division of several schools Owen founded for children of his factory workers in New Lanark, Scotland, in 1816. Because Owen believed young children's minds were malleable, in his words, they could 'be trained to acquire any language, sentiments, beliefs, or any bodily habits and manners, not contrary to human nature' (Owen 1817: 20).

Owen's idea of the free child was influenced by the eighteenth-century philosopher Jean-Jacques Rousseau. Owen agreed with Rousseau's concept of negative education, in which children were protected from what were judged to be harmful influences. This education was called negative because of what it did not include: It was matched to a child's stage of development by preventing children's exposure to certain elements. If, as Rousseau believed,

FIGURE 1.1 *The free and constrained child views*

young children learned through self-activity, they should be kept from having books. Rousseau (1762/1911) explained that children have no need for reading, because a child's 'whole environment is the book from which he unconsciously enriches his memory, till his judgment is able to profit from it' (167). Rousseau felt very strongly on this point: He called reading 'the curse of childhood' (177). A ban on books was meant for children aged two to twelve, the stage Rousseau called 'the age of nature'. In Owen's infant school, children were 'not to be annoyed with books; but were to be taught the uses and nature or qualities of the common things around them, by familiar conversations when the children's curiosity was excited so as to induce them to ask questions respecting them' (Owen 1857:140). A legacy of a philosophy of negative education was the bias against teaching reading in preschool that lasted into the 1970s.

Our ideas of development and image of the child influence both what counts as a material for learning and the relationship of the teacher and child. In the view of nature's child à la Rousseau, teachers do not use a 'hands-off' approach. Indeed, Rousseau's advice to the tutor of a fictional student, Émile, was to do the opposite:

> Let him always believe himself to be master, and always be master yourself. There is no subjection so complete as that which preserves the appearance of liberty; it is by this means that even the will is led captive ... Certainly, he should do only what he wishes, but he should only wish what you desire, he should not take a step which you have not foreseen nor open his lips to speak without your knowing what he is about to say. (Rousseau 1762/1964: 107–8)

This viewpoint gave rise to teaching practices supporting a pastoral relationship between teacher and student, in which teachers monitored children's behaviours in the interest of their protection and guidance. In nineteenth-century preschools called infant schools, surveillance required open-style classrooms as well as outdoor spaces with unencumbered sightlines. Even the outdoor privy located in the playground was monitored by teachers 'to inculcate habits of delicacy and cleanliness' (Wilderspin 1852: 149). In modern times too, surveillance and the regulation of children and children's bodies can extend to toileting routines, as found by Cliff and Millei (2011) in their study of bathrooms in a preschool in Australia, where toilets, apart from one which was partitioned, had waist-high glass walls to allow teachers to see inside. Children managed the situation by lining up at the partitioned toilet, leaving the other five vacant.

## The environmentalist view

In the environmentalist perspective (Figure 1.2), experience deriving from sensation or reflection leads to the growth of knowledge, an idea commonly

FIGURE 1.2 *The environmentalist view*

associated with the ideas of the seventeenth-century English philosopher John Locke. In contrast to the free/constrained child perspective in which the human mind is preformed by nonhuman forces, the environmental perspective is an optimistic, educationalist view (Ezell 1983). Locke conceived the mind as having powers or faculties for creating complex ideas from simple ones, which was the basis for faculty psychology and phrenology in the nineteenth century and Howard Gardner's theory of multiple intelligences in the twentieth century. In faculty psychology the mind is modular, containing '"inborn faculties" capable of translating sense impression into ideas' (Altenbaugh 1999: 135). A rich tradition of images of the child's mind reflects the environmentalist view – as a blank slate to be written upon, a sponge to soak up experiences, a twig to be bent, plastic to be shaped or clay to be moulded.

An example of an education approach drawing on an environmentalist image is Maria Montessori's system, which employed the metaphor of the absorbent mind to describe the preschool child (Montessori 1949). Montessori believed that for adults, 'impressions pour in, and we remember and hold them in our mind', but for children, 'impressions not only penetrate the mind ... but form it' (35). However, in this imagery, a child's mind is vulnerable to the effects of negative impressions. As Jenkins (1998) describes, there is always 'the persistence of these two contradictory strands' with 'one celebrating childhood freedom from adult control, the other insisting on the necessity of adult restraint' (18–19). Vaughn (2002) studied teachers in a Montessori classroom to understand how they made decisions about freedom and control, finding that they tailored their interventions according to their understandings of individual children's socio-emotional needs, information they gained through their observations and prior knowledge of the children.

## The conditioned child view

The conditioned child perspective (Figure 1.3) is based on behavioural principles of learning, in which the environment is understood to determine behaviour in ways that can be predicted and controlled. Behaviourism, the study of human behaviour as the subject matter of psychology, was popularized in the United States in the early twentieth century by John B. Watson. Watson responded to problems in early psychology by measuring subjective experiences such as conscience and feelings, arguing that psychology's sole focus should be human behaviour. He was highly influenced by the Russian psychologists Vladimir Bekhterev and Ivan Pavlov, the latter conducting experiments on dogs who were trained to salivate at the sound of a bell using classical conditioning. B. F. Skinner developed radical behaviourism, which he defined as 'the philosophy of a science of behaviour treated as a subject matter in its own right apart from internal explanations, mental or physiological' (Skinner 1989: 122). Radical behaviourism, now

FIGURE 1.3 *The conditioned child view*

called behaviour analysis, sought to explain and train behaviour through operant conditioning. Albert Bandura's social learning theory is based on classical and operant conditioning, but with the addition of observational learning, for example, learning in the absence of reward and punishment (Phares 2001).

Each formulation of behaviourism seeks to understand human behaviour in an effort to learn how to train humans to behave in ways that enhance the survival of the species. Through 'genuine behaviourism', behaviourists argue that we can increase our 'possibilities for direct, practical, effective action when it comes to promoting ... behaviour[s] of interest' (Moore 2011: 462).

Watson made a far bolder pronouncement in his book *Behaviourism* in 1924:

> Give me a dozen healthy infants, well-formed, and my own specified world to bring them up in and I'll guarantee to take any one at random and train him to become any type of specialist I might select – doctor, lawyer, artist, merchant-chief and, yes, even beggar-man and thief, regardless of his talents, penchants, tendencies, abilities, vocations, and race of his ancestors. (J. B. Watson 1924/1930: 82)

While Watson may not have had 'the foggiest idea of how to fulfil his guarantee' (Harris 1998: 6), he nevertheless upheld an image of the conditioned child as passive and of child rearing as a mechanistic process best left to experts. Indeed, his belief that 'no one today knows enough to raise a child' (Watson and Watson 1928: 12) motivated him to write a guide for parents on child rearing. Watson's approach appealed to a mother who used it as a manual for her daughter's upbringing in the early 1930s. She wrote in her diary:

> The world is a strange and marvellous and terrible place for children; they crave a guide line to take them safely through the maze ... Children want and need to imitate someone. They need the continued inspiration of pleasant and agreeable adult companionship. After all, childhood is simply the preparation for adulthood, it is not a state within itself. It is a stepping stone, a preparation for conscious living. (Talalay 1995: 56–7)

For this mother there was a clear image of the child as incomplete and passive, eager for their parent or teacher to lead their learning.

## The child and the species view

The child and the species perspective (Figure 1.4) is underpinned by unfoldment theory and recapitulation theory. Rousseau's belief that children developed naturally helped establish free play as the principal learning context in which the role of teachers was to follow children's lead. However,

FIGURE 1.4 *The child and the species view*

as with Rousseau's Émile, this did not mean that children played without constraints. Friedrich Froebel, who established the kindergarten system of education in Germany in 1839, believed children were complete beings from birth, capable of higher-order thinking but requiring guidance. While development unfolded naturally, it was preset, having been ordered by God. Some of the images reflecting the idea of the child and the species are benign (e.g. the child develops in the manner of photographic processing, in which the latent image becomes visible) or harmful (e.g. the child is racialized, as in colonial-era images of the child-savage).

Froebel's philosophy of education was influenced by his religious beliefs, his studies in mathematics, physics and architecture, and his observations at Johann Heinrich Pestalozzi's school in Switzerland. Like Rousseau, Froebel believed in the innocence of childhood. Like Pestalozzi, he understood the importance of connecting learning to real-life experiences, but he used materials with a much more symbolic and spiritual purpose. Central to his approach was his religious belief in the unity of all things.

Kindergarten activities were planned to enable children to make these essential connections. The credo of the kindergarten movement, 'come let us live for our children', did not mean that children took the lead in their own education but that teachers should show the way based on their understanding of the nature of childhood. Froebel believed that children's minds were fully formed at birth and capable of reason but were unfocused and disordered. The sensitive guidance of a female teacher – the ideal candidate being a sensitive mother or mother substitute – could bring children's reason to full flower by providing crafts and materials known as play-gifts and by engaging children in activities called occupations.

The materials could mediate these big ideas, helping children achieve an integrated understanding of their relation to the world and facilitating their natural development, or unfoldment, through which children's underlying powers were revealed. It is important to remember that the materials mediated children's development but could not change it.

While unfoldment theory has a deep spiritual basis, the related recapitulation theory is a biogenetic approach to child development in which each child's growth and development repeats the evolution of the species. Cultural recapitulation was called culture-epoch theory when it was applied to educational contexts by followers of the German educator Johann Friedrich Herbart. For Froebel, who was influenced by Herbart, as were many nineteenth-century educators, this meant a cultural and spiritual recapitulation in which children progressed from 'primitive' towards higher abilities. The theory, which was established on a racialized notion of child development, continued into the twentieth century, reflected in the ideas of American psychologists John Dewey and G. Stanley Hall (Fallace 2012) and Vygotsky's colleague, the Russian psychologist Alexander Luria (Scribner 1985).

Recapitulation theory is evident in some popular approaches to early education. Maria Montessori created educational activities to support what she believed to be children's instincts (Fallace 2015). Montessori considered her preschools, called *Casa dei Bambini*, to be a second womb for children who were at a stage of spiritual embryo (Montessori 1936). In her address to the International Kindergarten Union in 1915 on a visit to the United States, Montessori observed: 'All forms of imperfect development which we find in the child, bear some resemblance to like characteristics in the savage' (Montessori 1916: 109). Rudolf Steiner's Waldorf school curriculum is based on cultural epoch theory, and is another approach, in addition to Montessori's, based on sense impressions. For Jennifer Gidley (2016), Steiner's approach to teaching reading, beginning with pictures or pictograms, represents a 'soft version of recapitulation theory' (219).

## The loss of innocence view

The loss of innocence perspective is based on ideas from psychodynamic theory. Childhood innocence, as in the free child view, is revealed as 'a myth based on adult wishful thinking' (Cleverley and Phillips 1986: 60). Psychodynamic theory postulates that some of our behaviour occurs for reasons we cannot ourselves comprehend. The view highlights the importance of family in development. Images reflecting the loss of innocence perspective focus on childhood's complexity, sexuality, rationality and irrationality and fantasy.

Psychodynamic theories are associated with the psychoanalytic ideas of psychologist Sigmund Freud and his followers. Freud's psychoanalytic theory explained child development in terms of the emotional aspects of development, which are expressed as internal conflicts. Development was in stages, with progression between stages occurring after the successful resolution, or management, of the conflict. Because the stages described the development of sexuality and personality, they were called psychosexual stages. Freud's five psychosexual stages of development were oral (infancy), anal (18 months to 3 years), phallic (ages 3 to 5), latency (ages 5 to 12) and genital (adolescence). Freud's theory influenced a broader set of psychodynamic theories among his followers, for example, attachment theory (e.g. John Bowlby and Mary Ainsworth) and ego psychology (e.g. Anna Freud and Erik Erikson). Both Freud's theory and psychodynamic theories 'represent approximations of human experience, metaphors that have developed with particular cultures, during particular social times, and with particular social values' (Berzoff et al. 2016: 11).

Psychodynamic theory inspired influential experimental preschools in the 1920s. At the psychoanalytic laboratory kindergarten in Soviet Russia, led by the Froebel-trained Vera Schmidt, teachers were trained according to psychoanalytic principles. Children's sexual freedom was encouraged, a factor in the school's closure in 1925 (Valkanova 2016). Anna Freud, who trained as a kindergarten teacher before she became an analyst, established the Hertzing school in Vienna in 1927, combining the ideas of Froebel, John Dewey and psychoanalysis (Midgley 2008). The psychologist Susan Isaacs taught at the Malting House School in Cambridge in the same period, documenting her experience as an analyst and teacher in three books on child development. Like Anna Freud, Isaacs had trained as a kindergarten teacher. Isaacs was completely committed to her analytic interpretations of development in the experimental school. Her biographer noted of her book *Social Development* (Isaacs 1933): 'there is not a single occasion when psycho-analytic theory is questioned or when an observation is recorded that seems to run counter to such a theory' (Graham 2009: 233). This included her interpretations of behaviours such as spitting that were considered expressions of oral eroticism and sadism in the Freudian view of infantile sexuality (Isaacs 1933). A visitor observed a scene at the Malting House School:

> There's one particular boy (age 5) who domineers and bullies the whole set. His chief enjoyment is spitting. He spat one morning onto Mrs Isaac's face. So she said: 'I shall not play with you Philip' – for Philip is typically his name – 'until you have wiped my face'. As Philip didn't want Mrs Isaacs to play with him, that lady was obliged to go about the whole morning with the crachat upon her. (Graham 2008: 13)

The openness of sexual expression at the Malting House School and other experimental preschools in the period fit the analytic image of the learner. As Isaac's biographer observed, 'this freedom entails a certain amount of unpleasantness for grownups' (Graham 2008: 12). Deborah Britzman (2003) has articulated the more general discomfort and even hostility of teachers and teacher education students with the uncertainty of the analytic perspective when what is 'wished for' is 'a magical pedagogy' (80). Instead, a psychodynamic view complicates teaching in its orientation towards understanding a child's instinctual and unconscious motivations and supporting their healthy psychological and sexual development.

## The ages of man view

The ages of man perspective is grounded in a stage-based developmental idea of the normal growth of the child. In psychological theory, stages describe a normative model of behaviour. The character of a stage is qualitatively distinct from what comes before or after (i.e. previous or subsequent stages), and stages are progressed through in a fixed order, integrating the sequences of earlier stages. Abnormal development occurs when behaviour fails to progress from one stage to the next, called fixation in Freud's psychoanalytic theory and Piaget's epigenetic theory (Crain 2016). Stages are identified as such using scientific methods such as clinical methods, psychometrics and naturalistic observation. Examples of developmental stage theories include Piaget's cognitive stages, Kohlberg's moral stages, Erikson's social-emotional stages and Freud's psychosexual stages. Images reflecting the ages of man perspective depict the child as a little scientist, as vulnerable, or as bounded by fantasy, in line with the particular theoretical position.

Maturationist theories posit that the direction and rough timing of children's development are biologically determined. The American psychologist Arnold Gesell was a proponent of the maturationist view. While developmental stages were predictable and every child was understood to develop at their own pace, the natural unfoldment required guidance and environmental supports. However, training had limited impact on development, if the goal was to speed it up. Gesell and his colleagues carried out observational research in a clinical setting using motion pictures of children and frame analysis to identify developmental milestones or norms of child behaviour; they identified, for example, fifty-eight stages of grasping a pellet and twenty-three stages of crawling (Adolph and Berger 2006). Lev Vygotsky, who was a contemporary of Gesell, regarded the maturationist view as a 'theory of empirical evolutionism' (1998: 301).

Piaget's epigenetic theory described the development of children's thinking within a constructivist framework. His research involved a 'clinical method' in which children were observed solving problems using physical objects. Children's thinking, or intelligence, evolved within a known genetic epistemology and in four stages, called sensorimotor (birth to 24 months), preoperational (24 months to age 7), concrete operational (age 7 to 12) and formal operational (age 12 through adulthood).

In Piaget's theory, children's experiences with their environments facilitate the creation and building of mental representations within their brains, or 'schemas'. Schemas develop through two processes: *assimilation* (where new information is absorbed into the schema) and *accommodation* (where the schema develops or changes to allow for acquisition of new information). Schemas both guide children's use of experience in their behaviours and help them make sense of the outcomes of their behaviours. Experience and an enriched environment are essential for the child to test and develop a repertoire of schemas. A child faced with two contradictory views experiences disequilibrium. For example, a child who has experiences with a family's car may call a truck a car the first time she sees one. If her parents correct her, saying, 'no, it's a truck', she needs to make sense of this contradictory information by refining her existing schemas, perhaps noting that trucks are larger than cars or that trucks have a different shape (accommodation). Piaget was the first to attend to learners' ongoing efforts to revise their understandings of the world, especially when they found themselves in new contexts. The ability to revise their thinking and, in this way, advance and refine their knowledge was viewed as adaptation to the environment through achieving a state of equilibrium. Piaget described the experience of achieving equilibrium as a dynamic process that regulates behaviour. In so doing, he acknowledged the role of language and social factors in knowledge construction (Piaget 1995).

By operations, Piaget meant the mental operations that are increasingly characterized by abstract, logical thought. The first stage of sensorimotor development initially involves reflexive actions based on sensory input that develop into 'schemes', leading to circular responses and eventually to thought. The preoperational stage is characterized by the beginning development of symbolism and imagination, but children's thinking is limited by their egocentricity, that is, their inability to assume different perspectives. Children at the concrete operational stage think logically but not abstractly, that is, outside of physical or concrete situations. The formal operations stage, characterized by logical abstract thinking and reasoning, is the evolutionary ideal in Piaget's theory. However, not all adults reach this stage, and those who do may regress under stress when 'their thinking can become preoperational, egocentric, and sometimes animistic' (Sadock and Sadock 2007: 136).

The initial interest in Piaget's ideas by early childhood teachers in the 1920s and 1930s was brief (Beatty 2009): Piaget was rediscovered by psychologists and educators in the United States in the 1960s (Ripple and Rockcastle 1964). His ideas were adapted to be used in curriculum theory contributing to constructivist approaches to early childhood education, such as the HighScope approach (Hohmann et al. 1979) and the Kamii-DeVries approach (Kamii and DeVries 1973). The image of the child as learner in Piaget's genetic theory was as an epistemologist: Children are 'active builders of their own intellectual structures' in the words of Piaget's colleague Seymour Papert (1980: 19), who worked with him at the University of Geneva. Piagetian-inspired education theorists are more likely to employ the metaphor of the active learner (Hohmann et al. 1979). Those critical of developmentalism are more likely to regard the image of 'Piaget's child' as an adult in training (Sorin and Galloway 2006), deficient (Dahlberg et al. 2013), incompetent (Lam 2012) or primitive (Johnson 1995).

Genetic theory did not stray far from culture-epoch theory, described earlier, in which 'the development of each human being metaphorically repeats the development of the human race' (Schultz and Schubert 2010: 164). As Flynn and Blair (2013) explain, 'every child first learns to manipulate concrete reality. Every twenty-first-century child must learn to transcend concrete reality and exchange a pre-scientific for a post-scientific mind. Various groups have easier and more difficult paths in undertaking that odyssey' (787). C. R. Hallpike (1979), for instance, used Piaget's view of mental structures to advance a developmentalist view of thinking of collectives rather than individuals, suggesting that preoperational thinking characterizes people who are illiterate, unschooled and rural.

However, for Piaget, 'the child is the real primitive among us, the missing link between pre-historical men and contemporary adults' (Voneche and Bovet 1982: 88), as he described in a lecture at Columbia University in 1968:

> Of course, the most fruitful, most obvious field of study would be reconstituting human history – the history of human thinking in pre-historic man. Unfortunately, we are not very well informed about the psychology of Neanderthal man or about the psychology of *Homo siniensis* of Teilhard de Chardin. Since this field of biogenesis is not

available to us, we shall do as biologist do and turn to ontogenesis. Nothing could be more accessible to study than the ontogenesis of these notions. There are children all around us. (Piaget 1970: 13)

## An upbringing fit for society view

In the upbringing fit for society perspective, child rearing and education are directed towards preparation for citizenship. In the case of democratic citizenship, the view is closely associated with the ideas of John Dewey. Dewey placed a large importance on the school as a social context of learning. On a practical level, children engaged in cooperative projects and activities, including useful occupations such as cooking and woodworking. On a psychological level, children undertaking such activities were meant to develop habits of democracy, meaning dispositions that influence the development of thought. Images reflecting the idea of an upbringing fit for society are freedom, responsibility and self-activity.

Dewey (1899) claimed that play in infancy was based in motor and intellectual development and the increased coordination and discrimination that were purposefully aimed at gaining experiences. A second stage, called the play period, involved exploration of objects; it began at about age two and lasted to age six or seven. Dewey described the start of this stage as characterized by a 'growing freedom of activity'; however, a child's repetitive actions and the 'comparative poverty of the idea' placed it for him 'on the borderland of play' (196). Activities with objects become more purposeful over time and are often taken up through participation in productive activity in the family as preparation for citizenship, for example, by helping with baking, carpentry or gardening.

Dewey reasoned that because such productive opportunities were limited for children in cities, schools needed to 'compensate for the limitations' (199). However, he believed that even 'in more favoured surroundings the child is often relatively stunted because adults are not willing to take the time and effort required; or have not the intelligence necessary to supply proper conditions' (199), that is, child-centred teaching methods and curriculum. The teacher's role is 'about determining and crafting the kinds of environments where children are likely to learn themselves or craft good habits that enable further learning in the future' (Stitzlein 2017: 42).

While play had a place in psychological development, it had a key role in forming the habits needed for a social democratic life. Play and work were not necessarily distinct activities, but play was distinguished from work by agency. By this Dewey meant not just that we can choose to play, but that we are in charge of the outcome, whereas in work in industrial systems we are not in charge of the product (Phillips 2016). Work is therefore tied to economic conditions. According to Beatty (2017), Dewey 'wanted children to experience a sense of free agency within a teacher-guided environment in which they learned the kind of voluntary self-control needed in a democratic society. Teacher-guided free play, Dewey argued, could reconcile individual agency and social discipline, one of the central dilemmas of liberal democracy' (424).

Thomas Fallace (2015) pointed out that the idea of a child-centred education has its origins in recapitulation theory, evident in the curriculum Dewey's teachers worked out at his laboratory school at the University of Chicago at the turn of the twentieth century. The curriculum 'was based in part on the historical re-enactment of the social progress of the human race' (Fallace 2015: 92).

## The agentic child view

The agentic child perspective (Figure 1.5) is a rights-based view in which preconditions of the child's right of participation and the right to be heard are met (see Chapter 2). To have agency is to have the power to cause change (Hyman 2015). This perspective is distinguished from ones in which the child is acted upon, is preformed by nonhuman forces, limited by biogenetic presets, controlled by reinforcers, directed by unconscious desires, etc. The agentic child is a social actor, co-constructing the meaning and knowledge that form their own lives. The view is associated with critical childhood studies, postfoundational theory and reconceptualized perspectives on early childhood education (Bloch et al. 2014; James et al. 1998; Mayall 2002). Examples of images reflecting the agentic child view are captured in the descriptors capable, active and influential.

Children's agency is often used in early childhood education as an abstract concept and not clearly defined. Yet the meaning of human agency is complex, including its qualities as intentional, interactional, situational and located within social structures (Leonard 2016). David Oswell (2013) elaborates that agency is always understood within contexts of 'multidimensionality and multiscalarity' (269). Whereas agency is often examined in micro-level analyses, it intersects and is influenced by many factors. For example, children's interactions on a playground are influenced by the 'playground designs, teacherly interventions, government policy regarding school formations and the importance of play, the history of developmental psychology and the regulations of class and motherhood' (269). Children's agency is therefore a constructed identity position.

Oswell (2013) considered the recent interest in children's agency, at least in an abstract or theoretical sense. He wrote: 'The long twentieth century is, and has been, undoubtedly the age of children's agency. Children are not simply seen to be, but seen, heard and felt to do. Children are not simply beings, they are more significantly doings. They are actors, authors, authorities and agents' (3). For Oswell, agency is not possessed by an individual child or performed by them. Rather, it is 'distributed across human and non-human arrangements and infrastructures ... [and] rests as

FIGURE 1.5 *The agentic child view*

much on parts of children as whole children' (7). By this Oswell means that children do not have agency in all situations.

The agentic child perspective is often contrasted with perspectives reflecting an image of a passive child. However, agency and passivity are not dichotomous constructs (Clark and Richards 2017). Because agency is acting with purpose, passivity is not the opposite of activity; it is possible to choose to be passive or voluntarily inactive (Hyman 2015). Moreover, activity is not always voluntary; it is possible to be compelled to be active.

Nonhuman agency is grounded in posthuman theory, which is anti-anthropomorphic and antihumanist. In other words, posthuman theory rejects a human-centred view of the world while requiring a disidentification from the human species through a process of disengagement involving 'taking critical distance from familiar habits of thought' and a 'consciousness raising that sustains critical thinking' (Braidotti 2016: 16). Nonhuman animals are considered to have consciousness, language, the ability to learn and participate in knowledge production, and the capability of rational agency (Morris 2015).

Agency is also attributed to nature and materials. As an example, nonhuman others such as trees show agency as (1) routine action (growing, reproducing, colonizing), (2) transformative action (autonomous seeding, transforming places by their presence), (3) purposive action (via the plan in their DNA), and (4) nonreflexive action (eliciting emotions in humans) (Jones and Cloke 2008: 80–1). Pacini-Ketchabaw, Kind and Kocher (2017), with reference to typical ECE materials such as clay, blocks and paints, consider how such materials 'speak back' to children in agentic ways (12).

This was also Froebel's view of materials, as in the following account of the first play-gift, the ball, by the Froebelian Denton Snider. In imagery that was 'sexual in part' (Scully 1980: 19), Snider described the ball as the child's 'earliest friend who can talk to the new unspoken soul, itself incapable of talking'. He elaborated:

> There is something in the nature of affection in the Ball when taken into your hand, especially one of these soft, pliable, responsive Balls of the First Gift. Do you not feel its gentle pressure upon your palm? It is trying to join hands with you in friendship by its first act, and you cannot help responding with a slight caress; your very organism must give answer with a little kiss. You cannot blame your hand if it soon closes more passionately upon that Ball, with an eager embrace, to which the latter replies by a stronger and warmer osculation imparted to your palm and fingers. (Snider 1900: 5–6)

Critics have challenged Froebel's philosophy, and Snider's interpretation, as a mystical discourse of development, raising questions about its relevance in the face of what we know about children and childhoods today. Indeed, Froebelian principles concerning universal attributes of child nature run counter to many non-Western images of childhood, as described in the section below (Brison 2011; Jackson 1998; Lall 2011; Pacini-Ketchabaw and Taylor 2015). Froebel's child was not a natural phenomenon, as he believed, but a particular version of nineteenth-century childhood. Of course, the same is true of the agentic child. While children can have agency in their work, play and education, and in their families, agency is not the essence of childhood any more than innocence or sin.

Yet, as Leonard (2016) observed, 'given the enormous significance of the "new" sociology of childhood's claim that children are active agents ... it remains surprising that there has been so little attempt to articulate what agency actually means' (84). Sellers (2013) argues that agency is itself a culturally bound concept that is also essentialist: It is not the experience of all children. And James (2009) encourages a deeper discussion of agency, asking: 'Do children have a right to agency? Do all children have the same capacity for agency? and What might inhibit or prevent particular children from exercising it, and under what kinds of circumstances?' (44). Moreover, because preschool classrooms as 'environments for agentic action are provided but controlled by adults ... these settings represent an opportunity to learn the necessary skills required for neoliberal citizenry' (Clark and Richards 2017: 133).

## *Majority-world and Indigenous images*

Conventional images of the childhood with their roots in Western philosophy, psychology and theology reveal an ethnocentric bias towards the superiority of Western or minority-worldviews of childhood. The terms 'minority' and 'majority' world are used to emphasize the reality that the Western world, despite its hegemonic positions, represents only a small minority of the world's population. Bame Nsamenang (1999) urged us to attend to the children who live in majority-world countries:

> If we could learn to listen to, discuss with, or observe and learn from how the enormous diversity in the human condition breeds variability in worldviews and images of childhood across cultures, this might lead to a new way of seeing children and the various ways different cultures organise children's development. (160)

He continued, 'the science of developmental psychology is the story of efforts to understand the Western child' (160). By attending to Nsamenang's call to action, we can gain insights into the best ways to teach all of the children in our classrooms.

Roderick Zimba (2002) uses the term *indigenous* to refer to images of childhood and development that originate from particular communities to bring about and sustain specific ways of existence and being, activities which are typically referred to as child rearing or child socialization, or, as in Nsamenang's words, the cultural organization of children's development. While there are many variations of Indigenous images of childhood, as Nsamenang indicates, the common core of beliefs about childhood in southern Africa emphasizes human solidarity, oneness and orientation to others and childhood as prosocial and group based, with values of respect, obedience, cooperation, hard work, helpfulness, hospitality, honesty, peace and responsibility (Zimba 2002).

There is similarly a common core of beliefs about childhood socialization shared by many Native American peoples (Reagan 2018), including a spiritual aspect, focus on harmony and balance, communal responsibility and teaching through observation, imitation, symbolism, ceremony and storytelling (Marashio 1982). The common core beliefs are reflected in Janine Akerman's (2010) study of the images of Plains Cree children held by Plains Cree elders in Saskatchewan, Canada, which identified beliefs about:

- *The child's awareness in the womb*: prior to their birth, children are learning and forming memories.
- *The child as powerful and pure at birth*, coming with spiritual gifts to share.
- *The child as journeying through infancy*, during which they learn how to be patient and observe.
- *The child's spirit as connected to Mother Earth*, learning from her energy and being open to her teachings.
- *Listening to the child's voice*, which teaches the adult both patience and responsibility.
- *The child as a butterfly*, 'moving from one learning opportunity or thought to another' (74) and requiring flexibility and patience from adults.

Forms of traditional Native American conceptions of play are (1) imitation of adult activities, (2) play involving toys, which for older children were often used in imitative activities and (3) 'self-testing' games of skill played by adults and children (Reagan 2018: 250). A study of beliefs about play held by mothers in an Ontario First Nations community found that the idea of learning through play in formal early childhood settings was consistent with their traditional Indigenous cultural values about teaching, learning and play (Gillis 1992).

## How can images of childhood be used as frames for practice?

Identifying images of childhood is highly important for ECE, where images, whether articulated or not, are frequently used as frames for practice. Whereas conventional Western images of childhood reflect the ideal of an imagined child, an authentic image can only be identified by listening to actual children. In this way, writes Loris Malaguzzi (1994), who inspired the Reggio Emilia schools in Italy, the image 'is based on the child you see in front of you' (52). Listening in this way starts with teachers asking the children questions about teaching and learning and asking the same questions of themselves. This approach is discussed further in Chapter 9 in relation to the process of pedagogical documentation. Malaguzzi (1994) notes that it is important for teachers to consider each child's reality as well as their own, and to grow comfortable with the unknown. As he writes, 'it is important for the teacher who works with young children to understand that she knows little about children' (60). Teachers with this understanding can discover new ways of observing children.

The Reggio Emilia schools are an expression of reconceptualist thinking in ECE as opposed to traditional approaches to curriculum and childhood education. The reconceptualist ECE movement, which began in the 1980s, coincided with and was influenced by several events. One was the publication in 1986 of the position statement of the National Association for the Education of Young Children (NAEYC), *Developmentally Appropriate Practice (DAP) in Early Childhood Programs*, which was planned as a tool for teachers to disseminate DAP ideas. The DAP idea followed the tradition of ECE to continually redevelop its theory and practice to reflect behavioural, cognitive, psychoanalytic and neuropsychological ideas, and drew on many of the conventional images of childhood reviewed in this chapter. The reconceptualist movement coincided with the introduction to the United States of the Reggio Emilia schools, of which Malaguzzi was a founder. The Reggio Emilia schools appeared as a counterpoint to the academic kindergarten curriculum, which was itself a motivation for both the DAP framework and programmes and the reconceptualist movement.

Reconceptualists argued that developmental psychology was flawed as a theoretical foundation for ECE programmes and practice, with potential to contribute to serious harm, for example, by creating social inequities (Lubeck 1985). Reconceptualist scholars have challenged conventional approaches as discourses of development, raising questions about their relevance in the face of what we know about children and childhoods today. Indeed, scholarship in the last thirty years has worked to reconceptualize play- and child-centred methodologies, to 'denaturalize childhood' in the words of Affrica Taylor (2013), by drawing on Foucauldian, postcolonial, posthuman and poststructural arguments. The imagined child of Froebel, or Freud, or Piaget, was not a natural phenomenon, as they had believed, but a particular version of childhood.

## *Summary*

This chapter examined images of childhood and their influence on ideas of socializing and teaching children, on policy and, consequently, on children's experiences of childhood. Images of childhood were explained as being embedded in culture and representing ideologies of child development. Eight conventional images and understandings of childhood representing Western historical, philosophical and scientific traditions and assumptions were reviewed, such as the agentic child view, along with majority-world and Indigenous beliefs about childhood and socialization. The impact of nature, culture and society on the ways in which children develop and learn was described to highlight how images of childhood influence how educators think about teaching and learning. The chapter emphasized the need to go beyond child development theory as the primary knowledge base and source of curriculum and pedagogy, and to consider teaching and learning in a reconceptualist view.

# CHAPTER TWO

# Children Are Citizens

***Proposition: Children have rights as citizens and active members of their communities.***

This chapter explores what it means for teaching to understand children as citizens with rights contributing to life in their classroom, school and larger community. Meeting children's basic needs for survival, protection and development is required under the United Nations Convention on the Rights of the Child. Beyond basic needs, children's rights include participating in democratic dialogue and decision-making processes in their learning. This chapter reviews the challenges and possibilities of meaningfully involving children at each step of the teaching and learning process. We ask:

1. What is the nature of children's participation in their diverse social ecologies from a rights-based perspective?
2. How do children express citizenship rights in their cultural and national communities?
3. What is the teacher's role in supporting children to express their rights as learners?

For additional information, reflective questions and practical implications visit: https://www.bloomsbury.com/cw/learning-to-teach-young-children/chapter-2/

## What is the nature of children's participation in their diverse social ecologies from a rights-based perspective?

The United Nations Convention on the Rights of the Child (UNCRC) is a legal framework that delineates the responsibility of state governments to 'give priority to the best interests of children in all decisions, to set up governance processes to ensure children are a priority, to translate children's Convention rights into law, and to treat children equitably in developing laws, policies and services to help protect them and promote their development' (United Nations 1989). Our focus is on how children's rights are invoked in the diverse contexts in which they live, with a focus on their participation in learning.

Human rights are those rights that are universally held by each member of the human species. Human rights legislation necessarily applies to all, regardless of age, gender, social class, nationality, etc. Modern human rights are traced to the French Revolution and the pillars of dignity, liberty, equality and brotherhood (Ishay 2008). The exploitation of child labour during the Industrial Revolution stimulated reforms aimed at creating rights specific to children for protection and education. Rights-based legislation, for example, setting out maximum hours of work and minimum years of schooling, was framed by an image of children 'either as passive, weak, and vulnerable creatures, and therefore in need of protection, or as unruly and threatening and therefore in need of control' (Kosher 2016: 12). The Universal Declaration of Human Rights in 1948, following the Second World War, was the basis for the UNCRC in 1989, which included dual images of the child: that of the child in need (of protection rights) and that of a competent, agentic child as the frame for participation rights (Woodhead 2005).

The Convention, which defines children as persons under the age of eighteen, was subsequently ratified by all UN member states except the United States. States ratifying the Convention are legally bound to adhere to its fifty-four articles and separate regulations, eleven of which are procedural. The rights follow principles of human rights, meaning that the articles are indivisible, interdependent and interrelated – all articles are linked and none are more important than another (UNFPA 2005). While Articles 29 (right to education) and 30 (children from minority groups and cultures) specifically refer to schooling, others provide the conditions for children's participation in rights-based education: Articles 12 (the right to be heard), 13 (freedom of expression), 14 (freedom of thought) and 15 (freedom of association). A rights-based education includes the right of access to education, the right to a quality education and respect for children's rights in education.

A child's right to be heard was elaborated upon by the UN Committee on the Rights of the Child, a group of international experts in human rights responsible for monitoring the Convention's implementation and assessing penalties for noncompliance. The committee concluded,

1  States Parties shall assure to the child who is capable of forming his or her own views the right to express those views freely in all matters affecting the child, the views of the child being given due weight in accordance with the age and maturity of the child.
2  For this purpose the child shall in particular be provided the opportunity to be heard in any judicial and administrative proceedings affecting the child, either directly, or through a representative or an appropriate body, in a manner consistent with the procedural rules of national law. (UN 2009)

Children have a right to participation from the earliest age, and communication can be expressed through nonverbal means such as facial expressions, play and body language. Moreover, there is an obligation to ensure the right to be heard for children 'experiencing difficulties in making their views heard' – children with disabilities, minority group or Indigenous children, or those who do not speak the majority language (UNCRC). Under the Convention, training for teachers in the obligation of Article 12, to provide conditions for children's participation in their learning, is mandatory.

The language in the Convention has been used to frame many curricula for early education, in which children are viewed as citizens with rights to participation in their learning, evident in international curriculum frameworks such as *Aistear* ('journey' in English) in Ireland, which states: 'Children are citizens with rights and responsibilities. They have opinions that are worth listening to, and have the right to be involved in making decisions about matters which affect them. In this way, they have a right to experience democracy' (National Council for Curriculum and Assessment 2009: 8).

## *Rights-based education*

In a rights framework, the image of the child is as a capable and socially competent person who has agency, that is, is a social actor able to influence and even co-create her world (Esser et al. 2016). The image of the agentic child (see Chapter 1) is consistent with a sociocultural perspective. In formal teaching and learning contexts with young children, rights-based education is exemplified by the Reggio Emilia approach and, more broadly, by approaches that are called child centred. Indeed, the Convention 'insists upon the need for Education to be child-centred, child-friendly and empowering' (UNCRC). Ideas about child-centred teaching have deep roots in early childhood education and can be traced to Jean-Jacques Rousseau's notion of connecting teaching to understandings of children's development. However, attending to children's agency and participation requires more than what is typically understood by child-centred education, in which 'children's personal, social, physical, and learning needs were to be at the centre of the education process' (Woods 2015: 52). Ideas about child-centredness (see also Chapter 6) are complex and contradictory, involving assumptions about children's interests and capabilities, and are frequently based on deficit notions of development (Chung and Walsh 2010: 215–34).

Child-centred education carried out at John Dewey's historic laboratory school, described in Chapter 1, resembled current rights-based understandings. In the Dewey School, child-centred learning through play did not mean individually focused, but rather working together, in which individual rights were bound up with responsibilities. In *Democracy and Education*, Dewey (1916) set out to apply the ideas of democracy to educational problems. By democracy, he meant a 'mode of interaction between individuals who constitute a community' (Phillips 2016: 14). This tenet was applied at the Dewey School through the development of cooperation (Waddington 2010) and other habits for democratic living, such as the habit of listening and the habit of learning (Hansen and James 2016). Today, we can see the importance of developing democratic dispositions expressed in the Irish curriculum framework, which uses the style of a child's voice to state: 'Remember that I too am a citizen. Help me to learn about my rights and responsibilities. Model fairness, justice and respect when you interact with me and others' (National Council for Curriculum and Assessment 2009: 8). In a twenty-first-century rights-based approach, participation is central to the learning process. At the same time, we need to be mindful to ensure that children's participation reflects their rights rather than an opportunity for learning the skills needed as 'neoliberal citizens in the making' (Clark and Richards 2017: 129) such as individual and rational autonomy. This is an important caution in light of the findings of one study that teachers' ideas of participation centred on 'individual self-determination and choice, rather than cooperation' (Bae 2010), based on Western philosophical ideals of autonomy and free choice.

## *Bronfenbrenner's ecological systems' view of children's rights and development*

John Dewey observed, 'the school is not the place where the child *lives*' (Dewey 1899: 51). The basis for Dewey's statement was his unfortunate negative view of the influence of parents on their children, which does not reflect current thinking about the importance of teachers and parents working together. Dewey meant to highlight the role played by school in expanding children's knowledge and experience beyond their family and community context, which he considered limiting. But we can reinterpret Dewey's statement in a twenty-first-century rights-based framework as a call to consider the multiple contexts for children's development. Dewey's assertion, revised to reflect current thinking, shows that while both school and home are important influences on children, they are not the only ones. Children live in, and are influenced by, their engagement in a myriad of contexts (see also Chapter 5). Understanding children's diverse social ecologies is therefore a central step to teachers forming appropriate and effective educational experiences, thereby facilitating children's active participation from a rights perspective.

Psychologist Urie Bronfenbrenner provided a way to think about children's diverse contexts with his ecological systems framework of child development (Bronfenbrenner 1979a: 844–50). In his framework, cultural, historical and policy-related contexts interacted and mediated one another, and were influences upon and influenced by children's development in its immediate context of family, childcare and school. Bronfenbrenner's framework helps us to understand the relationship among children's diverse social ecologies. In biological science, *ecology* refers to the study of the organism-environment relationship called an *ecosystem*. It has the same meaning in human–context relationships, where ecosystems are known as social ecologies. Social ecologies vary in scale and complexity. In child development terms, schools, homes and neighbourhoods are separate but related ecosystems, which underscores the need to look outside of the child to fully understand development in its social and cultural context.

For Bronfenbrenner, the contexts for learning and development are systems nested within systems, analogous to a set of Russian dolls. The Russian or *matryoshka* dolls metaphor for development is often illustrated as a series of hierarchical concentric circles (Figure 2.1). The child is represented by the closest circle in an ecosystem, called a microsystem. Microsystems are those elements of the environment with which a child has direct contact, for example, their family. There are also systems within microsystems, for example, sibling groups within families, classrooms within schools or friendship groups within classrooms, which interact with and influence one another. The interface between two microsystems is called the mesosystem. The exosystem, corresponding to the next largest circle, is the layer of the environment that impacts development but with which the child does not directly interact, such as a parent's workplace, which can determine the amount of time a parent can spend with their child or the availability of family-friendly benefits and policies.

The largest circle represents the macrosystem, consisting of the policies, ideas, values and beliefs that direct our actions towards children as social beings, for instance, a preference for greater independence versus interdependence, or child versus parental rights. To elaborate, the UNCRC functions in the macrosystem. In the United States, which is a signatory to the Convention but has not ratified it, there is a continuing debate over 'whether children should be considered their own person or whether they are the property of their parents' (Vissing 2016: 74). A fifth element, the chronosystem, is the influence of timing on child development operating within all systems of the ecological relationships in relation to changes in environment. A child's age when a sibling is born is an example of the impact of timing on development within the microsystem. What is typically called birth or child spacing has significant effects on child and maternal health (WHO 2005).

There is not always congruence between interacting microsystems, for example, between the immediate system of the family and the school classroom. For example, an outcome of implementing play-based learning

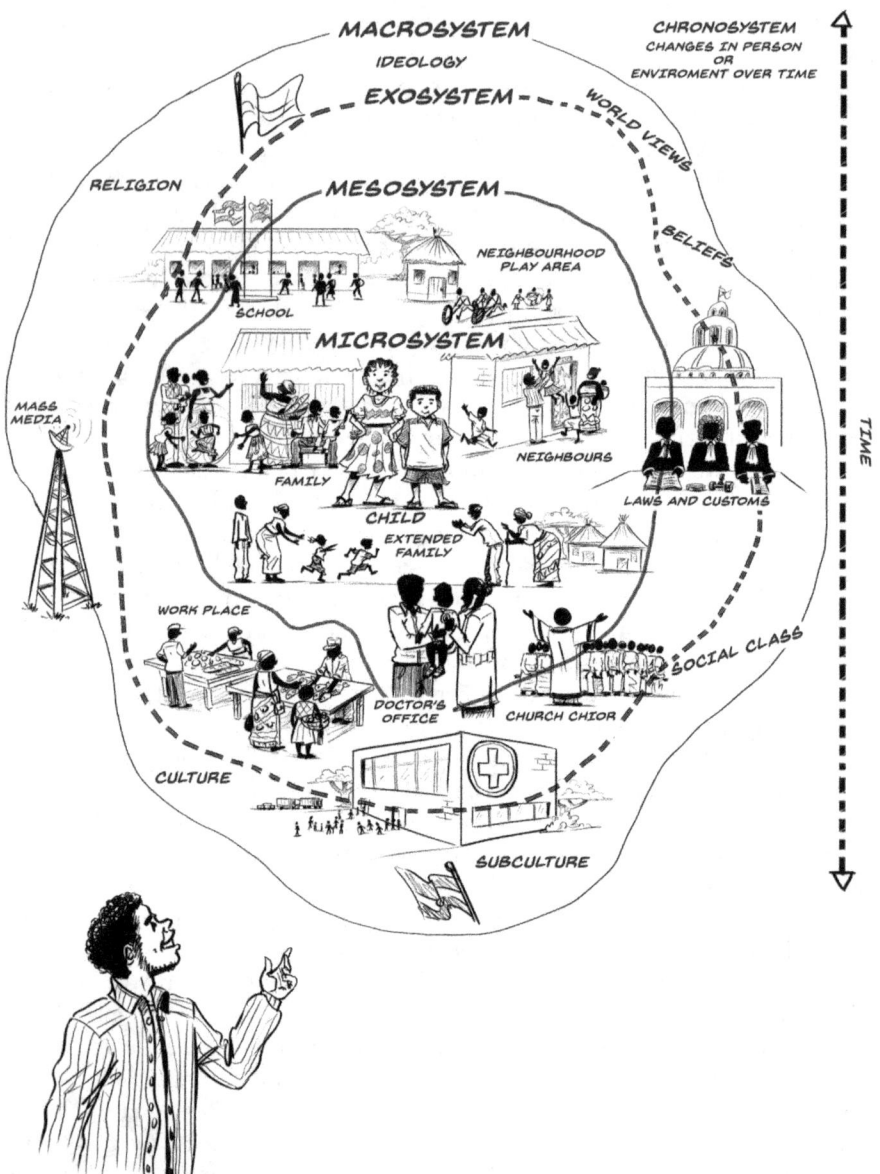

FIGURE 2.1 *Bronfenbrenner's model of development*

as a school district policy created in the spirit of Article 31 of the UNCRC, which sets out children's right to play, could be a change to classroom schedules (a function of a microsystem) to permit more free play time. However, this can bring to the fore differences with families' understandings and acceptance of such provision based on different cultural values, for example, the belief that children should play, but not in school.

FIGURE 2.2 *Children as responsible participants through shared values*

Young children's participation in the ecological system is mainly at the family and school ecological levels of the microsystem (Figure 2.2). Because behaviour in social situations has a reciprocal impact, it is important to consider the entire social system of a setting. Bronfenbrenner emphasized the importance of considering the multiple factors influencing development. Within a family, for instance, the social system includes family members, kin and other caregivers along with the physical and material factors of the setting that have direct and indirect influences on a family's social practices and children's participation. Cell phones, for example, can 'dissolve the boundaries that once separated work and home' (Wajcman et al. 2008: 638), impacting parents' time with their child. Additionally, the use of cell phones and other technologies for social networking can increase a child's autonomous participation in their own identity formation through the separation of the child's family and personal networks, but can also create risks and cause harm (Cochran and Brassard 1979; Simpson 2013).

## *Criticisms of Bronfenbrenner's framework*

Bronfenbrenner's notion of nested systems influencing child development has been adapted as an ecological metaphor across a number of disciplines to describe interactions within and between systems. Mariana Souto-Manning's ecological systems framework for understanding teacher development locates teachers at the centre, with their development 'influenced by culture and history through participation in a variety of communities' (2017: 26). Her trans/contextual cultural-ecological approach addressed a critique of Bronfenbrenner's framework by showing the permeability of the contexts and by challenging Bronfenbrenner's claim that the closer relationships (e.g. family) are always the most influential. Other criticisms of Bronfenbrenner's framework focus on (a) its complexity (if everything counts as an influence, which data and what amount of data are required to explain development), (b) its reliance on systems to understand all development and (c) its limited use for explaining change in development over time. Bronfenbrenner addressed the last point by distinguishing microtime, macrotime and mesotime within the chronosystem, corresponding to the influence of time on development in the three systems (Bronfenbrenner and Morris 2006). Another criticism of his framework is its anthropocentric approach to child, family and community and the absence of a spiritual domain (Souto-Manning 2017). Spirituality, along with a dynamic relationship with the natural world, is fundamental to Indigenous worldviews and ways of life and education of children.

## *Parenting style as a context for children's rights*

The way children's rights are expressed within families is influenced by parenting styles and parenting practices. Multiple and contradictory images of the child coexist: The image of a child held by a family may be quite different from the image held by the teacher. Children's role within families and their experience with decision making or participating in decisions varies widely and depends on many factors. Parenting practices may reflect a democratic style, using claims of fairness, with the final authority resting with the parents, or an authoritarian style in which obedience is expected. Children may have a role as a caregiver within a family, for example, for younger siblings, or be responsible for tasks or household work in line with their age and development. Parenting practices, which are a reflection of parenting identities, are highly related to cultural and social influences.

The minority-worldview of child socialization favours development of independence and autonomous agency (see Chapter 5). However, as social psychologist Çiğdem Kağitçibaşi (2007) has shown in her studies of majority-world childhoods in collectivistic cultures, agency can occur in social relatedness. Kağitçibaşi (2007) proposed three models of the family as contexts for self-development. The interdependence model is based on cooperative interconnectedness and is more common in traditional collectivistic cultures; the independence model is based on individual interests and needs and is more typical of higher socioeconomic-status minority-world families; the emotional interdependence model is an intermediate position having relational and autonomous socialization goals, characteristic of families living in a context of rapid social change (e.g. urbanization).

The differing child socialization in the models is reflected in the emphasis on making friends or focusing on family in a study of the views of parenting held by middle-class European Canadian mothers and Indigenous mothers (Cheah and Chirkov 2008). The European Canadian mothers, reflecting the independence family model, focused on extrafamilial social competence, emphasizing skills for children's relations with their peer group; Indigenous mothers, reflecting the interdependence model, emphasized interfamilial competence, including elders and Indigenous cultural values.

Psychologist Diana Baumrind (1966) used a psychoanalytic framework to study middle-class White parents in 1960s California, identifying three parenting styles and links with child qualities: authoritarian, authoritative and permissive styles. Subsequent research found four parenting styles defined on the dimensions of warmth and control: authoritative (high warmth/high control), authoritarian (low warmth/high control), permissive indulgent (high warmth/low control) and permissive indifferent (low warmth/low control). The authoritative parent – the style favoured by White, middle-class families – uses control to address the inherent tension between freedom and responsibility, which are aspects of citizenship and children's rights.

For the authoritative parent, whom Baumrind compared to a Montessori teacher, discipline is vested in the environment, 'which is controlled; in the teacher herself who is controlled and is ready to assume an authoritarian role if it is necessary; and from the very beginning it resides in the children' (1966: 890). In other words, discipline, or control, rests in a three-way relationship of the child, adult and environment. In parenting styles in Baumrind's typology, which is often extended to teaching styles (e.g. Wentzel 2002), children do not express their rights as individual agents.

Baumrind's original model, which is based on assumptions reflecting an individualistic minority world culture and is therefore ethnocentric (Lancy 2010), is a poor guide to understanding parenting in a diverse society. When cultural aspects of child socialization are considered, parenting identities reflecting authoritarian practices are seen as positive, for example, in some collectivist cultures (Choi et al. 2017). Moreover, research has often ignored the distinction between parenting styles and practices (Kerr et al. 2003: 395). The usefulness of the concept of parenting styles has itself been questioned (Ramaekers and Suissa 2012), as has the separation of style and practice. Child-rearing ideologies, including those that are culturally based, are increasingly seen as being 'negotiated by parents in a diverse range of contexts and from different intersectional positions' (De Graeve 2016: 111).

## How do children express citizenship rights in their cultural and national communities?

In political terms, citizens belong to a nation-state in which membership is associated with civic dimensions oriented to relations to other citizens, as well as political dimensions directed to the state. The ways children experience citizenship vary in their social ecologies and according to many factors, including age, gender, social class and race, with different aspects coming into play in different circumstances. The right to directly influence education policy and laws by voting, for example, is constrained by a minimum legal voting age. In the majority of nations, voting is restricted to persons eighteen years of age and older. Nor are children eligible to hold positions on school boards or other education decision-making bodies. Whereas children have a right to education, as stated in the UNCRC in Article 29, responsibility for ensuring the right is vested in others with that authority.

Children's participation in civil society is an element of citizenship, but participation is not the same as citizenship (Milne 2013). There are four basic elements of citizenship, all of which are relevant to child citizens (Howe 2005). The first is the possession of basic rights, for example, for survival and protection. The second is the exercise of responsibilities, which, for children as for adults, can place individual freedoms in tension with civic obligations. Compulsory school attendance, for example, is a civic obligation, whereas a child or a child's parent may desire an alternate form of education or none at all (Papastephanou 2014). Children have a right to learn, but there are limits to the degree young children can be learning refusers (Williams 2014), that is, possessing the right not to learn. Indeed, school refusers are generally believed to be troubled or suffering from an anxiety disorder. The third element of citizenship is active participation in civil society, and the fourth is differentiated citizenship, which allows for group differences, for example, for citizens who are members of Indigenous or other communities where cultural contexts are important considerations.

For the purposes of this chapter, the focus is on the broader meaning of citizenship, beyond the political one. For Dewey, children were future citizens. Their participation in the social world of home and school was education *for* citizenship. For young children in school contexts, this meant their involvement in productive activities mimicking work that would have been undertaken by children in family learning contexts, for example, baking, carpentry, gardening and housekeeping. This perspective contrasts with current understandings in which children are citizens in the present. In this view, teachers should plan for children's basic needs for care, support them as they undertake their responsibilities, ensure their democratic participation in the social world of the school and classroom, and use differentiated teaching to meet the requirements of diverse learners. Lee Jerome (2016) identified three roles for teachers in rights-based education. In the legal position, teachers follow the guidance of authorities to implement rights-based education in a technical way, attending training, following curriculum, etc. In the reformist role, teachers act as collaborative agents of rights-based education but may view it pragmatically as a means to achieve outcomes such as improved attendance or literacy. In the radical position, teachers act independently as change agents and are politically engaged with children's rights. The latter position is a rights-based teaching approach that is framed by an image of the teacher as agentic, able to influence as well as follow policy. The radical position does not reflect the experience of all teachers in every situation. As Jerome (2016) concludes, rights-based teaching is more likely revealed in 'a series of locally negotiated solutions, which address local problems in the context of local cultures, traditions and resources' (152).

## *Challenges for the UN Convention in relation to child education*

The complexity and lack of specificity of the UNCRC have led to numerous attempts to interpret rights for application in various contexts, for example, in relation to participation rights in school and community (Percy-Smith and Thomas 2010). Moreover, fundamental barriers to authentic participation are not always considered, such as the privileging of adult modes of communication, captured in the metaphor 'child's voice', which is often taken in its literal meaning (Jones and Welch 2010) and without consideration for ethical challenges (I'Anson 2013). The Convention is also difficult to enforce. Child policies may be consistent with the Convention, but practices have not necessarily changed. Helen Penn writes, 'the Convention on the Rights of the Child is an aspirational document, and interpretations of the protection, provision and participation rights of young children are still being developed' (Penn 2011: 106). Moreover, the majority of children in the world do not have even their basic needs met for survival, protection and development, and educational provisions for preschool-aged children are sometimes non-existent, inaccessible or of poor quality.

## What is the teacher's role in supporting children to express their rights as learners?

Our focus is on young children's education as citizens with rights as learners, and not their citizenship education as it is set out in official curricula and policies. Yet, it is important to remember that children are educated about their citizenship as they are engaged as active citizens. The rights-based early education frameworks referred to in the companion website, all emphasize children's participation in their learning from the earliest age, consistent with their status as citizens. Yet, we ask, in what ways do children actually participate in their learning, and what is the role of the early childhood practitioner to ensure their participation?

In Chapter 1, we described some of the limitations to defining children as learners, namely that it positions them as lacking in some respects, for example, in skills for school success. However, the learner image can be recast as strength based, focusing on children's potential and as active co-constructors of knowledge (Chapter 6). While the latter view of the child as a learner with agency informs this chapter, the passive view has frequently given rise to technologies of teaching and assessment that limit children's participation (Buchanan 2015). As Tom Popkewitz (2003: 451) explained: 'The child as learner has become so natural in the late twentieth century that it is difficult to think of children as anything else but learners; yet in a sociological sense, the "making" of the child-as-learner involved particular transformations in the social reasoning that we now associate with modernity.'

In this dominant view, when children are in any environment, it is necessarily a learning environment for them because they are children. Yet, children are full citizens across their diverse social ecologies, including learning communities in school contexts in which teachers are also learners. Children's rights as learners are rights shared amongst all persons in a given context, including teachers, and they are rights to both learn and participate in decision making about learning (Figure 2.3).

That a child has rights as a learner is different from the notion of self-efficacy, which is the term used by social psychologists such as Albert Bandura to describe a child's self-perception as a learner, that is, their 'beliefs about

FIGURE 2.3 *Children in democratic dialogue and as decision makers*

their capabilities to produce designated levels of performance that exercise influence over events that affect their lives' (Bandura 1997: 2). In Bandura's view, a child's self-efficacy is increased by their mastery experiences in controlling an environment. While this situation is enabled by rights, it relies on a child's collaborative and social engagement with others in a learning context. Put another way, in social-psychological terms a child's positive self-concept includes beliefs about their autonomy in the learning process, whereas in a rights-based framework, children simply *are* learners, with rights bestowed for participation regardless of their learning beliefs.

Teachers must therefore find ways to act on children's rights as learners in early childhood settings. The United Nations (2005) publication *Implementing Child Rights in Early Childhood* provides a start. It defines early childhood as birth to age seven, the beginning of formal schooling in many countries. The emphasis is on building strong relationships with caregivers and other children as the foundation for learning. Demonstrating 'respect for the views and feelings of the young child' (Article 14) includes ensuring children have the right to express themselves and be heard. Teachers can do this by creating 'opportunities for young children to progressively exercise their rights within their everyday activities in all relevant settings, including by providing training in the necessary skills' (UN 2005: 7). The UN document echoes the assertion of Reggio Emilia schools founder Malaguzzi that teachers need to listen to children: 'To achieve the right of participation requires adults to adopt a child-centred attitude, listening to young children and respecting their dignity and their individual points of view' (UN 2005: 7). In rights-based ECE settings, there is a notion of progressively exercising rights, based on the idea of 'evolving capacities as an enabling principle' (Article 17), which is related to developmental and individual factors. And finally, teaching in a rights-based framework means implementing 'child-centred care practices, curricula and pedagogies', with the right to play as a central activity (UN 2005: 11).

The Reggio Emilia approach to early education, named after the city in Italy where it originated, is a rights-based approach to ECE that embodies Dewey's ideas of democratic participation in education (Lindsay 2015). Teachers in Reggio Emilia schools hold an image of children as 'rich, strong and powerful' with emphasis placed on 'seeing children as unique subjects with rights rather than simply needs' (Rinaldi 1993: 102). Children learn to feel comfortable and competent in their multiple social worlds (New 2001). In this approach, curriculum necessarily emerges from observations of and conversations with the children; it revolves around their interests and is expressed and represented in multiple symbolic forms. Learning in Reggio Emilia schools is socially constructed, with parents, teachers and children collaborating in learning and listening to one another. Families are therefore central to helping the teacher gain an understanding of 'what counts as knowledge in their homes' (New 2001: 250), which has been theorized as funds of knowledge (see Chapter 5). This social constructionist view respects the child's alternative constructions of knowledge and situates the teacher as a collaborator in the creation of meaning (Dahlberg et al. 2013).

In the UNCRC, children have a right to express themselves in many languages, including their minority or home language, but also through alternative modes of expression (Bae 2010). Malaguzzi described some of these ways in his poem 'No way. The hundred is there', which was subsequently developed as the theory of the hundred languages of children. It has become 'an emblem of Reggio Emilia pedagogy, a theory in which children (human beings) are recognized as possessing many cultural possibilities', though only a few of the possibilities are supported by school or society (Cagliari et al. 2016: 104). Swedish educationist Gunilla Dahlberg, who was closely associated with the Reggio Emilia approach, explained Malaguzzi's poem as 'an important statement of an education characterised by connections and relations instead of dualisms, such as nature and culture, mind and body, subject and object, theory and practice. This poem also points to the importance of building a transdisciplinary way of working in schools' (in Cagliari et al. 2016: xi).

The Reggio Emilia approach, which has been a feature of the global early childhood scene for almost thirty years, has attracted praise as well as criticism. Although the schools were founded as populist institutions to counter elitism, the approach has been perceived as appealing to an intellectual and class-based elitism, with teachers from North America and elsewhere participating in costly study tours at the schools in Italy (Johnson 2000). These study tours have nevertheless been a main means of the diffusion of Reggio Emilia; over the years, thousands of education students, teachers and teacher educators have visited the schools and are now practicing locally inspired variations of the approach. A further criticism is that the schools reflect a culturally-based image of children rooted in a prosperous and relatively homogenous region of Italy. In 2016, 16.47 per cent of the population of the city of Reggio Emilia was classed as foreign born (Urbistat 2017), compared with 46.1 per cent in Toronto (Statistics Canada 2017). While it is a fundamental principle of the approach to reflect local culture, community and values, the experience and image of childhood in the city of Reggio Emilia have often been adopted as a guiding image for practice elsewhere in the world, leading some critics to argue that the approach represents a globalized hegemony regarding early care and education (New 2007). There is a similar critique regarding the universal character of the human/children's rights movement with its underlying concept of childhood and the global/local tensions it may create in diverse settings (Burman 1996). Indeed, in some cultural models of childhood, babies are not yet persons (Lancy 2014).

## *Summary*

This chapter explored what it means for teachers to understand children as citizens with rights who are active members of their families and communities, and the implications for classroom practice. The United Nations Convention on the Rights of the Child was described as a context for understanding children's participation and for developing a rights-based framework for teaching and learning. This approach was contrasted with conventional developmentalist approaches to child-centred education. Child development and education were explained in relation to Bronfenbrenner's ecological systems theory, parenting styles theory and Kağitçibaşi's social psychological theory. How children experience participation in their diverse social ecologies was outlined, along with teachers' key role in supporting children in classrooms based on a rights-based framework. The Reggio Emilia approach was presented as an example of rights-based early education with its focus on children's alternative modes of expression and means of participation.

# CHAPTER THREE

# Children, Communities and Cultures

*Proposition: Children's everyday life and participation in multiple communities influences their emerging social and cultural selves.*

The focus of this chapter is on children's cultural ecologies – their everyday lives and experiences in a range of social settings, including homes, preschools/kindergartens and schools, as well as in different social and cultural communities, that may or may not reflect and support diverse social and cultural beliefs and values. Children are positioned differently in the everyday practices of such settings, and interacting with members of different communities helps them gain knowledge about the social/cultural and natural worlds, and develop their social/cultural selves while negotiating transitions among the diverse contexts.

The chapter is organized around the following questions:

1 How do children become members of social and cultural communities?
2 How does children's participation in their communities influence their identity development?
3 How do teachers and parents partner in providing continuity of children's experiences across communities?

For additional information, reflective questions and practical implications visit: https://www.bloomsbury.com/cw/learning-to-teach-young-children/chapter-3/

## How do children become members of social and cultural communities?

Culture is deeply implicated in children's upbringing and development. It provides the setting for the activities children are engaged in, as well as the roles that the members of the culture play in them, their status within the group, the resources, both material and intangible, and the types/modes of interactions that are considered acceptable and desirable within the culture (Tudge 2008). Yet, perhaps because of its omnipresence in the everyday lives of its members, culture is one of the most difficult concepts to define. To capture the meaning of culture in human activities, scholars have focused on different aspects of culture, including culture as:

- Material artefacts: the 'entire pool of artefacts accumulated by the social group in the course of its historical experience' (Cole 2005: 2–3)

- A problem-solving toolkit: 'collective problem solving toolkits of individual social groups in response to their historical and ecological circumstances' (Cole 2005: 2–3)

- Customs, practices and parental ethnotheories (Super and Harkness 1994, 2002)

- Shared cultural models, expressed in everyday routines (LeVine et al. 1994)

- Shared beliefs and practices that are communicated to the next generations to help them develop a 'sense of identity of themselves as constituting a group' (Tudge 2008: 3–4)

- A context of psychological functioning and an 'organiser of meaning' (Kağitçibaşi 2007: 28).

The fact that scholars from different theoretical traditions and disciplines have focused on different aspects of culture does not mean that culture can be reduced to these aspects or their characteristics. Nor does it mean that all members of a cultural group are engaged in practices that have the same set of characteristics. Reducing the complexity of culture to its components conveys a misleading message that cultures are static, homogeneous and/or normative. How culture is understood, not only by researchers but also how it is lived in everyday lives of its members, has implications for approaches that are used in socializing and educating the youngest/newest members of the (cultural) group – children.

FIGURE 3.1 *Culture as pattern*

## *Culture as pattern: Socialization into a given cultural practice*

An approach to socialization into a given cultural context that views culture as a particular stable way of acting, behaving, knowing and mediating meanings, and relating to and communicating with other people is defined as 'culture as pattern' (Matusov and Marjanovic-Shane 2017: 311). From this point of view, members of a culture are not aware of the culture but rather see it as nature, necessity, logic, rationality, norm and tradition; it is '"culture-in-itself" – it does not know itself as culture' (Matusov and Marjanovic-Shane 2017: 315). The view of culture as pattern (Figure 3.1) is implied in two conceptual ecological frameworks of young children's family socialization presented briefly in this chapter: the paediatric vs. pedagogical model of early child care (LeVine et al. 1994), and developmental niche theory (Super and Harkness 1994).

## *Paediatric vs. pedagogical model of early child care*

The paediatric vs. pedagogical conceptual model of early child care emerged from a study by Robert A. LeVine and colleagues (1994) that examined and compared the way Gusii mothers of rural Kenya, Africa, and urban middle-class mothers of Boston, United States, parented and therefore socialized their infants and young children in the mid-1970s. Although a full description of the model is beyond the scope of this chapter, it is important to mention that the researchers used 'four points of view' to analyse parental behaviour: the first three points of view, 'organic hardware', 'ecological firmware' and 'cultural software' are then combined to form the fourth point of view, 'the cultural mediation model' (16). (See Table 3.1 in companion website.)

LeVine et al.'s (1994) seminal work challenged 'presumed universals' (15) of child development and has been very influential in understanding cross-cultural differences in child rearing. The study's findings provided insight into Western/minority-world and non-Western/majority-world visions of childhood via two distinct cultural models of child care – the paediatric and the pedagogical (see Table 3.2 in companion website). LeVine et al. point to very different conceptualizations of early socialization that tend to persist into later teaching-learning situations, both formal and informal.

LeVine et al.'s study explained that paediatric model is observed when a group needs to survive economically in a rural or subsistence economy. When the home environment is relatively impoverished, non-literate and non-Western, the prevailing model of child care will likely emphasize health and physical survival. The teaching of morality and other values may occur through oral storytelling, with little use of language between adults and children for encouraging or answering questions, reading stories or building vocabulary – the kinds of discourse patterns found in schools. Beyond infancy, one may observe a shift in focus to children's mastery of specific skills through observation and imitation via the respect-obedience model (LeVine et al. 1994), a model that suggests a culturally shared vision of the adult-to-be as one who can function within a hierarchical society in which the authority of a parent or other adult (such as a teacher) is not to be questioned.

The pedagogical model observed in the middle-class mothers of Boston was mainly concerned with the infant's optimal behavioural development and capitalizing on opportunities for educational interaction. The main goal for those American mothers was 'active engagement in social exchange' (LeVine et al. 1994: 249) where infant curiosity, such as exploration of surroundings, as well as verbal and visual communication, was encouraged and readily facilitated. The cultural script for those mothers was 'questions and praise' (252) meant to build the child's social interactions in both frequency and complexity. Each of the two models of parenting has its proponents and detractors; however, in school contexts, the pedagogical model is likely to prevail.

## *Developmental niche theory*

The 'taken-for-granted' nature of cultural models of parenting described by LeVine et al. (1994) is similar to what Charles Super and Sara Harkness (2002) called parental ethnotheories – the way in which parents' ideas about the 'natural' or 'right' way to think or act (270) is based on what a parent inherently feels is best for the child. Harkness et al. (2013) define parental ethnotheories as 'culturally constructed ideas about children's behaviour and development, about the family, and about parenting' (148). Parental beliefs, values and orientations towards daily routines such as play and work, as well as formal and informal education, are central to the developmental niche surrounding the child. Although developmental niche theory stems from the ecological systems theory of Bronfenbrenner (1979b; see also Chapter 2), it has a more distinct focus on the cultural influences in the daily lives of children and families.

Harkness et al. described three interdependent and interconnected subsystems of the developmental niche: (1) the physical and social settings of daily life, (2) the customs and practices of care and (3) the psychology of caretakers. Three corollaries result from the developmental niche that are premised on the assumption that the three subsystems of the developmental niche function interdependently as a system in a more or less consistent fashion. More consistency reflects a 'stable cultural environment' (149) in which the parental ethnotheories regarding the child are evident in the customs of care, as well as in the daily physical and social settings provided for the child. (Harkness et al. 2013: 147) (See Table 3.3 in companion website.)

Although useful in identifying observable differences in mothers' patterns of socialization in cross-cultural contexts, LeVine et al.'s (1994) study, like other studies of its kind (e.g. Harkness et al. 2013), did not pay sufficient attention to the heterogeneity that exists in every society. For example, the parenting goals of mothers in North America who live in poverty in urban settings may be more similar to those of the Gusii mothers of rural Kenya than to those of middle-class mothers of Boston. Such oversimplification could lead to generalizations about societal practices attributed to culture, without consideration of the intersection of culture with social class, gender and/or race, and may lead to dividing cultures into those that 'belong to modernity' and those that do not.

## *Individualistic and collectivistic cultures as ideological concepts*

Concepts such as individualistic (I) and collectivistic (C) cultures have been studied in cross-cultural and social psychology in terms of their values, social norms, conventions and rules (Kağitçibaşi 2007). From this normative I–C perspective, *Individualism* is seen as akin to modernity because it is associated with modern values such as sex role equality, human rights and freedoms, while *collectivism* is seen as embodying traditional, conservative ideology. Kağitçibaşi further elaborates that normative Collectivism emphasizes the group or collectivity that serves the person's in-group needs that have priority. It is combined with tradition and conservation and thus it creates 'power distance' and hierarchy. Some refer to it as 'vertical collectivism'.

The distinction between individualistic and collectivistic cultures can also be studied in terms of self-orientation. From this relational I–C perspective, the degree to which people in a society are integrated into groups can be measured. Adopting this approach, Greet Hofstede's (1997) study of fifty-three cultures resulted in a list of differences between individualistic and collectivistic cultures, not only in what people do, but also in how children's sense of self or identity is formed. Hofstede concluded that in collectivist cultures, 'identity is based in the social network to which one belongs ... Children learn to think in terms of "we" ... Relationships prevail over tasks' (67). He further explained that this is in sharp contrast with individualistic cultures, among which the United States ranked as the number one. In these cultures, identity is based in the individual; children learn to think in terms of 'I', and task prevails over relationships. However, the dichotomy – individualistic/collectivistic cultures – is not applicable to real-world situations in which people mix individualist and collectivistic values in their daily lives or behave in an individualistic way in collectivist cultures and vice versa. As Patricia Lather (1991) reminds us, 'dualisms which continue to dominate Western thought are inadequate for understanding the world of multiple causes and effects interacting in complex and non-linear ways, all of which are rooted in a limitless array of historical and cultural specificities' (21).

## Culture as pattern in school context

The view of culture as pattern – that is, as a relatively stable, taken-for-granted way of being and doing things in accordance with cultural expectations – influences not only families' socialization practices but also the overall function of schooling as socializing agent. Education can become a process of shaping people to allow them to participate in culture as pattern, socializing individuals into a given cultural shape (Matusov and Marjanovic-Shane 2017). Students can be viewed as objects of socialization, acculturalization and cultural shaping. From a narrowly interpreted Vygotskian perspective, for example, 'one of the major goals of education – formal as well as informal – is to help children acquire the tools of their own culture' (Bodrova and Leong 2013: 243). Based on this premise, parents and teachers share a common goal of helping children acquire cultural tools. The danger of such a vision of socialization and education is that it can aim at a 'deviation-free society' (Bauman 1991: 29) based on cultural conformity, which in turn emphasizes a deficit model in which anyone who deviates from or does not fit the cultural mould needs to be 'fixed' (see also Chapter 8). Such approaches can also support an assimilationist agenda through promoting the superiority of one particular culture that becomes the norm against which all other cultures are measured. The culture-as-pattern approach to education has been criticized as 'being expansionist, colonialist, and imperial, disrespectful to a cultural other' (Matusov and Marjanovic-Shane 2017: 315). Culture as pattern is also criticized for positioning children as passive recipients of culture who do not have any contributions to make or do not engage in any culture and/or meaning making of their own.

Children's acquisition of cultural mediation tools as part of their home culture may differ significantly from those they acquire in the school culture, which may result in a disconnect between the home and school (see also Chapter 6). Instead of resulting in a disadvantage for children who have been socialized at home in ways that differ from the school's cultural expectations, such discontinuity can be used as a creative culture-making opportunity. To use the example from LeVine et al.'s (1994) study, a child socialized according to the pedagogical model will have acquired the cultural mediation tools utilized in the education system prevailing in the majority world and is likely to have an advantage of familiarity over a peer who has been socialized according to the paediatric model in their country of origin and who find themselves in a school in the majority world. However, the education system can also be open to these children's life experiences and modes of socialization and engage them in a cultural exchange of ideas, practices and mediation approaches. In his work, Vygotsky (1987) distinguished between 'everyday concepts' (202) that children acquire in their home and community and 'scientific concepts' (203) acquired at school (see also Chapter 5). Both concepts are relevant to children's transition from home to school in that each child comes to school with their own communally influenced 'personal cultural tool kit' (Cole and Gajdamaschko 2007: 208) that will, or will not, to varying degrees, aid them in understanding the scientific concepts presented to them at school by the teacher. Consequently, two children may experience the same situation at school (or elsewhere) differently (Fleer 2017).

From a Vygotskian point of view, the subjective/personal and cultural/collective characteristics of the experience can be explained through the concept of *perezhivanie*, which may be translated as 'emotional experience', 'lived experience' or simply 'experience' (Esteban-Guitart and Moll 2014: 33). This concept explains how the same cultural/environmental characteristics are lived or experienced differently by different individuals and how these different lived experiences affect individuals' behaviours depending on how they understand them. Lived experience, therefore, is the subjective side of culture that mediates and organizes behaviour. In other words, cultural practices and factors are mediated by motivation, perception, memory and self-concept. Applied to educational contexts, *perezhivanie* emphasizes the unpredictability of the outcome of teaching as each child or student takes away from or learns differently from the content the teachers have taught. The unpredictability of educational outcomes indicates that education as socialization can be creative; it can modify shapes of cultural patterns and create new ways of being. Children, as newcomers to the communities of practice, have a tremendous potential to change cultural patterns (see also Chapter 6).

## Culture as both close and open socialization

From the perspective of sociocultural historical theory, stability of culture does not mean that they are static – cultures do change with time (Rogoff 2003). An individual's development is not simply a product of culture, nor is it an inevitable product of a preprogrammed developmental pattern, nor is it entirely a result of free choices by the individual, nor is it simply a compromise between the opposing forces of individual needs and socialization pressures. Children's participation in a given cultural practice or a 'community of practice' (Lave and Wenger 1991) also results in changes in both the practice itself and the person involved in it. Participation in the activities of the community allows the individual to gain access to the skills, understandings, tools and knowledges – the 'culture of practice' – needed to move from being a peripheral participant to a legitimate member of the community (Lave and Wenger 1991). Communities, from this perspective, are conceptualized as open systems that exchange information with their environment.

Luis Moll and his colleagues Amanti, Neff and González (1992) proposed approaches to curriculum and pedagogy based on communities'

FIGURE 3.2 *Culture as boundary*

and families' 'funds of knowledge'. They posited that these funds result from people's everyday life and daily activities and that individuals 'consume and use' them. They defined funds of knowledge as the 'historically accumulated and culturally developed bodies of knowledge and skills essential for household or individual functioning and well-being' (133). Esteban-Guitart and Moll (2014) point out that 'funds of knowledge do not exist solely within the mind of the individual, but rather they are distributed among persons, artefacts, activities, and settings' (36).

Communities are also grounded in associations between human and nonhuman actors, both of whom have agency. Human relationships that also include nonhuman agents (e.g. material and cultural artefacts/objects/things) hold together and modify these relationships and help groups/communities produce and maintain a sense of belonging as they move forward to an uncertain future. Hillevi Lenz Taguchi writes: 'We are all in a state and relationship of inter-dependence and inter-connection with each other as human or non-human performative agents' (2010: 15). Material objects function as a symbolic resource for an individual's sense of self as a member of a community.

Cultural communities therefore are more than their members' beliefs, values, practices and knowledges or their sum. Rather, they are 'simultaneously constituted by (1) dynamic and tenuous social bonds as people relate to each other and (2) the network or system of developing customs, practices, beliefs, symbols, etc. (collective culture) that are created' (Beckstead 2015: 386). Through participation in sociocultural practices, individuals learn to be members of these social and cultural communities and to experience themselves in a particular way.

## Culture as boundary

The central defining attribute of the concept of culture as boundary (Figure 3.2) is the relationship between cultures (Matusov and Marjanovic-Shane 2017: 314). As Zachary Beckstead explains, 'each group or community (e.g. group A) only exists as a particular group or community because of its relationship to other groups (e.g. non-A)' (2015: 382). However, these relationships may not always be harmonious; there may be disagreement, conflict and tension within a community of practice as the participants often bring diverse beliefs, values, experiences, skills, competencies and interests to their encounters. 'It is on the boundaries that culture learns about itself', Matusov and Marjanovic-Shane (2017: 315) write, which contributes in turn to denaturalizing the patterns of (cultural) behaviours, actions, values, etc.: They are no longer taken for granted but are recognized as arbitrary. The encounter with the cultural 'other' has a potential to become a *culturally recognized encounter* (Matusov and Marjanovic-Shane: 315) in which the other is acknowledged not only as other but as equal other. Therefore, central to this approach are human rights, including minority, women's, children's, gay rights, etc. Culture as boundary is implied in the acculturation development model (Sam and Oppedal 2003), which acknowledges the unique situation of immigrant and refugee children who are simultaneously socialized in two cultural contexts.

## Acculturation development model: Socialization and acculturation of newcomer children

Although culture as boundary is experienced by both citizens and newcomers to pluralistic societies worldwide, migrant, immigrant and refugee families and children are often described as living 'between' cultures, which creates unique challenges as well as affordances for the development of newcomer children. The acculturation development model, proposed by David Sam and Brit Oppedal (2003), recognizes culture as a driving force of these children's development and puts in the forefront the unique situation of immigrant and refugee children who are simultaneously socialized in two cultural contexts: (a) the heritage culture of their parents, which governs their home and ethnic community lives; and (b) the culture of the country in which they live and which they encounter at school. Socialization has been defined as 'the process through which children acquire the beliefs, values, practices, skills, attitudes, behaviours, ways of thinking, and motives of their culture that together help children develop into effective and contributing members of the group' (Gauvain and Parke 2010: 239). Immigrant and refugee children need to become familiar with the language, beliefs and behaviours of both their heritage and majority cultures if they are to develop a sense of belonging and participate successfully in both (Oppedal 2006: 97). The challenges these children face come from the different, sometimes conflicting, goals of their families and their schools as socialization agents.

Problems for immigrant and refugee children emerge when changes in the family's daily life are accompanied by structural and economic changes. This is especially noticeable in the case of immigrant and refugee families that come from rural areas in countries where the culture is characterized by close-knit relationships and the cultural socialization pattern adopted by the parents aims at developing socio-affective aspects of cognitive competence in their children (Nsamenang 2009). These parents' notions of children's competence and appropriate behaviour often conflict with those of the mainstream culture and the school (Kağıtçıbaşı 2007), which place disproportionate emphasis on cognitive competence as measured by standardized tests grounded in Eurocentric norms and expectations. Referring specifically to early childhood education practices, Cannella (1997) points out that 'child development theories have fostered dominant ideologies and created privilege for those in power. Examples include establishment of hierarchical stages and the privileging of logical thought' (63). In addition, class and race need to be considered as a structural variable in the process of acculturation and educational attainment of immigrant and refugee children.

To recognize the cultural socialization continuum that can support newcomer children's development, a model for intercultural practice (i.e. RAISED between two cultures) in the early years has been developed in consultation with members of multiple ethnocultural communities, NGOs and immigrant-serving organizations, academics and early childhood educators (see Georgis et al. 2017 in companion website). However, full integration into the host society as the most desirable acculturation strategy for immigrants in pluralistic societies (Berry 2007; see Table 3.4 in companion website) may not be equally accessible to immigrants from cultures that are perceived as extremely different from the host culture. These cultural differences are often described in cross-cultural and educational research terms of individualistic or collectivistic orientation of the culture, as well as religious practices and linguistic and ethnic markers of identity (see also Chapter 8).

## How does children's participation in their communities influence their identity development?

Identity, like culture, is part of our everyday vocabulary, yet as a concept, identity is often ambiguous, abstract and confusing. It is often used interchangeably with other terms, such as 'personality', 'character', 'self/self-meaning'/'self-awareness' and 'ego/ego identity', among others, derived mostly from Erik Erikson's work in the 1950s. The term 'identity' is also often paired with a range of adjectives to indicate a particular property of a category, including 'gender identity', 'religious identity', 'racial/cultural identity', etc. Such characteristics may contribute to a person's social subjectivity, allowing them to identify themselves in a variety of ways. Criteria for membership in any group can include, among other things, self-categorization or identification, descent, specific cultural traits such as custom or language, and a social organization for interaction both within the group and with people outside the group. However, being a member of a social category does not necessarily entail having the desire to act in accord with the norms associated with the identity.

For a child, becoming a member of any particular group is a complex developmental process that is intertwined across social situations with others, including relationships formed in social institutions like families and schools. Esteban-Guitart and Moll (2014) argue that identities created and recreated in interactions between people in a given context are lived experiences of self. 'In that sense', they write, 'identity is a conceptual artefact that contains, connects, and enables reflection over the emotional and cognitive processes of self-understanding and self-defining, in the past as well as in the present and the future' (34). Since the experience of the

FIGURE 3.3 *Culture, identity and school experiences*

self or one's identity is related to both the individual/subjective experience and the cultural experience, it is likely that multiple identities are formed through moment-to-moment negotiations with others in different social contexts (Adams and Fleer 2017). When we think of children's development in multiple social contexts – home, community, child care setting, school – we can also see the importance of temporality as a dimension of their developing identities (Figure 3.3). Adams and Fleer (2017) point out that 'temporality relates primarily to how individuals position themselves in time and use it as a resource for building their identity' (3). The use of terms like 'past', 'present', 'future', 'never' or 'always' as well as 'moment-to-moment' when used to describe not only the process of learning and development but also the lived experiences/*perezhivanie* (Vygotsky 1998) of children in different social contexts speaks to awareness of temporality. Identities then are not fixed; rather, they emerge as 'a kind of unsettled space, or an unresolved question in that space, between a number of intersecting discourses' (S. Hall 1991: 9). Stuart Hall elaborates: 'Identity is a narrative of the self; it's the story we tell about the self in order to know who we are' (14).

## *Worldviews and 'narratives of the self'*

The stories we tell ourselves are grounded in the worldviews that are dominant in the societies in which we are raised. Worldviews, as Michael Hart (2010: 2) explains, are 'cognitive, perceptual, and affective maps that people continuously use to make sense of the social landscape and to find their ways to whatever goals they seek. They are developed throughout a person's lifetime through socialisation and social interaction'. However, a worldview, although held by most of the members of any given society, may be expressed in a very personal way by individual society members, who may hold alternative worldviews.

Peter Giordano (2017) explains that the dominant Western worldview is essentially an ontology of Being, in contrast to the Becoming ontology of the East (he capitalizes the terms Being and Becoming in his work). Deriving from the classical Greek philosophy, Being is based on an understanding of the world as a static, fixed and relatively permanent entity. Giordano writes: 'The prevailing models of persons that have developed in Western culture reflect this way of thinking – the autonomous rational self that is the backbone of Western cultural experiencing' (504). The Western conceptualization of self therefore is a separated self (Kağitçibaşi 2007) aware of itself ('I', 'me') as separate from the outside world. A 'culture of separateness' refers to the contexts (cultural-familial) and interpersonal relational patterns characterized by relations between separate selves, with clearly defined boundaries (making the self contained). In the pedagogic model of LeVine et al. (1994), socialization for independence can be observed in the cultivation of individualistic attributes through praising children's individual achievements so that they learn self-enhancement of their own performance.

In contrast, the Becoming ontology of the East (i.e. Chinese and East Asian cultures), deriving from the philosophical traditions of Daoism, Confucianism and Buddhism, construes the world, including persons, in terms of transitions, change, impermanence, emergence and novelty (Ames 2015). The Becoming worldview, according to Giordano, '"locates" personality *between* persons and anchors it in the always dynamic, contextual process of *interpersonal* relations' (2017: 507, italics in original). This relational conceptualization of the self, where individuals are known not as individual persons but rather by the roles they are assigned in society, is known as a connected or interdependent self – a 'self in process' or 'personality-ing' (Giordano 2017: 507). Examples of connected/interdependent selves include the Filipino concept of *kapwa* as a unity of self and other, the Chinese *yin* and *yan*, the West African concept of social selfhood and the familial self of the Japanese and Indians, where the self is experienced as 'we-self' (Kağitçibaşi 2007).

Although in a very different way, in 'Cultural Identity and Diaspora' Stuart Hall (1990) also identified two ways of thinking about cultural identity: 'oneness' and 'becoming'. Oneness positions cultural identity in terms of one shared culture, a sort of collective 'one true self'. He explained that 'within the terms of this definition, our cultural identities reflect the common historical experiences and shared cultural codes which provide us, as "one people," with stable, unchanging and continuous frames of reference and meaning, beneath the shifting divisions and vicissitudes of our actual history' (225). Hall pointed out that such a conception of cultural identity played a critical role in all the postcolonial struggles that have so profoundly reshaped our world. To Hall, cultural identity was a matter of both becoming and being. In his non-binary view, cultural identity 'belongs to the future as much as to the past; they are subject to the continuous "play" of history, culture and power' (225). This 'play' has a profound impact on those who have been subjected to colonizing powers. For example, part of Indigenous identity is defined in relation to the colonizing culture and state government (Loring and Ashini 2000). As a group of people, Indigenous people share a history of genocide, a collective trauma, a history of dispossession of land, disenfranchisement, poverty and ill health due to lack of access to quality health care. However, the ultimate claims to Indigenous identity do not derive from contemporary nation-states. Indigenous identity is not granted by the nation-state and does not derive from colonial legal proclamations or the decisions of courts. Rather, it derives from Indigenous peoples' 'relationship with the Creator, their occupation of the land and from their self-government according to their own way developed over the years' (Frideres 2008: 321).

Indigenous worldviews are regarded as networks of relationships – all things are interconnected, and relationships among people are also critically important. The notions of religion and spirituality have a communal, rather than an individual, basis. For example, Indigenous people know and respect immanence (Graveline 1998), that is, unseen powers that sustain the universe. This worldview provides people with a distinctive set of values, a feeling of rootedness, of belonging to a time and place: a distinct identity. Indigenous peoples' collective values are invested in land, not as an individual property right, but as a right from the Creator (Frideres 2008). Frideres further explains that 'Aboriginal people have multiple positionings in the family, home community and state, which means they have multiple identities. The interplay of multiple identities is important and must be fully understood to appreciate Aboriginal identity' (321). According to this author, while Aboriginal (Indigenous) identity is complex, it ultimately refers to 'Band, linguistic or cultural collectivities, and not personal identity' (322).

## *Ego identity and personality*

Working within the social psychological tradition in sociology, James Côté (1996) attempted to resolve the 'culture-identity link' problem by providing a theoretical model with three interrelated levels of analysis: (1) social structure, including political and economic systems; (2) interactions, 'comprising patterns of behaviour that characterize day-to-day contacts among people in socializing institutions like the family and schools'; and (3) personality, 'which encompasses terms like character, self and psyche, including subcomponents like ego identity' (417). In this theoretical model, ego identity is a subcomponent of personality, embedded in everyday interactions with socializing agents that function in larger societal structures and systems. In other words, sociocultural processes and individual responses to these realities are interconnected in a complex and dynamic interplay that influences one's identity formation. At play are ever-present poles of tension between society and individual. As Erikson's theory of identity formation describes it, it is a 'process "located" *in the core of the individual* and yet also in *the core of his communal culture*, a process which establishes, in fact, the identity of those two identities' (Erikson 1968: 22, italics in original). (See Table 3.5 for Erikson's theory in companion website.)

The sociocultural approach to identity formation is represented in the works of Erikson and Vygotsky who asserted the importance of social organization, as well as the cultural and historical context, in building a coherent identity. While both Erikson and Vygotsky pointed to the importance of cultural and historical tools in identity formation, they put different emphasis in their theories. As William Penuel and James Wertsch (1995) explain, Erikson primarily focused on the dynamics of the individual self, as in the choices people make as individuals from the cultural tools available to fashion a coherent identity. Vygotsky gave primacy to sociocultural processes, that is, the social origins of people's mental functioning and the role of signs and tools in mediating actions (see also Chapter 5). From this perspective, identities are formed 'in local activity settings where participants are actively engaged in forming their identities; to examine the cultural and historical resources for identity formation as empowering and constraining tools for identity formation; and to take mediated action as a unit of analysis' (Penuel and Wertsch 1995: 83).

Building on cultural-historical theory, Esteban-Guitart and Moll (2014) propose a new concept – 'funds of identity' – that emphasizes the distributed and mediated nature of identity understood as being essentially social in origin. They define identity as a 'box of tools and signs' (35), a socially constructed product and a cultural device that is 'an internalised and externalised set of meanings, practices, and distributed resources embedded in ways of life and contexts of learning' (37). The critical components of their definition of identity include all skills, knowledge, practices and resources that people have acquired and use through their involvement in their various activities with various people; the social institutions and practices (work, school, church, sport) that work as hubs of activities, resources and patterns of identity that are available to children; and children's active appropriation, through explicit or implicit educational processes, of discourses, narratives and visions or models of identity.

Comparing their concept of funds of identity to Moll's earlier concept of funds of knowledge, Esteban-Guitart and Moll explain: 'Funds of knowledge are repositories of identity to which people have access. Consequently, the funds of knowledge are funds of identity when people use them to define themselves. Specifically, what we understand by *funds of identity* are historically accumulated, culturally developed, and socially distributed resources that are essential for people's self-definition, self-expression, and self-understanding' (2014: 37, italics in original). In other words, funds of knowledge can become funds of identity as individuals internalize specific resources provided by the social and cultural worlds in which they live.

# How do teachers and parents partner in providing continuity of children's experiences across communities?

The discussion so far has been about the influences of culture on parenting, parental beliefs and practices, as well as how different approaches to culture influence both home and school as socialization agents in young children's learning and development and, more specifically, the development of their identity or sense of self. One view of the role of different institutions in children's lives is that of *sequential responsibilities* of institutions that emphasize 'the critical stages of parents' and teachers' contributions to child development' (Epstein 2011: 26). This view is grounded in the belief that the early years of a child's life are critical for later success. As discussed in Chapter 1, Piaget's stage theory of development still dominates the field of early childhood education practice and contributes to its division into two distinct subfields: (1) early childhood care, in which preschool teachers and other professionals support or guide parents in teaching their young children skills to prepare them for school, and (2) early childhood education, which is marked by children's formal entry into school, when the teacher assumes the major responsibility for educating them.

Building on ecological, educational, psychological and sociological theories, Epstein (2011) developed an integrated theory of *overlapping spheres* of influence which posits that students learn more when parents, educators and others in the community work together to guide and support student learning and development. In this model, the three contexts of home, school and community 'overlap with unique and combined influences on children through the interactions of parents, educators, community partners, and students across contexts' (Epstein 2011: 43). The model emphasizes the need for partnership, which Epstein defines as a shared responsibility of home, school and community for children's learning and development based on reciprocal interactions of parents, educators and community partners to understand each other's views, identify common goals for students, and appreciate each other's contributions to student development. Although the model recognizes the agency of the students in developing such partnerships, it mainly stresses the need for educators to acquire, as part of their professional preparation, the knowledge and skills to organize and implement effective partnerships with all students' families. In increasingly diverse school settings, such an approach is essential in creating positive learning environments. However, the model highlights differences between 'school-like families' and 'family-like schools' (38), which disregards the influences of culture, traditions and worldviews on families' child-rearing and socialization practices by emphasizing the educational level of parents. Furthermore, research into families' and schools' different socialization and education goals is the basis for the claim that although parents' educational backgrounds differ, 'both more- and less-educated parents have similar goals to those of the school for their children's education' (Epstein 2011: 39). When differences among families are presented in such a one-sided way, the relationships among schools, families and communities are reduced to information exchange between teachers and administrators, and families and communities, or to types of parental involvement and school communication strategies with different types of families. As a result, partnerships with families and communities, especially in pluralistic societies, diminish schools' potential to play a significant role in strengthening the social inclusion discourse, which focuses on the power relationships between those who are excluded and those doing the exclusion.

There are a number of educational approaches that, although not developed specifically for forming partnerships among families, schools and communities, have very important implications for such relationships because they attempt to address cultural differences in educational settings. For the purposes of this chapter, we focus on three of these approaches – multicultural, intercultural and culturally relevant/sustaining education philosophies and practices – specifically considering their different views of culture.

## *Multicultural education as theory and practice*

The primary goal of multicultural education is to develop awareness of and respect for cultural diversity (Portera 2011). Culture as pattern (Matusov and Marjanovic-Shane 2017) is exemplified in attempts to preserve culture and cultural diversity through cultural museums, appreciation of cultural cuisines and celebration of cultural (as opposed to religious) holidays such as the Chinese New Year, for example. This form of multicultural education advocates for acceptance of all cultural perspectives as equal – a central concept in cultural relativism. The positive aspect of this view of culture, according to Matusov and Marjanovic-Shane, is that 'in the celebration of diversity model, a cultural other is viewed as a legitimate and equal human being with alternative but equal quality' (2017: 315). The concept of culture as boundary is also inherent in multicultural education philosophy in its respect for human dignity, promotion of social justice and greater equity within society by reducing discrimination, promoting, enhancing self-understanding through expanding one's cultural lens, and liberating individuals from the restraints of cultural boundaries (Banks 2008).

The limitations of multicultural education are many, including ignoring the impacts of time and change on culture (i.e. its dynamic nature); the emphasis on exoticized, knowable (other) cultures, which solidifies the boundaries between majority and minority cultures; and the view of the self/culture relationship that reiterates the cultural hegemony associated with Eurocentrism (Kirova 2008). Specific shortfalls regarding diverse families' engagement in their children's schooling are that they are typically seen as sources of 'exoticized' cultural knowledge who can mainly contribute to 'cultural' celebrations – an add-on to the 'core' curriculum. Thus, family and community participation is often reduced to tokenism.

## *Intercultural education philosophy and practice*

Unlike multicultural education that is focused on cultural retention, intercultural education aims to create a common space through dialogue. However, as we have stated elsewhere, 'while openness to difference and the expansion of understanding through cross-cultural dialogue is central to intercultural education, blanket acceptance of all cultural perspectives and practices is not'

(Kirova and Prochner 2015: 392). Open, respectful dialogue among cultures is not only about diverse cultures encountered but about one's own and the general influence of culture on how we perceive and interact in the world. In this sense, intercultural education philosophy goes beyond what Matusov and Marjanovic-Shane (2017) call culture as boundary; it is 'culture as authorship', which is 'constantly on the move of transcendence of the given recognized and valued by others in dialog' (317). From this perspective, 'every person is an authorial culture maker. The life of every person is culture making' (317). Thus, the creative authorship of culture making is dialogic; it involves a 'third space' in which cultural boundaries are perceived as a tension to be resolved. For Homi Bhabha, in the third space, 'the meaning and symbols of culture have no primordial unity or fixity; even the same signs can be appropriated, translated, historicised and read anew' (Bhabha 1994: 37). In a classroom in which there is a tension between the teacher's official school culture and the minoritized students' counter-culture, creating a new or hybrid culture can be a result of a creative authorship of both the students and the teacher. The culture as authorship involves an authentic meaning-making process.

An example of the dialogic nature of culture as authorship is provided by Hennig and Kirova (2012) where, in an intercultural early learning classroom, the 'third space' was created not only by the ongoing dialogue among the educators in the room, who came from diverse cultural backgrounds, but also by the deliberate introduction of cultural artefacts as nonhuman agents in the intercultural dialogue. In the intercultural programme, families and communities' strength-based partnership was established and maintained through cultural brokers – members of the community who were also members of the classroom teaching team that allowed children to consolidate their learning from both home and school environments in a manner consistent with their cultural background. In the language of culture as authorship, this case demonstrated how authorial education is 'always unpredictable in several aspects: whether it happens, when it happens, with whom, about what, what outcomes will come out of it, what sense to make out of it, by whom, and finally, whether it is good or not – questions embedded in dialogue, that define meaning making' (Matusov and Marjanovic-Shane 2017: 320). Therefore, intercultural education theory and practice have potential to disrupt the taken-for-granted dominance of minority-world educational values reflected in the education standards, curriculum and pedagogy.

## *Critical race theory and culturally relevant/sustaining pedagogies*

Although both multicultural and intercultural education theories and practices emphasize culture in their approaches to cultural diversity in school settings, they both pay insufficient attention to other markers of difference (e.g. race, language, social class, gender) that intersect with culture at both individual and group/societal levels (see also Chapter 8). Building on critical race theory (CRT; Ladson-Billings 1998) and using intersectionality as a conceptual lens, Souto-Manning and Rabadi-Raol (2018) have proposed four design principles that help redefine quality in early childhood education in a way that will result in 'counterstories to Whiteness, monoculturalism and monolingualism', which they assert have been 'pervasive and ingrained features of DAP across time' (216), resulting in increasing oppression of multiply marginalized linguistically, culturally and racially diverse children. These four principles are as follows:

1 Children's development is social, cultural and historical; it will not follow discrete trajectories or certain timelines.
2 All children, families and communities have rich cultural and linguistic assets and are 'at promise'.
3 Quality early childhood education must positively engage intersectional identities.
4 Quality early childhood education must centre the voices, values, practices and experiences of the global majority. (217–18)

It is the application of these principles in everyday practices in ECE institutions that will position culture 'as critical dialogue' (Matusov and Marjanovic-Shane 2017: 320) in which each culture is self-critical and nothing is taken for granted, where 'everything is legitimately questionable, and everybody is legitimately answerable' (321). Only then can ECE practices genuinely originate in the voices, experiences, practices and values of all children, families and communities.

## *Summary*

This chapter considered how culture is understood and practiced in different contexts, and how it influenced children's socialisation. 'Culture as pattern' is presented in relation to two ecological theories: the paediatric and pedagogical models of early child care, and developmental niche theory, which considers parental ethnotheories. Individualist and collectivistic cultures are discussed. 'Culture as boundary' is discussed in relation to the socialisation and acculturation of newcomer children navigating different expectations at home and in school. The relationship between culture and identity formation is explored with respect to the impact of worldviews on narratives of the self and sociocultural approaches to identity formation, including the concept of funds of identity. A critical review of several approaches that have attempted to address the diverse needs of families and children is described, highlighting the need to develop strength-based partnerships among schools, families and communities.

# CHAPTER FOUR

# Experience, Learning and Development

***Proposition: Early experiences influence children's development and learning.***

For John Dewey (1916), meaning making involves 'a backward and forward connection between what we do to things and what we enjoy or suffer from things in consequence. Under such conditions, doing becomes a trying; an experiment with the world to find out what it is like; the undergoing becomes instruction – discovery of the connection of things' (164). Dewey believed children shape their world and are shaped by it, being in turns active and receptive, agentic and passive. The concepts of experience, learning and development therefore are understood in relation to both the child and the world. This chapter explores the concepts in relation to three questions:

1. What is environment?
2. What is development?
3. How do children's experiences in the environment influence their learning and development?

For additional information, reflective questions and practical implications visit: https://www.bloomsbury.com/cw/learning-to-teach-young-children/chapter-4/

## What is environment?

The term 'environment' derives from the French word for surroundings. In a human-centred definition, the environment consists of the surroundings of a person or people, but with attention to particular aspects of the surroundings (McShane 2012). Environment holds another meaning with reference to the natural world and nonhuman natural surroundings (Sutton 2007). What we count as environment has shifted over time, is influenced by culture and reflects multiple realities. While the environment can be categorized as natural, supernatural and human-made, our focus is on human-centred environments along with human–natural world relationships.

The interactions of an infant as a biological organism are mainly within its proximate or near environment, which is mediated by the infant's family and community. As anthropologists explain, there are features of human biology that make rearing children a 'cooperative breeding activity' (Bogin et al. 2015). Human infants' helplessness, according to Courtney Meehan and her colleagues, along with their extended period of child development and 'short interbirth intervals, compared to other apes, results in the cost of child rearing being more than what a mother alone can provide. Thus, development requires significant energetic contributions from others' (Meehan et al. 2015: 200–1), which creates a context for prolonged learning and socialization coinciding with an infant's rapid brain growth. The constraint of infant helplessness is therefore interpreted as an evolutionary development providing the optimal conditions for the transmission of culture (Trevathan and Rosenberg 2016).

Human-made environments are created to meet human needs. As such they are informed by cultural beliefs and practices which guide behaviours and interactions within the environment. Human-made environments include built environments, that is, the modified physical surroundings in which we live (Moffatt and Kohler 2008). While the built environment 'can only be defined in contrast to the "un-built" environment, or the ecosphere' (Moffatt and Kohler 2008: 259), the distinction between built and un-built is not always clear. As Moffatt and Kohler point out, a forest preserve requires planning by humans, including plans for its protection from humans.

The relation of humans to the natural world is a philosophical question – or, some would say, a spiritual, moral, legal or biological one – of what it means to be human. An anthropocentric answer to this question places humans at the centre, defining humans by what they are not. However, as Rob Boddice asserts, 'the process of acquiring these world perspectives is to us invisible, and we therefore operate with and within them, unaware that we overlay cosmology with ideology at every step' (2011: 7). Understandings of the human–nature relationship are also shaped by models of science, for example, the attempt to measure, classify and categorize nature in the scientific revolution of the Enlightenment as a way to make sense of the world. The nineteenth-century German scientist and explorer Alexander von Humboldt, who travelled with vast sets of scientific instruments into jungles and to rims of volcanoes, was said to have 'invented nature' (Wulf 2015) in this way. However, von Humboldt's understanding of nature as organic was imbued with German idealist philosophy, with its emphasis on the question of the self and the not-self. For von Humboldt, nature (the not-self) could be comprehended only by linking scientific empiricism with human creativity and emotion. Similar ideas characterized the thinking of Froebel, shaping his kindergarten approach to education (Allen 2000), and German idealism, evinced in Hegel's notion of 'grades of development', influenced the ideas of Piaget (Limnatis 2008), who proposed an essentially philosophical view of the 'life-form of childhood' (Patocka 2016). For Piaget, Hegel's question 'of how to direct the development of the society in the service of progress [became] the question of how to direct the development of an individual in the service of progress. The imperative of such a position, then, is to understand what stages of development the individual traverses such that it can best be directed' (Mulryan 2008: 317).

In a relational bioecological developmental systems perspective, development is 'a joint function of process, person, context, and time' (Bornstein and Leventhal 2015: 1). Developmental contexts, that is, environments, include microsettings such as the home, which are influenced by actions outside the settings, such as family policies and workplace policies. Homes as microsettings are environments with 'specific physical and material parameters' (Bornstein and Leventhal 2015: 1). Schools are another microsetting for learning and development (Hamm and Zhang 2010). Formal learning environments are arranged to focus learners' attention on particular surroundings. In Rousseau's idea of negative education (see Chapter 1), children needed protection from what were judged to be harmful influences. The learning environment was therefore designed with constraints in mind, limiting children's access to books and or skills such as reading. While this approach does not fit current thinking about children's literacy development, teachers – and in some cases, school districts, in the form of censorship – make decisions about which books to make available to children (West 2006). As microsettings, schools include people, space and materials linked by a model of teaching and learning and the structure of a curriculum. And the school environment is not neutral. As Foucault explained, the built environment of the school includes mechanisms of discipline, of bodies and minds, such as school chairs oriented forward to the teacher's gaze (Rubio and Fogué 2015), or, in early years classrooms, the seating of children in a circle. In a Foucauldian analysis, discipline is also achieved using soft power through the use of language or regulation of emotions. In an early childhood setting, this can involve managing children's feeding behaviours and learning about food through racializing and civilizing strategies (Albon and Hellman 2018; Nxumalo et al. 2011).

A relational understanding of the natural world is part of many Indigenous knowledge systems, in which humans are part of nature. In these views, there is 'reciprocity between human actions and nature' and knowledge in all things (Landry 2018: 22). Indigenous worldviews are therefore characterized by notions of interconnectedness and a dynamic relation with nature. Among the Chagga people of Tanzania, for example, 'everything is alive. Stones and mountains, rivers and lakes, clouds and rain, are all alive in their intrinsic meanings and in their active partnership to people and everything else' (Mosha 1999: 213).

FIGURE 4.1 *Agentic materials – clay*

Phenomena which cannot be explained by scientific investigation are sometimes categorized as supernatural. For example, African ways of knowing include three types of cognition – supernatural, natural and paranormal – which, when analysed, result in 'a logical explanation of reality' (Ngara 2017: 346). Supernatural cognition includes knowledge obtained directly from dreams or indirectly by possession or diviners. Places can also be associated with stories and be performative, that is, have agency. As Valk and Savbörg (2018) describe, 'the storyworld, landscape and people all participate in the creation of the ... supernaturalisation of places' (10).

Many historical approaches to early childhood education had supernatural elements. Froebel's kindergarten reflected his ideas of the relationship among the natural, supernatural and spiritual (MacVannel 1905); the Waldorf schools were based on Steiner's occultist beliefs and metaphysical theories called anthroposophy (Ullrich 2014); Montessori's educational ideas were influenced by a spiritualist movement called theosophy (Kramer 1988) and the American kindergarten was infused with the mysticism of the transcendentalism movement (Mott 2010; Ronda 2017). As one result, agency in these historical early childhood education programmes was expanded to apply to materials, which were believed to have a supernatural relationship with children (Figure 4.1). As Froebel (1904) described, the child and blocks develop a relationship, in which the blocks are seen 'as a worthy, an appreciated, and a loved comrade' (195). Moreover, '*the surroundings should speak to the child by their qualities and attributes so as to be understood*' (95, emphasis in original). A humanist view of agentic materials is represented in current thinking by some posthumanistic perspectives (Pacini-Ketchabaw et al. 2012), for example, the notion that clay, blocks and paint 'speak back' to children, as discussed in Chapter 1, and the role ascribed to nonhuman animals (Pacini-Ketchabaw et al. 2017; Taylor and Pacini-Ketchabaw 2018) as fourth educators in an early childhood setting in addition to the people, materials and space (Bone 2013) (Figure 4.1).

## *What is development?*

Concepts of development are applied in many situations, to understandings of children, of countries, and so on. However, the meaning of development varies according to its associated theoretical lens. From the standpoint of Piaget's epigenetic theory, for example, children develop in a stage-like process of growth towards a finished and known state, or, as explained by classical economic theory, countries are categorized as developed or developing based on economic criteria (Dang and Pheng 2015). These sorts of notions of development of children and of countries have been subjected to a similar critique of developmentalism, whereby ideas about development form the basis for ideologies of development. Childhood ideologies are different from ideologies of child development; the former express culturally specific values and ideas regarding child socialization (Hoffman 2003), while the latter describe child development in normative and universal terms. In early childhood education, developmentalism refers to 'a set of ideas and practices that are particular to the sector and have unique meanings associated with them, largely shaped by Piaget, Gesell, Vygotsky, and Erikson' (Kilderry 2015: 119). The sector's attachment to developmentalism as an ideology occurred with its move towards positivistic science and the professionalization of teaching in the early twentieth century (Bloch 1992). Developmentalism is manifest in the approach to teaching called developmentally appropriate practice (DAP). In biological terms, 'development refers to systematic changes in the organisation of an organism, an organism that is seen as a functional, adaptively oriented, relatively open system throughout its life' (Lerner 1979: 276). Human development is therefore marked by changes in physical, social and intellectual functioning over time. And as an individual develops in relation to a changing environment, they modify the environment in a reciprocal manner.

Factors influencing development are typically explained according to the roles played by culture and biology: Children are reared in ways that support development according to the priorities of the culture in which they live. The weight of scientific opinion regarding the dominance of socialization or biology, often expressed as nurture and nature, has shifted over time and is a continuing debate. Yet, as the philosopher of science Evelyn Fox Keller (2010) points out, what we call nature is inseparable from nurture; the existence of a space between them is an illusion rooted in the established (Western) worldview in which nature and nurture are disjoined. As Keller describes, a gene, which is often taken to represent nature, has no causal role without environmental factors. Moreover, it is impossible to distinguish with precision among the causes of development. As discussed in Chapter 2 in relation to Bronfenbrenner's ecological framework, if everything counts as an influence on development, it is difficult to understand which aspect of our surroundings explain developmental outcomes (Figure 4.2).

In the view of development favouring biology, children's growth has been metaphorically compared to that of plants. Friedrich Froebel, for example, used a horticultural metaphor in his kindergarten approach to education in which teachers were kindergartners (child-gardeners). The idea is that children mature according to a predetermined plan. In this view, although their development can vary within a range according to environmental conditions and their genetic inheritance, children play a relatively passive role in their own development. A contrasting metaphor depicts development as the assembly of building blocks, suggesting that intellect, along with other facets of development, is constructed from materials set out in proper relationship with one another to create a solid structure. While children have a more active role in this process, developmental changes also involve maturation. These metaphors are associated with groups of theories that are broadly characterized as maturational and constructivist, with both

FIGURE 4.2 *Environmental factors and development*

corresponding to the 'ages of man' view of childhood (see Chapter 1). In each of the two groups of theories, development occurs in stages that are more or less discrete.

Child development theories have changed over the past one hundred years, from generalized theories based on evolutionary laws of development (Tracy 1909), to ecological approaches concerning the 'whole' child in a social and cultural context (Bronfenbrenner 1979a, 1979b). However, a key debate continues to be the degree to which human development is fixed or changeable. In the past, plasticity in development was thought to be more possible in the early years, with older persons less easily influenced by environmental influences. For this reason, interventions focused on changing the course of development through various social, moral and educational interventions. Current thinking is that humans are able to change, within limits, at all stages of the lifespan, while at the same time aspects of development are robust, meaning that 'the general characteristics of each individual develop in much the same way irrespective of environment' (Bateson and Gluckman 2011: 1). Ideas from brain science have influenced education and social policy. For example, the notion of prolonged plasticity is partly responsible for increased attention to adult education, along with social justice theory and other factors, while the idea of greater plasticity in the early years has stimulated the burgeoning of preschool programmes such as nursery schools, Head Start programmes, kindergartens and specialized programmes for children with special needs. Concepts of plasticity and robustness cannot be considered independent of one another. While learning is 'the archetype of plasticity ... learning processes are highly regulated by robust mechanisms' (Bateson and Gluckman 2011: 46).

## *Biology-based theories of development*

Ethological theories describe the adaptation of behaviour in relation to the social environment in the context of evolutionary history (Bateson 2015). The classic example is the imprinting of ducklings to follow their mother triggered by her movement. John Bowlby's attachment theory applied ethological ideas to the development of an infant's relationship with their mother, in which they would form an attachment for survival reasons 'regardless of the treatment they receive from them' (Martin and Fabes 2009: 32).

In the early twentieth century, evolutionary theories suggested there were clear genetic limits to human potential linked with race and ethnicity. A person's social or economic circumstance, such as poverty, was attributed to their weak genetic material. Intelligence was associated with different races, with humankind ranked according to racial categories (Jensen 1969). The continued publication of works that hold this point of view (Miele 2018; Rushton 1997) highlights the way old ideas coexist with new ideas, as well as the resilience of a belief in the fixity of human nature. The same ideas fuelled the eugenics ideology that advocated the planned development of the human species eliminating weaker individuals. Eugenics – which was a mainstream movement among academics and the political class in the 1920s and 1930s – was used as the basis for educational and reproductive policies around the globe (Bashford and Levine 2010). This ideology continued to influence government policy long after competing theories of development gained sway.

The durability of eugenics relates to the beginnings of the discipline of developmental psychology, which coincided with the popularization of evolutionary theory. The influence of evolutionary theory is found in the ideas of many psychologists, including G. Stanley Hall and Jean Piaget. In this view, children are competent yet primitive (in relation to adults) in terms of their cognitive functions. As described by Hall (1904), individual human development (ontogeny) repeats or recapitulates the development of the human race (phylogeny) from savage to civilized (see Chapter 1). Race theory was partnered with recapitulation theory, in which humans were distinguished and ranked according to racial characteristics. In this scheme, the cognitive, moral and social development of 'Negroid' adults was ranked with European children (Cole 1996). While it was expected that most European children of normal intelligence would reach the highest stages of cognitive development by mid-adolescence, the development of 'Negroid' adults was fixed at a lower level.

Developmental theory is translated in programs to guide or change development. Where limits of development were considered part of a child's genetic, social, racial or ethnic inheritance, intervention programmes focused on those factors amenable to change. For this reason, removing children from high-risk environments, including their homes and communities, was seen as an appropriate move to fight against social contagion. This kind of reasoning, together with racist government policy of forced assimilation, was behind the development of systems of residential and boarding schools for Indigenous children in Canada, the United States and Australia.

If children were at risk of school failure due to their cultural and social circumstances, it made sense to educational planners in the 1940s and 1950s to use schools as a way to give these children a head start. The forms this strategy took were matched to the school culture that children would experience in the first grade. Reinforcing home culture and language was not a viable option: They were named as a primary source of children's difficulties. This idea was captured in the term *cultural deprivation*, which was coined by social scientists in the 1960s (Banks 2015).

## *Contextual theories of development*

Erica Burman (2008) urges us to be critical but to think carefully about developmental theory, to not 'throw out the baby (of developmental theorising) with the bathwater (of changing conditions)' (145). Indeed, the 'bathwater', she argues, 'is crucial to the baby's flourishing and well-being' (145), while it is essential to contextualize developments (plural), to think about childhoods instead of individual children, to consider the influence of gender, politics and economics, and intersectionality and childhood studies (Konstantoni and Emejulu 2016). We can consider the bathwater to be 'a resource, something we can analyse for clues as to what this baby is all about, including what we think it should not contain' (Burman 2008: 161).

In contrast to evolutionary theories, the currently popular contextual or ecological theories of development consider the way biological, family and cultural factors combine with political and ideological movements to influence children's growth and learning (Bronfenbrenner 1979; Rogoff 2003; Tudge 2008). This extends to physical development as well as cultural learning and cognitive development. At the same time, ecological theories recognize biology and heredity as playing a large role, representing a developmental systems approach within which there is a bidirectional influence across the two systems (Lerner 2018). The image of development, in comparison with growing plants or building blocks, is one of concentric circles emanating out from the child and family at the centre, to political forces and ideologies at the circumference, as in Bronfenbrenner's framework. The timing of biological and social events is a key debate in ecological theories. Early experience is generally thought to be crucial for later development, with the limits of adult potential relatively fixed by adolescence at the latest.

In contextual theories, the role of culture is established as an important factor directing children's development. The subdiscipline of cultural psychology is concerned with the relationship between the 'psychological foundations of cultural communities and the cultural foundations of minds' (Shweder et al. 1998: 867). Cultural psychology is a useful way to think about the impact on the development of Indigenous children of government removal from their families, as was undertaken in Canada, Australia, the United States and other countries in the nineteenth and twentieth centuries. Banning children from speaking their home language and enforcing changes in clothing and food were blunt tools used by residential school teachers and administrators for assimilation. Institutional life in a boarding school was also constructed to interrupt children's cultural socialization in more subtle ways. Child rearing by Indigenous parents is noted to reinforce interpersonal values and interdependency. In traditional child rearing, children were not left alone, were not spoken to directly by adults and were not expected to speak in the company of adults. Children learned via storytelling and observation, and gained experience in providing care for younger siblings and relatives according to the 3 Ls: look, listen and learn (Hookimaw-Witt 1998). While there may have been many opportunities for children to observe adults and others in the institutional context, their activities were regulated by institutional life and unsupported by family relationships. They were embedded in a pedagogical mode of child socialization (LeVine et al. 1994, see Chapter 3) as opposed to socialization approaches that emphasized 'social intelligence and responsibility toward the community' (Gauvain 2005: 16). Various other cultural traditions reinforced interdependence, for example, communal sharing of food and resources. Boarding school practices were inconsistent with traditional family-life practices, and moreover they were designed to disrupt the latter. Family relations, providing support for the psychological foundation of the community, were impossible to sustain in the same way in boarding schools, where children were separated from their siblings as well as their parents.

Other contextual theories that are currently popular help us understand this process. Vygotsky's (1986) sociocultural theory of development gives an important role to language and social interactions in thinking. David Wood's (1998) description of this process highlights the critical role of family and community:

> Instruction – both formal and informal, in many social contexts, performed by more knowledgeable peers or siblings, parents, grandparents, friends, acquaintances and teachers – is the main vehicle of the cultural transmission of knowledge. Knowledge is embodied in the actions, work, play, technology, literature, art and talk of members of a society. Only through interaction with the living representatives of culture ... can a child come to acquire, embody and further develop that knowledge. Children's development thus reflects their *cultural* experiences and their opportunities for access to the more mature who already *practice* specific areas of knowledge. (27, emphasis in original)

Barbara Rogoff (2003) and others (e.g. Tudge 2008) have expanded on the relation between culture and development in the tradition of Vygotsky, and there has been considerable interest in the educational application of his ideas (e.g. Fleer 2010).

# How do children's experiences in the environment influence their learning and development?

The aim of early childhood education is often stated in terms of facilitating development, but the question 'Whose development?' is seldom asked. In their seminal article, 'Development as the Aim of Education', Lawrence Kohlberg and Rochelle Mayer (1972) argued for a progressive view of education based on what they called a 'Piaget-Dewey concept' (457). Kohlberg and Mayer claimed that such a notion of 'education for development and education for principles' is 'liberal, democratic, and non-indoctrinative. It relies on open methods of stimulation through a sequence of stages, in a direction of movement which is universal for all children. In this sense, it is natural' (494).

Development as the aim of education was also identified as the foundation of the prescriptive pedagogy known as DAP. However, as we have discussed, development is a complex biocultural phenomenon, and we recognize views such as DAP as examples of developmentalism. Turning to Dewey's (1916) own words, we can see that he did indeed believe that development was the aim of education. He wrote: 'Since growth is the characteristic of life, education is all one with growing; it has no end beyond itself' (62). Garrison et al. (2016) clarify his meaning: Although Dewey meant growth in a biological sense to mean development, he was also concerned with psychological, social and cultural growth. And insofar as Dewey considered that education is the reconstruction of experience, what is needed is a theory of experience to support development, which is to say, a theory of education. Indeed, as Barbara Schecter (2011) observes, 'it is precisely because development is NOT natural, not inevitable, that we must pay close attention to the kinds of experiences which foster it' (257).

Approaches to ECE attach meanings to the relationships among experience, learning and development, and the meanings inform teaching practices supporting the interactions. Development is expressed in biological terms as the dynamic and spontaneous interaction between the internal systems of the organism and the demands of the environment, through which the processes for returning to a normal state of homeostasis or balance are activated (Salkind 2004). In this case, the child, as the organism, is agentic in their own development as they seek to maintain balance; experience is the interaction with the environment; and learning is an adaptive activity called accommodation in Piaget's terms. Constructivist teaching practices emphasize the role of children in their learning, the place of authentic and purposeful interactions and the importance of children and teachers engaging in academic work (Dangel et al. 2004).

In the Reggio Emilia approach, development is believed to be subject to social influences and rooted in culturally based values. Moreover, Reggio Emilia's proponents criticize the concept of development as being problematic due to its issues of power and equity and its foundation in Western ideas of psychology (Dahlberg et al. 2013). Reggio Emilia teaching practices position the teacher as a researcher, advocate, collaborator and facilitator immersed in teaching and learning relationships that are both community based and political (McNally and Slutsky 2017). Learning in the Reggio Emilia approach reflects Dewey's concept of experience, whereby learning arises from practical real-world experiences through a cyclical process of meaning making.

## *Relationships with the human world*

Ideas of development and education place demands on the environment for particular elements to be in place in a particular way. The people, materials and space that make up formal early childhood settings are planned to focus learners' attention on certain aspects of the environment. For example, teachers use documentation procedures (see Chapter 9) to isolate specific aspects of learners' engagement with the environment in order to facilitate their reflection and further engagement in a cyclical process to lead to learning. Noah Sobe's (2004) historical analysis of a Montessori demonstration preschool examined the role of the educational settings in 'fixing attention' and developing 'subjects of attention'. Fixing the learner's attention is accomplished by the arrangement of space and materials, for example, in the ways the setting indicates what is and is not preschool (Figure 4.3). Rituals reinforced the transition from outer to inner contexts. As an example in current times, in many Japanese preschools children change into a uniform when they arrive at school. In this way, the 'school or classroom entranceway marks a divide not only between a literal inside and outside, but also between children's sense of being at home and being at preschool and between the compartments each of these contexts requires' (Hayashi and Tobin 2015: 84). In the historical preschool, attention was also developed through habits which eventually became internalized; in this sense, repetition was a learning strategy. Materials such as Montessori's didactic apparatus were also designed to fix attention and guide learning in a particular direction.

Developing 'subjects of attention' refers to the ways children in early childhood settings take on roles as learners. This is accomplished through a number of processes, including in routines, such as mealtimes, used as an opportunity for civilizing children's bodies (Albon and Hellman 2018). As Sobe (2004) reminds us:

> The objects of schooling are anything but incidental and untheoretical. Things ... that are to be manipulated, touched, and thus learned through construct subjectivity. They represent strategies for organizing human perception that rely upon a theorizing of attention as deliberate, cultivated, and affirmative of certain truths about the subject. (295)

Attention is an individual and a social process. In cognitive science, attention is explained in relation to the development of voluntary attention, self-regulation, including emotional regulation and the ability to focus. Voluntary attention is a higher mental function that is 'the product of social connections and environment' (Leontiev 1932: 53), developing from involuntary, that is, directed by external stimuli (e.g. words of others) to voluntary attention, that is, self-regulated by thought (Gredler and Shields 2008). However, while 'self-regulation is a property of living matter' it does not mean 'self-aware' (Lewis 2015: 22). The development of a consciousness occurs through a child's actions with the social world. Self-awareness requires the child to 'assume an outside point of view' or 'to look back at themselves' (Lewis 2015: 25). Aspects of self-awareness

**FIGURE 4.3** *Role of space and materials in fixing the learner's attention*

such as self-referential behaviour – for example, for a child to literally look back at themselves through self-recognition in a mirror – depend on brain development.

Self-regulation involves emotional and cognitive processes – 'the ability to modulate one's own emotions and to respond appropriately to the emotion of others' (Raver et al. 2012: 248), works alongside the ability to stay on task and includes neurological, behavioural and cultural dimensions. In education settings, the term 'self-regulation' is used to mean different things, including learners' engagement, delay of gratification (thought suppression) and behavioural regulation such as attention and impulse control (McClelland et al. 2015). Self-regulation is different from compliance, in which a child controls their behaviour in relation to an external requirement, for example, a classroom or school rule. There is a strong correlation between self-regulation and academic achievement in early childhood, especially in the areas of literacy and math. Motor processes also involve self-regulation, including in the midst of environmental distractions. Cultural differences in self-regulation 'direct attention toward culturally driven practices that may support or hinder self-regulatory behaviour' (McClelland et al. 2015: 22), for example, differences in attention span and working memory based on home training and expectations.

Self-regulation is a core concept in Vygotsky's theory of cognitive development; it is required for the higher mental functions and therefore school success (Bodrova and Leong 2018). Vygotsky's stages of the use of symbols are also stages of self-regulation, which he called volition, or 'the mastery of one's behaviour with the help of cultural instruments' (Vygotsky 1925, quoted in Zavershneva and van der Veer 2018: 118). He wrote: 'The history of a child's attention is the history of the development of the organisation of his behaviour' (Vygotsky 1997b: 153), which involves neurological processes and cultural developments. Margaret Gredler (2009a) outlined three stages of mastery/self-regulation, with each representing a transformation of thinking towards self-regulation, from pre-mastery to external regulation and culminating in internal regulation. Preschool-aged children, who are typically in a stage of external regulation, benefit from supportive teaching strategies such as play planning (see also Chapter 7) and scaffolded interactions (see also Chapter 5). As discussed at this chapter's start, early childhood settings manifest a view of development and image of the child. In the model of teaching called participatory pedagogy in Finland, studied by Kangas et al. (2015), self-regulation was supported by the environment through routine opportunities created by teachers for discussion, negotiating and reflection.

## *Relationships with the nonhuman world*

Nature-based early childhood education prioritizes human and nonhuman relationships as essential for optimal human development and the sustainability of the 'natural world'. Nature education is a pedagogical approach combining open-ended play with environmental education. Nature pedagogy can range from learning in a classroom using materials drawn from nature, for example, 'pinecones and pebbles' instead of 'plastic math manipulatives' (Sobel 2016: 33), to immersive experiences in nature with a stress on outdoor education. Nature preschools in Germany and Scandinavian countries are based on several models: urban-based schools with regular opportunities to visit outdoor areas, preschools that have nature as a main element of their attached play area and the German *waldkindergarten* (forest preschools) located in natural settings with no fixed buildings (Lysklett 2017).

Rationales for nature education are based in humanist and posthumanist ideas. Humanist arguments draw on the child development ideas of Rousseau, Pestalozzi and Froebel, Montessori's notions of sensory education, Dewey's idea of the importance of active and engaged learners, Gardner's multiple intelligence theory (1999) that identifies a naturalist intelligence and Vygotsky's learning theory highlighting learning in the social world (Williams-Siegfredsen 2017). Nature education proponents with humanist orientations also emphasize developing children's eco-consciousness and responsibility for the natural environment (Lysklett 2017) and, conversely, are concerned about the impact of a 'nature deficit' on the well-being of children and the planet (Louv 2010).

Whereas European nature preschools generally have safety and behavioural rules and routines to 'restrict the children and to ensure they do not run away' (Lysklett 2017: 8), a study of children's activity in a forest preschool in Canada found them engaged in various types of 'risky play', for example, playing out of sight of the teacher (Coe 2017). The idea of risky play is based on notions of the biological and evolutionary purpose of play for survival and skill learning combined with ideas of nature education. As Hawkins (2017) describes, because children's authentic engagement with the environment necessarily includes risk, there are benefits for teachers to plan for risky possibilities for play involving elements and materials of nature such as rocks, fire, air, earth, plants, water and wood (Hawkins 2017: 87). When children are involved in risky play, or the subcategory of 'free-range, wild play' in which they encounter their environment from heights or at speed, 'nature becomes the third teacher' (Bailie 2016: 217).

Reconceptualist scholars challenge humanist perspectives for being discourses of development, raising questions about their relevance in the face of what we know about children and childhoods today. Posthumanist arguments for the benefit of children's encounters with nature are based on scholarship that has reconceptualized play- and child-centred methodologies, aiming to 'denaturalise childhood' in the words of Affrica Taylor (2013), drawing on Foucauldian, postcolonial, posthuman and poststructural arguments. Developmentalist perspectives claiming universal attributes of child nature also run counter to many Indigenous perspectives on child development.

Fikile Nxumalo (2015) employed a posthuman and postcolonial perspective to analyse the way nature is socially, materially and historically situated and is therefore not natural. She suggests using children's encounters with nature, for example, nature walks, as opportunities for 'refiguring presences' by restorying the forest in the context of settler colonial history and the history of Indigenous people. Aspects of Indigenous views of the human–nature relationship are compatible with reconceptualist views. As Carol Rowan (2017) described in her description of early childhood education in an Inuit community in northern Canada, learning with and on the land with the help of Elders can be a means of accessing Indigenous knowledge. Rowan explains that 'Inuit knowledge is made possible in relation to the land', which is considered a teacher and not just a learning resource (Rowan 2017: 7).

Human and nonhuman animal encounters in school classrooms take several forms. Live animals can be kept as classroom pets or for observation, dead animals or parts of animals can be used for science learning, and/or the products of dead animals can be studied. Cole and Stewart (2014) call these practices *anthroparchal*, meaning they advance human primacy and privilege. Moreover, they are examples of speciesism – 'discrimination based on species membership' (Cudworth 2014: 25) – which, in an intersectional analysis, works alongside other forms of stratification, such as class, race, gender and disability, to maintain systems of power. Taylor and Pacini-Ketchabaw (2017, 2019) describe the potential for developing a new ethic whereby child–animal relations can highlight the complex connectedness of the species. They contend that close consideration of urban child–wildlife relations, in which children share a common world with animals such as raccoons or kangaroos, can lead to insights into common world ethics practice.

## *Summary*

This chapter described how early experience influences children's development and learning and how children shape their world and are shaped by it. Experience was described in terms of the role played by human and natural environments, cultural beliefs and educational practices. An idealist view of nature was contrasted with a relational perspective in which a diverse range of environments are seen as developmental contexts having agentic qualities. The concept of development was examined as a childhood ideology rooted in a Western discourse of stage theories and developmentally appropriate teaching practices. Diverse perspectives on development were reviewed, including the contextual theories of anthropologists and sociocultural thinkers. Characteristics of human-designed learning environments were outlined, including the role of educational materials and space. Development and learning were explained in relation to the nonhuman world through nature pedagogy and the concept of 'common worlds' drawing on posthuman perspectives.

# CHAPTER FIVE

# Partners in Learning

***Proposition: Children and adults are co-constructors of knowledge and partners in learning.***

The capacity for continuous learning has always been viewed as important for both the individual and the society. However, our understanding of the relationship of learning, development and instruction/teaching has changed over the history of human societies and, more specifically, in philosophical and educational thought. The idea that children and adults are partners in children's learning and co-constructors of knowledge is relatively new in the history of educational thought. We explore this idea through the following questions:

1. What does it mean to learn?
2. Do children and adults learn in the same way? How do different theories view children's learning and development?
3. What does it mean for teachers to co-construct knowledge with children?

For additional information, reflective questions and practical implications visit: https://www.bloomsbury.com/cw/learning-to-teach-young-children/chapter-5/

## What does it mean to learn?

Broadly defined, learning is 'any process that in living organisms leads to permanent capacity change and which is not solely due to biological maturation or aging' (Illeris 2007: 3). Therefore, learning is not exclusive to our species. Like most living things, humans use their perceptual systems (sight, hearing, smell, touch, etc.) to discriminate between one object and another in their environment in order to adapt to it. However, unlike other living things, humans have extended the tendency to perceive details into a conceptual habit. As Brent Davis (2004) points out, that habit is vital for our human 'processes of self-definition and collective identification – to our having a reality. One tool that has greatly enabled our abilities to discern – our intelligence – is language. We use this flexible and powerful tool to weave possible worlds through naming, contrasting, likening, and other acts of association and dissociation' (7). For example, a young child who is offered two unfamiliar kinds of fruit might first touch the outside and feel the textures and then smell and taste them to learn more about them. However, the child's learning about each type of fruit is expanded when each is named as well as compared and contrasted in terms of its size (large and small), colour, shape (round, cylindrical, etc.), feel (smoothness, hardness, etc.), texture (juiciness, etc.), taste (sweetness, bitterness, sourness) and other key properties.

Learning language, as well as learning through and with language, as one of many symbolic forms (e.g. musical notes, numbers, signs, letters and other symbols) is what makes human learning unique (see also Chapter 6). When these symbolic forms are organized in systems, individual assumptions, beliefs and values can be shared with others. That is, humans can pass their knowledge and understanding of reality from one generation to another in one (instructional) form or another. Over time, the acquired knowledge and understandings can be transformed into a system of beliefs, assumptions and knowledge about reality that form worldviews shared by members of different groups/cultures. Therefore, human learning is more than a change in one's own capacities; it is also about becoming a member of a group/culture that holds a distinct worldview (see also Chapter 3). However, there are also similarities among worldviews, as in the case of Indigenous worldviews based on Indigenous peoples' relationship with the land/environment (Rice 2005). Summarizing several perspectives taught by elders, Leanne Simpson (2000) lists seven principles of the Indigenous worldview:

1 Knowledge is cyclical, holistic and dependent on relationships and connections with living and non-living beings and entities.
2 There are many truths, depending upon individual experience.
3 Everything is alive.
4 All things are equal and related.
5 The land is sacred.
6 There is an important relationship between humans and the spirit-world.
7 Humans are the least important beings in the cosmos. (171)

The outlined assumptions of Indigenous worldviews, Simpson explains further, form the foundation for the generation, communication, transmission and characterization of knowledge in Indigenous cultures in general. While historically one of the goals of learning has been the transmission of the worldview held by the (cultural) group from generation to generation, gaining or conforming to already existing knowledge is only one side of the process. If this were the only goal of learning, every new generation would simply adopt the same beliefs, understandings and skills as adults in previous generations. It would be impossible to advance knowledge. Creating new knowledge, then, is an equally important goal of learning and one that transforms human societies.

## *Traditional sources of knowledge*

In preliterate societies, folklore was the main source of knowledge about customs, beliefs and life itself that was to be passed from generation to generation. Folklore represents a repository of deep insight, cultural memory, traditional customs and biological history (Thompson 1989) as well as collective traditional wisdom. Typically gained from experience, stories, legends, proverbs and maxims, folklore provided a way of organizing one's belief system (Gredler 2009b) and was acquired by the young members through word of mouth. In Native American cultural life, legends 'gave concrete form to established beliefs and traditions that linked generations of people together' (Friesen 2013: 9). Indigenous knowledge defies categorization and relies on the knowledge and teachings of Elders and knowledge keepers (Battiste 2005). The learning spirit within the self is central to the Indigenous belief system about education. Enhancing and developing the learning spirit, which is tied to one's self-concept, is a key measure of success (Tunison 2007). Marlene Castellano (2000) described the characteristics of Indigenous knowledge as personal, oral, experiential, holistic and conveyed in narrative or metaphorical language, while Mahia Maurial (1999) identified three characteristics of Indigenous knowledge: it is local, holistic and oral. As Margo Greenwood (2009) notes, 'the importance of stories for many children today, and for Aboriginal children in particular, is critical – stories offer pathways to their Elders, their history, their knowledge(s) and ultimately to their identity as individuals and members of the collective' (67). While stories are still seen as central to Indigenous belief systems and have kept their significance in other ethnic and cultural groups, Eurocentric views of what constitutes knowledge have positioned them, at best, as 'additional' sources of knowledge. This marginalization or blinding of Indigenous knowledge 'has been and continues to be one of the major tools of colonization' (Walker 2004: 531).

## *European philosophical thought*

Philosophy became a major source of knowledge from 400 BC to nineteenth-century Europe (Gredler 2009b). 'In its most general terms', Gerald Gutek writes, 'philosophy is the human being's attempt to think speculatively, reflectively, and systematically about the universe and the human relationship to the universe' (1997: 2). Classical philosophers developed differing theories about the nature of the world which was to be known. The major figures in the ancient Greeks' philosophy – Plato and his pupil Aristotle – held contrasting views about the nature of reality and the world as a source of knowledge. Their ideas had a lasting impact on later learning theories. Plato, for example, saw reality as a creation of the mind and objects were reflections or flawed copies of perfect, timeless forms that exist in an ideal (Platonic) realm. He viewed learning as a process of developing innate/inborn ideas into a knowledge system (Gredler 1997: 6). Similar views of learning were held by the nativists in the nineteenth century who insisted that humans inherit abilities. Plato's idea of development as a movement towards an increasingly complete state of being was taken on by the maturationists (e.g. Arnold Gesell), who believed that children's learning results from an innate internal drive towards adulthood. For Gesell, however, children's inborn drive towards adulthood was a result of genetics and millions of years of evolution. From both nativist and maturationist perspectives, maximizing children's learning means listening to nature rather than nurture (see also Chapter 1). The idea of development as a linear progress was also adopted and advanced by the field of developmental psychology, and it still dominates early childhood theory and practice through the proliferation of developmentally appropriate practices.

By contrast, Aristotle defined reality as the relationships found in nature and the physical environment. He understood learning to occur through contact with the environment. In his view, knowledge is 'initially acquired by forming images of sensory experiences, and associations are then made among the images' (Gredler 2009b: 5). This idea was used, though modified, by behaviourists who described learning as a process of associating responses with objects or events defined as stimuli. Based in the practice of accumulating 'facts' through carefully designed experiments, the field of behavioural science/behaviourism was predominantly concerned with learning as the acquisition of skills, facts and concepts through practice. Through the use of rewards for compliance with preferred responses and punishments to deter undesirable responses, one can be conditioned/taught any desirable behaviour. The use of tokens as a reward system in a classroom is an example of such understanding of learning.

The Western idea that knowledge is created, not discovered, can be traced to Giambattista Vico, a philosopher from the Enlightenment era. Unlike many of his contemporaries (e.g. John Locke), Vico believed that knowledge making is not a progression towards certainty (i.e. Truth). Rather, 'scientific truth was not totally created in the mind, but through experimentation that bridged mental constructs and physical constraints' (Davis 2004: 116). The idea of knowledge creation took a more central stage more than a century later when Charles Darwin's radical proposal of an 'origin of species' defined a new reality – a reality that is in constant change rather than static and/or predetermined. Vico's view of knowledge as created influenced a number of philosophical traditions, including constructivist theories of learning seen in both Piaget's and Vygotsky's work. These influences are evident in the philosophy of Reggio Emilia schools, as first formulated by their founder, Loris Malaguzzi.

Collectively, the Western philosophical traditions have contributed to privileging 'scientific truths' about child development and learning and have become the dominant foundation of ECE theory and practice. Such 'truths', Jayne Osgood says, are 'linked to a modernist desire for certainty, order, rationality, standardisation, and universality' (2015: 157). These dominant truths directly shape pedagogical or curriculum frameworks and create narrowly defined notions of 'quality' early childhood practice (Dahlberg et al. 2013) by prescriptions based on exclusion and selection. Through the discursive power of globalization, the dominant discourse of the West that privileges certain topics and objects of knowledge has normalized particular understandings of the nature of children, childhood, motherhood and ECE professional practice. These ways of framing practice have led to the exclusion of majority-world/Indigenous systems of knowing and being in the world, as well as ways of relating to other beings, both human and nonhuman. Indigenous ways of knowing and being are seen as 'old fashioned and unscientific to dialogue with the voice of the dominant discourse of the "West" that seems appealingly rational, scientific and modern' (Gupta 2015: 154). Indigenous knowledge contrasts starkly with minority-world dominant discourse or theory in ECE that is rooted in the developmental psychology of the nineteenth century. Recognizing that most of the theories still in operation in ECE are 'neither culturally neutral nor politically innocent' (Taylor and Pacini-Ketchabaw 2015: 2) is an important step in rethinking ECE theories and practices.

# Do children and adults learn in the same way? How do different theories view children's learning and development?

## *Cognitive constructivism: Piaget's theory of learning*

Constructivism is a theory of knowing that emphasizes 'the role a person plays in constructing his or her knowledge rather than absorbing it directly from the environment' (Branscombe et al. 2003: 10). The constructivists' theory is grounded in the view that our knowledge of the world is rooted in our experience. Cognitive constructivists such as Piaget advanced the idea that knowledge is built inside the individual learner's mind as they interact with objects in their environment. From Piaget's perspective, in the process of developing new knowledge, the individual and the environment cannot be separated. Rather, the physical world shapes and constrains which meanings can be constructed in any given context. Individuals act on their environments based on what they already know and have experienced – their history of

FIGURE 5.1 *Children's interactions with different environments influence their development*

experience – therefore, a person's knowledge is uniquely developed. Piaget rejected the idea of learning as knowledge transmission because such a model reflects the understanding that knowledge is fixed and ignores the process of knowledge formation.

Piaget saw childhood as a necessary and important phase when children's thought patterns undergo changes as they develop the ability to think logically. He challenged the behaviourists' view that the same principles of learning apply to both children and adults. Piaget described children as having distinctive and changing patterns of thinking. His theory of cognitive development advanced his belief that cognitive development follows a series of stages and sub-stages that the child must progress through. A child cannot skip a stage or return to a previous stage. The metaphor most commonly used to capture this understanding is a child climbing a ladder or stairs (Figure 5.1) beginning from the sensorimotor stage and climbing to the formal operational stage of cognitive development (see also Chapters 1 and 4). In Piaget's view, therefore, children's learning followed their cognitive development.

Although Piaget's theory viewed children's growth of intelligence as influenced by four factors – the physical environment, social environment, maturation and equilibrium – he saw the child as a solitary knower/learner, constructing knowledge *within* their head.

## Criticism of Piagetian views and their implications for classroom practice

Piaget's concept of readiness – that children's stage of cognitive development determines what the child can and should learn – has resulted in pedagogical practices focused on matching the environment to children's presumed (age-related) developmental level. Therefore, the goal of education was to engage children in age-appropriate learning tasks. There are three main areas of critique of Piaget's theory: the concept of readiness, the idea of child-centred practice and the role of the teacher.

Piaget's concept of readiness suggests that there is very little that adults can do to enhance children's thinking. The assumption that readiness can be identified often leaves the teacher waiting for the child to be 'ready' to learn. As a result, the teacher is 'either too early and they [children] can't learn it, or it is too late, and they already know it' (Duckworth 1987: 31). Despite numerous studies' findings demonstrating that preschool children are capable of performing concrete operational tasks successfully three to four years prior to the time indicated by Piaget's stage theory (e.g. Meadows 1993), dividing up childhood development into stages is still a common practice in organizing the Western education system (Fleer 2010). Feminist poststructuralists have criticized early childhood practices based on Piaget's view of development for encouraging educators to wait to raise issues of equity and diversity when children are cognitively ready to deal with such complex concepts (MacNaughton 2003; see also Chapter 8).

As Sean MacBlain (2014) notes, Piaget believed the role of the teacher/practitioner was to nurture children's emotional and social development by removing any barriers to their engagement in practical activities. This view was similar to that of Froebel, Montessori and Dewey (see also Chapter 1). From a critical postmodern perspective, the concept of child-centredness is highly problematic because it has become a dominant way of framing practice in which children 'require freedom from adult authority to explore ideas independently and make sense of their world' (Ryan 2005: 99).

The taken-for-granted notion of child-centredness (Fleer 2003) has resulted in ECE practices in which children are further removed from the day-to-day lives of their families and communities by providing them with child-sized equipment, 'safe' toys and other play materials and universal age-appropriate activities. Such institutionalized practices are even more detrimental for children from non-Western family backgrounds, including Indigenous communities where children are an integral part of the everyday life of the family and the community, which is not 'centred' on them.

Child-centredness incorporates another aspect of Piaget's cognitive constructivist theory of learning – the process of learning through discovery. He described the child as a lone scientist who creates their own sense of the world is able to make their own mistakes and find solutions on their own or in interactions with their peers. Piaget asserted that true logical thinking is constructed by the learner in self-directed or peer-collaborative research on topics that are of interest to students, mostly in science and mathematics.

Piaget (1973) saw the role of the teacher as being attuned to the spontaneous mental activity of the child, accomplished through observing children's experiments in their environments and keeping track of these observations through note taking. Because the role of education, in his view, was to support the child's spontaneous research, he recommended engaging children in active enquiry of topics of interest to them to stimulate that spontaneous research. This view, Valerie Walkerdine (1990) argued, led to the construction of the child in a child-centred environment as active, free, autonomous, omnipotent and essentially male, which in turn positioned the female teacher as passive. Paul Connolly (2004) states that in Western ECE practices, Piaget's notion of child-centred development and his concept of readiness have 'relegated the role of adults in the children's learning to the "sidelines"' (4). Elly Singer (1996) suggested that child-centred methods separate children from adults, leaving 'nothing to talk about together' (32).

From a postmodern perspective, to overcome the outcomes of child-centred pedagogy, the early childhood educator needs to become a co-constructor of knowledge and a resource for children as they make sense of and co-construct their knowledge of the world (Dahlberg et al. 2013). It is this role as a thinker and reflective practitioner (see also Chapter 9) that would allow for 'decentring' the child.

## *Dialectical/social constructivism: Vygotsky's sociocultural theory of learning*

Social constructivism emphasizes 'the importance of culture and context in understanding what occurs in society and constructing knowledge based on this understanding' (MacBlain 2014: 45). In Vygotsky's social constructivist theory of learning, knowledge is viewed as being actively constructed by learners as a result of their interactions with others in meaningful activities (Figure 5.2). He 'extended the concept of environment beyond the physical context to include social and affective activity, products of cultural development such as speech and other symbol systems, and social systems and formations' (Mahn 2003: 130). His theory made a radical shift in understanding learning not just as an individual learner's activity but as a sociocultural undertaking. Signs, symbols, texts and other symbolic artefacts (see Table 5.1 in companion website) of the culture in which an individual learner is situated are mastered in collaboration with other, more knowledgeable members of the cultural group. These symbolic artefacts are the psychological tools that help individuals to enhance psychological functions such as perception, memory and attention, among others. Vygotsky identified language as the main psychological tool, or the tool of the mind that helps the learner acquire or appropriate other psychological tools.

Vygotsky's child, therefore, is situated in a specific context and develops knowledge and understanding through interactions with and participation in the everyday meaningful tasks of the family and cultural community (Fleer 2003). Vygotsky (1978) addressed the social dimension of learning as follows: 'Every function in the child's cultural development appears twice: first, on the social level, and later, on the individual level; first *between* people (*interpsychological*), and then *inside* the child (*intrapsychological*)' (57, italics in original). Vygotsky suggested that human cognitive development relies on both biological and cultural (or social) lines; that is, it is a sociogenetic process. He drew an important distinction between lower- and higher-order thinking and maintained that the social activities experienced by children can be seen as bridges across which children move from lower- to higher-order functions (see Table 5.2 in companion website).

The interdependence between children's individual growth and development and the sociocultural contexts in which they are situated is defined by Vygotsky 'as a process that is characterized by a unity of material and mental aspects, a unity of the social and the personal' (1998: 190). This unity is not only specific and unique to the age of the child; it is also experienced, perceived and interpreted in different ways by different children. As discussed in Chapter 3, Vygotsky (1994: 339) introduced the term *perezhivanie* to define the particular way in which social experiences are appropriated and internalized by children. Vygotsky saw this phenomenon as children's experiences of meaning making (see also Chapters 3 and 6).

FIGURE 5.2 *Children co-construct knowledge*

Vygotsky underscored that young learners' independent exploration of their environment could lead to the development of immature concepts that might not serve them well in school contexts. He therefore came up with the theory of mediation, according to which the development of children's higher mental functions depends on the presence of mediating agents in their interactions with their environments. These mediating agents can be one of two types: symbolic and human (Kozulin 2003).

## *Symbolic mediators*

Vygotsky (1978) made an important distinction between experiences that result from individuals' direct contact with the environment and experiences shaped by interactions that are mediated by symbolic tools. One example of the function of such mediators is 'counting fingers' (Vygotsky 1978: 127) in which one's body parts, such as fingers, can serve as external (primitive) symbolic tools that organize cognitive functions involved in elementary mathematical operations. Higher-order symbolic mediators include speech, different signs, writing, formulae and graphic organizers. Tools and signs differ primarily in terms of their mediating functions, as tools mediate human activity or action while signs mediate 'human social processes and thinking' (Vygotsky 1981: 135).

It is important to note that symbols may remain useless unless their meaning as cognitive tools is properly mediated to the child by an adult or more experienced member of the culture. In other words, the mere availability of symbols such as written signs, pictures, diagrams, maps or other advanced organizers does not mean that they will be used by the learners as psychological tools. The relationship between human and symbolic mediators is at the core of Vygotsky's sociocultural theory of learning (Figure 5.3).

## *Human mediators*

While Vygotsky (1978) was concerned with internalization of the tools, subsequent theorists contend that appropriation more accurately reflects the learning process. As Rogoff (1995) explained, internalization suggests a transfer of knowledge, while appropriation suggests that students co-construct shared understandings with their teachers and achieve an understanding of the tool that reflects their mutual engagement. In other words, not all interactions lead to internalization/appropriation of psychological tools or signs. They have to have mediational quality in order to play this role. Mediational concepts such as scaffolding (Wood et al. 1976), apprenticeship (Rogoff 1990), guided participation (Rogoff 1990), cognitive apprenticeship (Collins et al. 1989), appropriation (Rogoff 1990) and reciprocal teaching (Palincsar and Brown 1984) are elaborations on Vygotsky's initial ideas

FIGURE 5.3 *Mediating children's learning*

of the mediational quality of human interactions. Some of the common methods of scaffolding originally identified by Wood et al. (1976) included recruitment (or engaging the learner's interest), reduction in degrees of freedom (simplifying the task), direction maintenance (keeping the learner motivated), marking salient or relevant features of the task, controlling the learner's frustration, and demonstration or modelling (see companion website for examples). Explicit and implicit mediators can also function as means of scaffolding. In using explicit mediators, the teacher might insert concrete objects into a learner's ongoing activity that would help the child complete the task. In the case of implicit mediators, the teacher introduces more abstract mediators such as oral speech, mnemonic devices, actions or gestures into the learner's ongoing activity (Wertsch 2007).

## *Relationship between human and symbolic mediators*

When examined cross-culturally, the relationship between human and symbolic mediators appears to be culture specific rather than universal. Rogoff's (1990) comparative ethnographic research demonstrates that guided participation of children in activities with adults serving as human mediators depends on the sociocultural goals considered important by a given community (see also Chapters 2 and 3). It is important to note that the use of different mediational practices based on the goals and priorities of different communities does not mean that one community is superior to another. Rather, it means that children who are raised in communities that use symbolic mediators (e.g. literacy) differently from the way they are used at school do not have a high level of success in school-based learning. To use the examples from Chapter 3 (i.e. LeVine et al.'s 1994 study), children who are socialized in the pedagogical model are likely to succeed in a school context where reading, writing and questioning are praised and reinforced. In the same context, children socialized in the paediatric model, where adults might be reading but emphasize children's participation in everyday activities and use storytelling as moral guidance, may be seen as lacking interest in written language and 'at risk' for failing in school (see also Chapter 8).

## *Vygotsky's view on everyday/spontaneous and school/ scientific concept development*

The differences between children in what they know and can do as they begin formal school are related to their families' and communities' everyday life and practices. Children's development of everyday concepts is based on the 'families' cultural practices associated with their experiences with objects outside of an integrated system of knowledge' (Hedegaard 2007: 248). This view of learning is consistent with many Indigenous cultures in Australia, for example, in which learning does not happen in designated spaces, such as schools and ECE settings, but rather is embedded in everyday life of the family and the community (Fleer 2003). In contrast, scientific concepts are connected to children's activities in settings with conventional symbolic systems that the child learns at school (literacy, numeracy, etc.). Therefore, these concepts are organized in an integrated system of knowledge in relation to other concepts about academic disciplines. In early childhood, everyday concept formation dominates over scientific concept formation. The change occurs around school age (i.e. seven years of age), when scientific concept formation begins to dominate and enriches the child's everyday concepts (Hedegaard 2007: 249). However, 'there is no sudden discontinuity in human development from the natural to the sociocultural. Rather, there is a series of accommodations in the individual's organisation of experientially derived knowledge to conventional knowledge systems as learning in and through language progresses' (Nelson 1995: 240).

It is important to stress here that Vygotsky viewed everyday concepts as a foundation for the development of scientific concepts, explaining that 'the link between these two lines of development reflects their true nature. This is the link of the zone of proximal development and the actual development' (1987: 220). (See Table 5.3 in companion website.) Using a number of Vygotsky's works in which he elaborates on the concept of zone of proximal development (ZPD), Seth Chaiklin (2003) provided an overview of critiques and common (mis)conceptions about ZPD (see Table 5.4 in companion website). In Chaiklin's view, terms such as 'scaffolding' and 'assisted instruction' are more appropriate than ZPD when referring to teaching/instructional practices aimed at learning specific subject matter concepts or skills.

## Criticisms of Vygotskian views

Due to his untimely passing in 1934 at age thirty-seven, many of Vygotsky's theories were not fully developed and have been criticized by many for lacking specific guidelines for implementation. In addition, in the process of translating his works into English, some of the Marxist influences on his theories were lost or there was an overemphasis on the ZPD not found in his original works. One of the most controversial aspects of his theory has been that he put disproportionate weight on language/speech as a tool for cognitive development while understating the role of other, nonverbal types of symbolic representation (Bodrova and Leong 2007). Particularly problematic were the claims that language precedes thought and that spoken language is the primary means for developing higher-order thinking (see also Chapter 6). His emphasis on the role of adults and more capable peers in mediation and more specifically in shared activities has led to criticisms that he did not sufficiently stress the importance of the child's active participation in such activities, resulting in an oversimplification of the messiness of adult–child interactions and the complexity of learning within the ZPD. He also did not acknowledge the power relationships between adults and children; thus his sociocultural theory has not resulted in ECE practices in which context-bound, culturally specific ways of thinking about and being with children are encouraged.

Pedagogical practices based on the main point of sociocultural theory – that learning leads development – demand that teachers structure learning/teaching interactions in ways that lead children's development. The focus on the pedagogical task of promoting and constructing learning does not eliminate entirely the overarching goal of early years' education – the achievement of children's optimal development. Therefore, the sociocultural frame did not abandon developmentalism but rather reconfigured it (Buchanan 2017: 184). In addition, neither Vygotsky nor post-Vygotskian scholars have problematized the assumption that scientific/disciplinary knowledge is objective and neutral, therefore implying that knowledge is 'an absolute or final nature ... instead [of] a selecting out, among the many readings and possibilities present in a concrete instance, of those characteristics and aspects that will promote the goals of the individual or group doing the selecting' (Ransom 1997: 19). By choosing what to emphasize and what to present in a positive or negative light, John Ransom argues, 'knowledge shapes the world it describes' (1997: 19). Therefore, by presenting children's acquisition of scientific concepts as the ultimate goal of education, Vygotsky and post-Vygotskian scholars contributed to the perpetuation of educational practice that did not question the established 'regimes of truth' (Foucault 1980) that promoted the view of a single reality and that shaped a universal, single subject/person. The power relationships that shape the scientific understanding of the world and our relationship to it therefore were not questioned.

## What does it mean for teachers to co-construct knowledge with children?

Vygotsky's work on the interdependence of individual and social processes in children's meaning making has had a long-lasting impact on educational practice. He used the term 'collaboration' to capture the relationship between teacher and student in school settings, where, he said, 'the teacher, working with the school child on a given question explains, informs, inquires, corrects, and forces the child himself [sic] to explain; when the child solves the problem, although the teacher is not present, he or she must make independent use of the earlier collaboration' (Vygotsky 1987: 216).

Vygotsky's theory also brought to the forefront the understanding that thinking with language and other symbolic tools is culturally shaped and influences how children in that culture learn to think. Language and interaction between individuals, both adults and peers, create what Vygotsky called shared activity – an activity in which mental functions are shared. The role of the teacher in a shared activity is either as a participant in the activity or as a person who promotes, plans and creates opportunities for shared activities to develop between children and their partners, or both. Teachers participate in shared activities by engaging in educational dialogue in which their questions guide the students towards specific goals they have set for the activity. In such a dialogue, teachers model strategies for problem solving and construct a template for learning that the students can use in other contexts. As Elena Bodrova and Deborah Leong (2007) point out, 'in monitoring a child's engagement in an educational dialogue, the teacher must answer two questions about the child's thought process: (a) how the child arrived at this answer, and (b) will the child's answer ultimately fit into the system of concepts for this area?' (85–6). Depending on the answers to these two questions, the teacher determines the level of support within the child's ZPD. Vygotsky defined his concept of the zone of proximal development as 'the distance between the actual developmental level as determined by independent problem solving and the level of potential development as determined through problem solving under adult guidance or in collaboration with more capable peers' (1978: 86). Scaffolds that the child needs to achieve a higher level of independent performance will be gradually removed as they internalize the concepts (see companion website for an example). Shared activities and scaffolding are not limited to adult–child interactions but also include peer interactions (see companion website for an example).

The recently introduced concept of sustained shared thinking occurring in play-based environments (Siraj-Blatchford 2007) builds on Vygotsky's conceptualization of everyday and scientific concepts. It also sets the stage for transformative pedagogy in the early years based on a deeper understanding of concept formation in children's everyday lives. Hedegaard and Chaiklin (2005) suggest that the most powerful learning contexts are those in which educators keep in mind both the everyday concepts children have experiences with in their real-world lives and the scientific concepts within the subject matter they are being taught in the school context. Consideration of both concepts builds on and expands students' funds of knowledge (Moll et al. 1992). Hedegaard and Chaiklin (2005) call this the double move in teaching – teaching in which both the school subject knowledge (scientific concept formation) and the importance of everyday cognition (everyday concept formation) become explicit in the teacher's mind. Because play naturally creates a ZPD, play can become a pedagogical tool. More specifically, an imaginary situation allows the teacher to explore what the children already know and/or introduce scientific concepts relevant to their play (Fleer 2010).

The double move in teaching rejects the Piagetian idea that children will develop scientific concepts on their own by exploring the materials provided by the teacher. Rather, teachers need to actively create a 'contextual intersubjectivity' (Fleer 2010: 15) between themselves and the children.

Teachers might do so by moving in and out of the imaginary situation, which engages the children in sustained shared thinking. In the example Marilyn Fleer provides, a teacher helps a child develop scientific knowledge of an ecological ecosystem and habitat by building on the child's everyday knowledge of the danger of being bitten by a bull ant. By providing the child with a map, a magnifying glass and a paper clip, the teacher helped him adopt, in his pretend play, the role of a scientist who explored the lives of ants. In the process, both the child and the teacher stepped in and out of the role of a 'scientist', which created an imaginary situation and allowed them to develop their ecological understanding of the playground area in general, not just the life of the ants. In Vygotsky's theory, imagination is grounded in the real here and now; it is a conscious act (Bodrova 2008) that is seen as central to both play and learning (Hakkarainen 2010). As Vygotsky pointed out, 'the processes of invention or artistic creativity demand a substantial participation in both realistic thinking and imagination. The two act as a unity' (1987: 349).

Therefore, 'teaching from an educative play perspective (compared to more open uses of play-based learning) assumes that encounters or interactions and communication with more knowledgeable others would be necessary to support learning through play' (Edwards and Cutter-Mackenzie 2013: 57). From a sociocultural perspective, play-based learning in early childhood education is now commonly described as requiring adult interaction to support children's access to content knowledge in relation to their culturally situated home and community experiences (see also Chapter 7).

## *Influence of constructivist theories on the Reggio Emilia philosophy*

Fleer (2003) describes the practices of Reggio Emilia schools as being based on the sociocultural orientation to learning that has three main characteristics: '(1) the boundary of the learning environment extends well into the community and the centres themselves are created with a community orientation in mind; (2) the spaces within the centres do not follow the traditional early childhood environment; and (3) the equipment and materials available to children are real, representing what is available in the adult world' (68). Malaguzzi (1998), however, acknowledges the influences of both Piaget's and Vygotsky's theories of learning on Reggio Emilia's pedagogical approach, and stresses Reggio's unique take on these theories. This is not a surprise given that both Piaget and Vygotsky viewed the child as active participants in the learning process – actively seeking meaning and striving for understanding. The focus on the process, rather than the product, of learning is also common to both Piaget's and Vygotsky's views. Vygotsky's influence is most noticeable in the Reggio practice of learning as collaborative and interpersonal. However, in his Vygotskian commentary on the Reggio Emilia approach, Jake Stone (2012) points out the dissonance between the Reggio Emilia approach and Vygotskian theory in relation to the role of the educator in children's learning. Like Piaget, Reggio's pedagogical approach puts an emphasis on discovery learning that strengthens children's potential to explore and discover for themselves or with a group of peers. Children are seen to develop their own concepts and methods of discovery with minimal guidance from the teacher, who simply provides technical support for the children's own ideas. The objective of education, according to Malaguzzi (1998), is to increase possibilities for the child to invent and discover. Regarding the relationship between learning and teaching, he declares the priority of the former over the latter: 'It is not that we ostracise teaching but that we declare, "Stand aside for a while and leave room for learning, observe carefully what children do, and then, if you have understood well, perhaps teaching will be different from before"' (82). Malaguzzi is critical of teachers who, though democratic in their intentions, use unidimensional, 'undemocratic teaching strategies' (83) that can damage children's creativity. For him, the 'central act of adults is to activate, especially indirectly, the meaning-making competencies of children as a basis of all learning. They must try to capture the right moment, and then find the right approaches, for bringing together, into a fruitful dialogue, their meanings and interpretations with those of the children' (81). Malaguzzi appears to support Piaget's concept of readiness and insists 'it is useless to assert that readiness of children is too hard to observe' (84). Furthermore, he (1998) is quite critical of Vygotsky's concept of the ZPD as being 'ambiguous' and suggestive of 'the old ghosts of teaching that we tried to chase away' (83).

The emphasis in the Reggio approach is on the agency of the child to follow their interests and seek to make sense of the world through engagement with the environment and with others in it. This emphasis seems to differ substantially from Vygotsky's view of pedagogy, according to which children also need to be introduced to the practices, concepts and ideas of their cultures – coherent cultural tools that provide a conceptual frame for understanding their experiences. As Stone (2012) suggests, even if Reggio teachers are not conscious of it, they constantly make cultural tools available to the children through various means, one of which is the so-called provocation. Janice Novakowski (2015) states that 'a provocation is beautifully presented and is an invitation to explore, investigate, learn, represent and create' (4). Provocations also require the teacher and others to listen closely to children in order to devise a means to provoke further thinking and action (Fraser 2012). Along with presenting provocations, teachers ask questions and initiate conversations to bring about action. Provocations do not come just from the teacher, but often arise from conversations and interactions with other children, parents and adults (Figure 5.4).

The philosophy of Reggio Emilia is considered exemplary in terms of giving children power and seeing them as capable, competent and with

FIGURE 5.4 *Using provocations*

great learning capacity (see also Chapter 1). It is argued, however, that the approach has become 'a new foundational truth about children and parts of their selves that should be the focus of early education' (Buchanan 2017: 173).

## *Summary*

This chapter explored the role of adults in children's learning according to constructivist orientations, both cognitive (Piagetian) and sociocultural (Vygotskian) constructivism. Sources of knowledge are outlined from classical Western philosophical and Indigenous worldviews. In accordance with dialectical/social constructivist view, the expert or adult role is conceptualized as one of actively engaging with and mediating children's learning about the world and themselves. Approaches to co-construction of knowledge with children, such as scaffolding and guided participation, are discussed. Recent critiques of constructivist theories of learning and development from various theoretical perspectives have raised issues of power in adult–child relationships, as well as children's contribution to knowledge creation. These theories emphasize the need to recognize Indigenous knowledge(s) as a means of decolonizing ECE practices. The chapter also discussed the influence on Piaget's and Vygotsky's theories of learning on Reggio Emilia's approach.

# CHAPTER SIX

# Meaning-making and Representing Knowledge

***Proposition: Children make meaning and represent knowledge in a variety of ways.***

Meaning-making is inseparable from the symbolic systems utilized by the culture in which children are situated. Children and adults use imagery, art, music, drama and other ever-changing forms of making and communicating meaning. Both meaning-making and knowledge representation are enabled *and* constrained by language, as well as by history and traditions. Children make sense of the world when their minds are actively engaged in meaningful, shared interactions with adults and peers in a range of social, historic, cultural and linguistic contexts. The diversity of meanings and representations of children's knowledge reflects the nonlinear dynamics of their understandings of the world. We organize these ideas around the following questions:

1 How do children make meaning of the world?
2 What does knowledge representation mean?
3 What is the role of language as one of the symbolic tools through which humans make meaning and construct knowledge?
4 What is the role of children's art and art making as significant ways of knowing, problem solving and creating that allow for the construction of multiple meanings?

For additional information, reflective questions and practical implications visit: https://www.bloomsbury.com/cw/learning-to-teach-young-children/chapter-6/

# How do children make meaning of the world?

Learning involves the active construction of meaning by the learner, and it can be transformative to the person experiencing it. In learning, Peter Jarvis says, 'we experience the process of becoming' (2009: 29). The notion of learning as a personal change is related to meaningfulness – 'a personal intentional striving towards something meaningful' (Wiberg and Qvortrup 2017: 14). Learning also involves the whole person – both body and mind – whose experiences in the world begins with sensations that gradually acquire meaning through interactions and relationships with other human beings. Many Indigenous cultures share a holistic view of learning, often represented as a circle divided into four equal, interconnected and balanced parts: intellectual, emotional, spiritual and physical. Although on the surface these parts are similar to 'Western' holistic views of learning that include 'body and mind', the meaning Indigenous peoples have for each of the parts is quite different. For example, the intellectual segment of the circle is about life-long learning and teaching; the emotional segment is about inner reflections and flexibility to adapt and change; the physical segment is about the necessity of physical well-being and the spiritual segment includes interactions with others, both humans and nonhuman beings and a higher purpose in life other than oneself (Toulouse 2011).

## Cognitive constructivist views

Constructivist theories recognize knowledge construction as a way in which individuals make sense of the world. From this perspective, meaning-forming (meaning-making) is defined as 'the activity by which we shape a coherent meaning out of the raw material of our outer and inner experiencing' (Kegan 1994: 44). Therefore, meaning-forming/-making involves not just perceiving the world around us but also simultaneously interpreting what is being perceived. Similar to cognitive constructivists such as Piaget (see also Chapter 6), Robert Kegan (1982, 1994) contends that an event does not have a particular solitary meaning attached that simply gets transferred to the individual. Instead, meaning is created between the event and the individual's reaction to it. Kegan calls this process meaning-making.

Kegan's theory of meaning-making proposed that there is a 'zone of mediation' – 'the place where the event is privately composed, made sense of, the place where it actually becomes an event for that person' (1982: 2). This zone where meaning gets made is also referred to by personality psychologists as the self, the ego or the person. Kegan states: 'The activity of being a person is the activity of meaning-making. There is no feeling, no experience, no thought, no perception, independent of a meaning-making context in which it becomes a feeling, an experience, a thought, a perception, because we are the meaning-making context' (1982: 11). His theory of meaning-making explains how individuals' understanding of their experience, of themselves and of their interpersonal relationships evolves over their lifespan; it is a path of self-development towards self-authorship.

In reviewing Kegan's (1994) theory, Ignelzi (2000) explains that Kegan calls the major places along the path of self-evolution 'orders of consciousness' (7). As a person's development proceeds through these orders, meaning-making undergoes changes that affect the person's view of the self, relations to others and understanding of experience. Kegan maintains that there is consistency in an individual's meaning-making at any particular point in time. That is, how one understands knowledge or experience is directly related to how one understands others and the self. However, each order is a qualitative shift in meaning-making and complexity from the order before it. Kegan explains that we do not give up what we have learned in a previous order; we move the elements of the earlier meaning-making system. In so doing, we transform, changing the actual form of our understanding of the world. Like Piaget's theory, Kegan's meaning-making theory is developmentalist in nature (Ignelzi 2000). This means that the internal structures individuals use to organize meaning-making, and therefore the self, change and evolve in regular, systematic and predictable ways over time and experience. Unlike Piaget's theory, Kegan's theory maintains that no order is inherently better than any other order, just as a more complex idea is not necessarily more valuable than a simple one. (See Table 6.1 in companion website for Kegan's orders of consciousness and examples.)

Similar to Piaget, who saw effective instruction as being at the child's current level of cognitive development, Kegan viewed the role of educators as building developmental bridges that are meaningful to students' current meaning-making and that facilitate a more complex way of understanding. For him, learning should aim at both *what* we know (informational learning) and *how* we know it (transformational learning). As a whole, Kegan's theory privileges the traditionally Western orientation towards autonomy over other kinds of orientations towards connection to community. Moreover, it implies a progression towards an 'ideal person', moving towards a particular desirable norm, a standard of some sort that is set by the society and facilitated by parents, educators and others along the way.

## *Social constructivist views*

According to a social constructivist theory of learning (i.e. Vygotsky), children make meaning of the world by co-participating in a collective with others. More specifically, meaning-making is the participation in an activity system about which participants share understandings concerning what they are doing and what that means for their lives and their communities.

Meaning-making occurs in a process of interactions among individuals in shared activities in the context of sociocultural circumstances, including language and other symbolic tools, disciplinary knowledge and other culturally shaped knowledge systems (see also Chapter 5). The learner's coherence of understanding or meaning-making is therefore embedded in a group, the members of which develop meaning. Social constructivists emphasize interpersonal processes, norms and cultural tools and how these help individuals become integral part of collectives – groups and cultures. They believe therefore that 'cognition is always collective: embedded in, enabled by, and constrained by the social phenomenon of language; caught up in layers of history and tradition; confined by well-established boundaries of acceptability; defined by joint interests, shared assumptions, and common sense' (Davis et al. 2008: 103).

From a social constructivist perspective, the concept of situated learning focuses on the process through which individuals, including children, enter into a number of communities of practice. These communities are defined as a 'set of relations among persons, activity and the world, over time and in relation with other tangential and overlapping communities of practice' (Lave and Wenger 1991: 98). Preparing food is an everyday activity in which children are likely to be part of. Although food is commonly prepared in a family, the cultural practices of food preparation are evident in family members' ways of approaching the task. The role of the adult/educator is to mediate, mentor and model in the process of interactions that helps the child to become a member of an established community of practice and make sense of that practice (see also Chapter 3). Language used by the parents in the process helps the child understand the significance of the different actions associated with the task and make sense of what is observed. It is important to stress that within the social constructivist theoretical orientation, cultures are not replicated systems. That is, they do not copy themselves inflexibly from one generation to the next, but rather modify themselves. Learning within any given culture then also aims at modifying it. In the example of food preparation, the availability of new cooking tools, food techniques and fusion of spices can modify the overall process of food preparation the child would engage in later years.

## What does knowledge representation mean?

Most Western philosophers since Plato (see also Chapter 5) have attempted to construct a system in which 'something Real would and could be represented through thought. This Real is understood to be an external or universal subject or substance, existing "out there" independent of the knower. The philosopher's desire is to "mirror", register, or make present the Real. Truth is understood as correspondence to it' (Flax 1990: 34). The postmodern perspective rejects this reflective approach to representation and asserts that there are multiple realities, depending on the power relationships that shape the experiences, beliefs and perspectives of those who use different sources of knowledge to make sense of the world around them. From this perspective, therefore, 'construction replaces representation' (Dahlberg et al. 2013: 25). Constructivist approaches do not deny the existence of the material world; they stress the role of the 'social actors who use the conceptual systems of their culture and their linguistic and other representational systems to construct meaning, to make the world meaningful and to communicate about that world meaningfully to others' (Hall 1997: 11).

Randall Davis, Howard Shrobe and Peter Szolovits (1993) point out that the notion of knowledge representation can be understood in terms of five distinct roles it plays, one of which is defined in psychology as intelligent reasoning – a distinct characteristic of human behaviour. From this perspective, representation and reasoning are intertwined: We cannot talk about one without discussing the other. The understanding of knowledge representation as intelligent reasoning has given rise to both the extensive work on human problem solving and the large collection of knowledge-based systems. However, very different views of the nature of intelligent reasoning are possible. One of these views, found in the work of Jerome Bruner among others, is embedded in the idea of artificial intelligence.

The question of knowledge representation is at the heart of Bruner's theory. He asked, 'What is meant by representation? What does it mean to translate experience into a model of the world?' (Bruner 1966: 10). He suggested that individuals represent their learning and the world in which they live through three modes: enactive (action based), iconic (image based) and symbolic (language based). The first, an enactive mode of representation, is developed through action in cases when using imagery or words does not translate into action. For example, teaching a child to ride a bicycle by explaining how to do it or showing pictures will likely not lead to the child's learning how to do it unless they can try to use an actual bicycle. Enactive representation is based on learning 'responses and forms of habituation' (Bruner 1966: 11). In infancy, events and objects are defined in terms of actions taken towards them. For example, an infant might associate the sound a rattle makes with the motion required to produce the noise. Thus, if a rattle is the same as the movement needed to produce the 'shake', the infant would believe that moving their hand in a particular way would produce a sound. In later childhood, objects develop autonomy and are conceivable without taking action. The second mode of representation, the iconic, is generated by images. The child recalls or represents understandings using pictures and diagrams. Like the enactive mode, the iconic mode has its limitations. For example, the images formed by the child are initially restricted to observable characteristics of the objects, such as colour and shape. Images associated with higher-order concepts, such as friendship and kindness, can be represented only through language. The formation of the third mode of representation, the symbolic, is based on translating

FIGURE 6.1 *Iconic or symbolic representation?*

experience into language. 'Its hallmark', Bruner explained, 'is that it is symbolic in nature, with certain features of symbolic systems that are only now coming to be understood' (1966: 11; see also Figure 6.1).

These modes, Bruner emphasized, do not follow one another, as in Piaget's or Kegan's stage theories, but are integrated with one another. Children's development of symbolic representations once they enter school influences their enactive and iconic representations. Bruner also indicated that children repeatedly return to these modes of representation of ideas if needed. This account of the development of representation fits in with Vygotsky's description of the change from children's perceptual orientation to imagination, and later, their ability to act on a symbolic level (Vygotsky 1978).

The mode of knowledge representation has an impact on learners' abilities to master the domain of knowledge presented to them. Bruner points out that these abilities are also impacted by the *economy* of representation (the amount of information that needs to be held and processed in the mind in order to achieve comprehension) and the *power* of representation (its capacity to help the learner connect matters that, on the surface, seem quite separate). According to Bruner, 'mode, economy and power vary according to age, to different "styles" among learners, and to different subject matters' (1966: 44).

## *Representation as communication of knowledge*

Davis et al. (1993) identified another way of understanding knowledge representation – as a medium of expression and communication. They elaborated that knowledge representations are the means by which we express things about the world and the medium of expression in which we communicate to one another about the world. This understanding of knowledge representation leads to the following questions: How well does the representation function as a medium of expression? How general is it? How precise? An underlying belief behind these questions is that the central task of knowledge representation is capturing the complexity of the real world. From this perspective, representations make it possible to communicate and understand things. However, we may also misunderstand the representation, or not know how to use it. A representation is the 'language' in which we communicate, and therefore we must be able to 'speak' it. Yet there are cases when we truly cannot express some things.

Bruner (1996) viewed knowing and communicating as inseparable and believed therefore that the individual's quest for meaning-making is ultimately aided by the culture's symbolic system. It is the culture that provides the tools for organizing and understanding our worlds in communicative ways. Similar to Vygotsky, Bruner stated that 'learning and thinking are always situated in a cultural setting and always dependent upon utilisation of cultural resources' (161). Therefore, he too understood children's meanings to be integrated in cultural practices and symbol systems, including languages. In *Acts of Meaning,* Bruner (1993) proposed that there are certain classes of meaning to which human beings are innately tuned and for which they actively search. Prior to the development of language, he wrote, these classes of meaning existed 'in primitive form as protolinguistic representations of the world' whose full realization depended on the cultural tool of language (72). In his view, humans are initially equipped, if not with a theory of mind, then with a set of predispositions to construe or view the social world in a particular way and to act on our construals.

## *Theory of mind*

An essential part of making sense of the social world is to understand others' intentions and respond accordingly. This sense making is known as theory of mind (ToM), which Olivia Saracho (2014: 13) defines as the ability 'to assign mental states (e.g. beliefs, desires, pretending knowledge) to oneself as well as to be aware that others have beliefs, desires, and intentions that are different from their own'. Current approaches to ToM understand culture in relation to symbolic meanings, cultural practices, values and the importance attributed to these meanings.

The core principle of social understanding is not the intrinsic cognitive trait of a socially isolated child (Naito 2014). When we view the child in isolation, we cannot understand their emotional exchanges with others or their motives in a relational context. Therefore, although 'humans have representations that are reflected in language and thought, human representations are neither decontextualised nor emotionally colourless; rather, from their onset, representations are coloured with emotions and motivations for social interactions' (Naito 2014: 385). Furthermore, the development of social understanding could vary depending on culture, regional or periodic variation within the culture, and even particularities of infant–caregiver interaction in a given family or community. There are variations in the socialization of ToM, especially in terms of the extent to which adults emphasize beliefs and desires during their everyday interactions and communications with children (see also Chapter 3). The sociocultural approach to ToM stresses the need for children and their families to be understood within their sociocultural context. Social understanding and its development are not simply an increased understanding of the mind's function but a result of a sense-making process in a given sociocultural environment.

The ability to understand beliefs is the most sophisticated part of social understanding (Ames et al. 2001). However, Bruner (1991) explained that it is not just the shared beliefs about what people are like and what the

FIGURE 6.2  *Children playing cultural scripts*

world is like or how things should be valued that make a coherent cultural community. In addition, the existence of interpretive procedures for evaluating the different views of reality are inevitable in any diverse society makes an important contribution. Bruner proposed that one way in which these different views are developed in societies is through narrative. In his view, reality is narratively constructed, that is, through stories representing a version of reality.

Very early in life, children begin using narrative to make sense of their experiences. Infants, even before they can talk, 'begin to construct a mental model of their world' (Wells 1987: 196). Family events such as birthdays, vacations, celebrations or rituals, as well as parents' and other family members' conversations about them, help children develop oral narratives and relate incidents to themselves and others in their lives. Stories help children make sense of the world, because both culture and mind are narratively constructed (Bruner 1991). As Katherine Nelson points out, 'toddlers construct their knowledge of the world in terms of familiar events, a process of "world-making" or model building of "what happens" in the general case' (1996: 17). Within these 'mental representations of events', individuals follow scripts; actions are organized sequentially and can involve objects, though both actions and objects can vary. Since scripts are usually organized around meeting goals, certain invariable actions become part of the script. For example, eating is a central invariant action in a meal script. However, the actions that surround it are variable, as is the sequence, thus different pathways within the script are possible (Figure 6.2). Such cultural scripts are often enacted in children's play (see Kirova 2010 in companion website).

## What is the role of language as one of the symbolic tools through which humans make meaning and construct knowledge?

Meaning is profoundly connected to language when language is seen not just as a system of words and grammatical rules but as a social interaction. Practices, things and events in the world are inseparable from the language, and the primary means of understanding among members of a society is the everyday language. Although there is a consensus among researchers and philosophers alike that a relationship exists among language, communication and meaning-making, this relationship is understood differently based on the theoretical perspective used. Sue Robson (2006) summarizes these possible relationships as follows: (a) language shapes thought; (b) thought shapes language and (c) language and thought influence each other.

## *Language shapes thought*

Prevalent in the first half of the twentieth century, the idea of linguistic determinism proposed that differences between languages influence the ways people think and even the ways in which whole cultures are organized. This position's best-known proponents are Benjamin Lee Whorf and his teacher Edward Sapir, who claimed that the members of any speech community ascribe significance to different parts of nature and codify it in language. In Sapir's view, 'human beings ... are very much at the mercy of the particular language which has become the medium of expression for their society' (1929/1963: 162). This view found support in more recent research (e.g. Stephen Levinson's) that distinguishes between languages that describe spatial relations in terms of the body (like English right/left, front/back) and those that orient to fixed points in the environment (like north/south/east/west in some Aboriginal Australian languages). As Bernard Comrie (2012) explains, discussing Levinson's work,

> In a language of the second type one would refer, for example, to 'your north shoulder' or 'the bottle at the west end of the table'. So, in narrating a past event, one would have to remember how the actions related to the compass points. Thus, in order to speak this type of language, one always has to know where one is located with respect to the compass points. ('Investigating Language and Thought', para. 3)

However, linguistic determinist views are strongly challenged or rejected by most psychologists and linguists, who point out that language is only one factor influencing cognition and behaviour. Furthermore, research indicates that humans are incredibly creative (and less determined by language alone) and that even babies demonstrate a sophisticated ability to distinguish between concepts before having the language to express it (Fernyhough 2008). In addition, both adults and children can think in images or in what Steven Pinker (1994) calls 'mentalese' – a language of thought that is in some cases richer and in other ways simpler than any spoken language.

## *Thought shapes language*

For Piaget (1959), language is a system, a medium for representing thought. His theory defined four stages of cognitive development for children, which also included the development of language. Since children are seen to construct their own understandings of the world through their direct interactions with their environment, they first must understand a concept before they can acquire the language that explains that concept (see also Chapters 1 and 5). Therefore, it is impossible for a young child to use words to describe concepts that are unknown to them. Once a child learns about their environment, they can map language onto their prior experience, so thought shapes or leads children's language. From Piaget's perspective, language has 'no formative effect on the structure of thinking' (Wood 1998: 28). For example, an infant has learned that a dog is a four-legged animal that barks, is furry and eats from a bowl in the kitchen; hence they develop the concept of dog first and then learn to map the word 'puppy' onto that concept. Cognition therefore develops independently from language.

Piaget's cognitive theory states that there is a consistent order of mastery of the most common function morphemes – the smallest meaningful unit of a language (e.g. cat, house) – and simple ideas are expressed earlier than more complex ones even if they are more grammatically complicated. Children's language reflects the development of their logical thinking and reasoning skills in stages (Piaget 1959). (See Table 6.2 in companion website.)

## *Language and thought influence each other*

Since the 1960s, a new understanding of the social nature of language has influenced the study of language and its relationship to cognitive development. Psychologists, including Bruner, were interested in the processes occurring in the joint activity between adults and children that made it possible for young children to become language users. According to Bruner (1985), language as part of a culture is governed by rules and passed on to children through a process that is socially constructed. He proposed an interactionist or social interactionist theory of language development and argued that language enables children to internally represent their learning in sophisticated ways that facilitate abstract reasoning. He further suggested that engagement in basic language interaction with others, such as speaking and listening, has no significant effect on children's representation of their thoughts. By contrast, creating written symbols even as simple as making marks to represent their own and others' thoughts has a transformative effect on children's thinking.

Although Bruner made a significant contribution to developmental psychology by providing an explanation for how children come to learn – and how they learn how to learn and use a language – critics such as Newman and Holzman point that 'rule-governed-ness has become how we learn, understand, think and speak' (2014: 115). From Bruner's functional/instrumentalist point of view, human beings are similar to computer-modelled logical systems that engage in 'input' and 'recognition routines' that do not produce meaning (Newman and Holzman 2014: 114). From this critical perspective, Bruner's understanding of self-reflexivity of the learning process – learning how to learn as being culturally inducted – positions the learner as only instrumentally active in acquiring and using tools and the rules of their use. In Newman and Holzman's view, this is a misuse and misunderstanding of Vygotsky's theory, which is based on a dialectical worldview. Bruner emphasized the transaction of rule-governed behaviours that lead an individual to conform to the environment. Therefore, he overlooked the riches of the joint/shared activity intended by Vygotsky, for whom meaning-making was also disrupting, reorganizing and transforming the environment, not just conforming to it. For example, in the ZPD, the child, guided by adults' socially determined behaviours, is capable of doing more than they can do on their own.

The study of meaning for Vygotsky was not limited to the study of socially mediated appropriation of word-meaning relations. In *Thinking and Speech*, first published in Russian in 1934, he presented an important distinction between communicative language and language used for conceptual representation. He considered word meaning as the unit that expresses both thinking and speaking:

> The word without meaning is not a word but an empty sound. Meaning is a necessary, constituting feature of the word itself ... It is the word viewed from the inside. In psychological terms, however, word meaning is nothing other than a generalisation, that is a concept ... Thus, word meaning is also a phenomenon of thinking ... it is a unity of word and thought. (Vygotsky 1987: 244)

Vygotsky stressed that the structure of speech is not a mirror image of the structure of thought and does not merely serve as the expression of developed thought. Rather, 'thought is restructured as it is transformed into speech. It is not expressed but completed in the word' (Vygotsky 1987: 252). Vygotsky's view that meaning-making leads to language-making helps us understand how children's participation in play and activities such as language games is a condition, not only for children's language making, but also for completing thinking in the process. Thus, the distinctly human unity of meaning-making, language-making and thinking is produced in social interactions. (See Table 6.3 in companion website.) For Vygotsky, social interaction proper (communication) required understanding and intention.

Vygotsky's view of the development of children's speech is therefore markedly different from Piaget's (Figure 6.3). For Vygotsky, the initial function of speech is social: 'The notion that speech is socialised is incorrect in that this implies that speech was originally non-social, that it becomes social only through development and change' (Vygotsky 1987: 74). In contrast to Piaget's theory, according to which the egocentric stage of speech and thinking is regarded as transitional from private and personal to social, Vygotsky stated that private speech develops in a social process that involves the transmission of social forms of behaviours developed in collaboration with the child's sphere of individual mental functions.

Vygotsky's theory of speech and thinking viewed the child's needs as inseparable from the human reality, which is fundamentally social.

FIGURE 6.3 *Egocentric or private speech?*

Therefore, he did not present speech as the only way of communicating meaning and developing thinking. Although not as well developed as his theory of the connection between thought and speech, Vygotsky (1987) also considered other forms of communication, such as symbols, signs, drawing and writing, as mediating systems that, like language, served as a way of making and communicating meaning (see also Chapter 6). He emphasized that 'thought is not only mediated externally by signs. It is mediated internally by meanings' (282).

## *Indigenous and minority-language children's linguistic rights and linguistic genocide in education*

Because language has such a key role in both making and communicating meaning, identifying the unique challenges faced by linguistic-minority children as they enter the school system needs special attention. Although Indigenous peoples and minorities are the main depository of the linguistic diversity of the world (Skutnabb-Kangas 2002), children from these communities who are developing their language in a majority-language context are in danger of losing their home language(s). Many children enter schools too young to be fluent speakers of their home language, and as a result they lose the little they know of their home language very quickly. Those who enter school fluent in their home language are quickly discouraged from using it by the intentional or unintentional messages they receive from both the adults and their peers in these environments. Children interpret these messages to mean that only the 'official' language of the school is legitimate and they are forced to adapt to the majority language environment. UNESCO Ad Hoc Expert Group on Endangered Languages (2003) estimates that, 'in most world regions, about 90% of the languages may be replaced by dominant languages by the end of the 21st century' (2). In recognition of the importance of maintaining cultural and linguistic diversity, it adopted an action plan that recommends that Member States, in conjunction with speaker communities, undertake steps to ensure the linguistic diversity of humanity and give support to expression, creation and dissemination of the greatest possible number of languages.

The use of an official language as a tool of assimilation is defined as linguistic and cultural genocide. Skutnabb-Kangas (2002) makes a strong case for use of the term 'cultural and linguistic genocide' by drawing from the UN International Convention on the Prevention and Punishment of the Crime of Genocide (E793, 1948), Article II(e), 'forcibly transferring children of the group to another group' and Article II(b), 'causing serious bodily or mental harm to members of the group'. Likewise, most minority education is guilty of linguistic genocide according to Article III(1): 'Prohibiting the use of the language of the group in daily intercourse or in schools, or the printing and circulation of publications in the language of the group'.

The residential schools in Canada, Australia and New Zealand are examples of such practices (Buti 2002).

It has been documented that Indigenous peoples knew the dangers of assimilation, as stated by Handsome Lake, who was born in the Seneca village of Ganawagas on the Genesee River in 1735:

> We feel that the white race will take away the culture, traditions, and language of the red race. When your people's children become educated in the way of white people, they will no longer speak their own language and will not understand their own culture. Your people will suffer great misery and not be able to understand their elders anymore. (as cited by Thomas 1994: 41–2)

The education of Indigenous peoples and minorities in large parts of the world today is still organized in direct contradiction to the current scientific knowledge of how it should be organized to protect the linguistic rights of linguistic minorities and persons of Indigenous origin. Although Article 30 of the 1989 United Nations Convention on the Rights of the Child is very clear about the rights of children who belong to ethnic, religious or linguistic minorities, public education in many immigrant-receiving countries has not accommodated the needs of the children from minority communities, nor has it supported the development of their talents and capacities so they can become valued, respected and contributing members of society (Kirova 2012). Instead of trying to reprogramme children in terms of basic language–thought relationships, replacing earlier formed word–thought connections with new ones, W. E. Lambert suggested that the 'remedy for the language minority child is to root him/herself thoroughly in the likely to be bypassed heritage language, bringing the infant language-thought connections to fruition, and when solidly literate in the first language then, and only then, start the transformation from a subtractive to a thoroughly additive outlook on being bilingual' (1990: 218).

In addition, the pursuit of educational goals related to global competitiveness rather than human rights perpetuates linguistic colonialism or 'lingoracism' in many immigrant-receiving countries (Gounari 2006: 77). In the context of globalization, which demands a common international language and a common set of knowledge and skills, the linguistic and cultural capital of minority children and their parents and communities has been systematically invalidated. Education systems reproduce the cultural values of the upper classes who dominate societies, which puts children from lower economic classes at a disadvantage and further marginalizes individuals from these classes (Bourdieu 1986).

Although evidence in support of conceptual and academic skill transfer across languages is becoming more readily available, educational systems around the globe have 'failed to address in a sufficiently positive way the dual language reality of emergent bilingual children' (Cummins 2012: x).

FIGURE 6.4 *Supporting home languages in the classroom*

However, innovative early childhood practices, including linguistically appropriate practices that draw on cumulative knowledge about bilingual language use or children's 'translanguaging', are gradually replacing outdated and damaging practices that were overtly assimilative, such as forbidding children to speak their home language at school and strongly suggesting to parents that speaking the home language with their children will hamper their academic success (Chumak-Horbatsch 2012; Kirova 2012). To recognize and account for how multilingual children use language within and across systems, we adopt the definition of translanguaging as 'an approach ... that considers the language practices of bilinguals not as two autonomous language systems ... but as one linguistic repertoire with features that have been societally constructed as belonging to two separate languages' (García and Wei 2014: 2). (Figure 6.4.)

Recently, Indigenous language revitalization programmes in Canada, Norway, Sweden, Finland and New Zealand, among others, aim to extend the use of threatened languages among younger generations by drawing on the proficiency of the remaining speakers of a language. Such programmes facilitate 'language reclamation and promote the relearning of a language on the basis of historical documentation and archive materials' (Lo Bianco 2012: 501).

# What is the role of children's art and art making as significant ways of knowing, problem solving and creating that allow for the construction of multiple meanings?

Vygotsky (1997a) argued that signs' main function is the formation of meaning; he wrote, 'Meaning is everywhere where there is a sign – meaning is inherent in the sign' (1997a: 134). The implications of Vygotsky's view on cultural signs and symbols can be seen in two distinct but related areas (Gredler and Shields 2008). First, cultural diversity in symbols leads to differences, across cultures, in the way that members of the culture think. Second, as new discoveries and technologies are included in the culture, new symbol systems are created and added to the existing cultural repertoire of signs and symbols. As a result, new ways of thinking emerge. For example, unprecedented advances in technology in the late twentieth and early twenty-first centuries have led to the rapid growth of visual forms of cultural communication. Visual images are becoming a primary means for accessing information about the world. In the field of education, this tendency is captured in the term visual literacy, a skill that is described in a number of ways, including 'the interpretation and critique of images, the ability to understand images, and the ability to produce images and use them to express oneself' (Gredler and Shields 2008: 215). Because of the rapid changes in communication and in our ways of using communication technologies, several fields have emerged within literacy education that address how we can adapt to the shifts in literacy in the twenty-first century's communicational landscapes. One term that reappears in literature in the field of literacy education is *new literacies and multiliteracies*, which are understood to involve visual, audio, spatial, behavioural and gesture modes, including the body-as-text (Lankshear and Knobel 2003). Multimodality, like multiliteracies, has emerged in response to the changing social and semiotic landscape. Multimodality 'attends to meaning as it is made through the situated configuration across image, gesture, gaze, body posture, sound, writing, music, speech, and so on' (Jewitt 2008: 246). From a multimodal perspective, Carey Jewitt (2008) writes, 'image, action, and so forth are referred to as *modes*, as organised sets of semiotic resources for meaning-making' (246, italics in original).

Children from a very young age are makers and users of language and signs, and they intentionally use a wide range of modes when constructing meaning. Young children's selections of modes (e.g. drawing, singing, gesturing and dancing) are rooted in and controlled by the social and cultural tools made available to them (Kress 1997). The concept of *modal affordances* (Jewitt 2008) refers to 'what is possible to express and represent easily' (247). For example, images are understood by the logic of space and simultaneity, while sounds, as in speech, are governed by the logic of time and sequence. Increasingly, researchers and language arts educators have adopted the multiliteracies/multimodality perspective that recognizes art, music, dance, drama and film as vital modes of representation, meaning-making and communication. These modes play an important role in viewing children's multiple ways of understanding the world around them. Critical to this perspective is 'the understanding that symbol systems other than language are not "tack-ons" but rather relevant options for creating and expressing meaning' (Kendrick and McKay 2009: 54).

## *Multimodalities: Drawing, music, dance and movement and the creation of meaning*

Children's art, drawing, mark making, painting, building and constructing models and artefacts have been documented, researched and written about for centuries from a variety of different perspectives: psychological, philosophical, educational and aesthetic. However, in the last several decades of the twentieth century, the developmental psychological framework has been used most often when trying to understand children's art and image making (Kind 2005). Within this framework, children's drawings have been seen to be a direct reflection of the child's cognitive functioning, their emotional world, their developmental maturity (Hallam et al. 2014) and their physical control – gross and fine motor – over materials and tools. Young children's artistic representations have been understood to pass through chronological, sequential and predictable stages or milestones of development (Pente 2011) until they are able to produce a 'visually realistic' or 'correct' representation of the world (Matthews 2003). The 'evolution' of preschool children's drawings has been described as following a developmental sequence: from 'random scribbling' (ages 1–2), to 'shape making' (ages 2–7), to 'symbolic making' (ages 3–5; Cornett and Smithrim 2000: 143). However, since the focus was on the output (the drawings) as a way of getting insights into children's cognitive or emotional processes, located inside the child (Potter 2000), the wider context that shaped the creation of the artwork was not examined.

This developmental orientation has been used to assess what children can or cannot do artistically (Kind 2005). It has also been used in developmental psychology to measure intelligence, which can result in viewing those children who were unable to re-create 'correct' representations or endpoints as deficient or atypical (Ring 2003). John Matthews cautions that 'by doing this, a great misunderstanding is made of children's art and its meaning and significance is lost, to the detriment of children's intellectual and emotional development' (2003: 3). This orientation ignores that art making is a personally, socially and culturally constructed act.

Building on Vygotsky's work on signs and symbols, Kindler and Darras (1997) explored the communicative potential of children's art. They proposed a model grounded on the assumption that 'artistic development is a phenomenon which occurs in an interactive social environment and that artistic learning involves a social component' (20) that is typically overlooked by development theories, which put too much emphasis on culture-free psychosocial determinism of artistic development. Kindler and Darras's model rejected the stage theory of artistic development because of its concentration on realism and its linearity, which does not account for the diversity of work produced by children. They concluded that 'realism-centred stage theories seem to use an irrelevant baseline for consideration of artistic growth' (18). More relevant, they argued, is pictorial production as an integral part of a plurimedia process in contexts that include not only words but also drawings, sounds and gestures.

Children's drawings, from a Vygotskian perspective, serve a very similar function to oral and written speech – they communicate meaning to others and to oneself. Vygotsky argued that children's drawings 'capitalise on the narrative impulse that emerges in their earliest representational drawings, on their tendency to create stories in drawings, and on the talk that surrounds and supplements drawing events' (1978: 174). The development of representational skills through drawing acts as a nonverbal tool that helps children to analyse objects and their parts (Chang 2012). Drawings also teach the cultural tool of representing three-dimensional objects in two-dimensional space, following the cultural conventions of their context.

Drawing on Vygotsky's understanding of the relationships between thinking and speech, Margaret Brooks (2009) proposes that drawing mediates between thought and action to support progressively complex ideas. She suggests that drawing informs the development of visual thought following parallel forms of meaning: (a) meaning as reference and abstraction, and (b) meaning as contextualized personal sense. 'When drawing informs thought and thought is given life through drawing', Brooks writes, 'we can begin to see the connection between thought and drawing and the value of drawing in the creation of meaning' (12). She further points to a couple of significant differences between speech and drawing. First, drawing is seen as a whole and simultaneous to the thought, while speech is seen as following a more linear and temporal order. Brooks suggests that 'the power of drawing for children (and adults) is that it more closely represents thought' (12). Second, the materiality and relative permanency of the drawing as compared to speech offers children an opportunity for an extended dialogue around ideas it represents as a mediating tool for collaboration. For young children, these activities occur during play and playful contexts (Ring 2003, 2009). As Matthews (2003) points out, '*play* makes all this possible. Play is implicated in the development of all forms of representation' (27, emphasis in original).

Perret and Fox (2004) identify similarities between music and language, particularly in their reliance on processing and assembling features that are associated with unique symbols – notes in the case of music and letters in the case of language. Both music and language are 'multisensory', the authors write, 'and separate parts of both are processed in different parts of the brain and reassembled to experience them as either music or language' (120). In many majority-world cultures, singing, when part of everyday tasks, is a culturally meaningful way of being with young children. Songs involve instructions (e.g. how to complete a task at hand) or expressed particular emotions, most commonly affection. Songs filled with traditional morals were used to both praise children and scold them.

Patricia Whitfield (2009), who employed dance to teach narrative writing, maintains that 'in dance, children interpret ideas and feelings through the use of their bodies in an open-ended search for a unique movement vocabulary' (159). Dancing is a very important aspect of the way in which children in Indigenous and other majority-world cultures participate in adult culture and make sense of rituals and traditions through shared activities. For example, in North America, powwow dances are beautiful expressions of Indigenous spirituality, history and culture. A variety of regional dance styles are performed by men, women and children across the continent. There are also dances that are specific to certain First Nations or that commemorate certain events or elements of nature. Drum music, singing and regalia are sacred elements of the celebration, meant not only to entertain, but also to tell important stories about personal and cultural history, such as in the Anishinaabe hoop dance. In many cultures, therefore, children's participation in singing and dancing as cultural activities is a way of making sense of the world.

## *Reggio Emilia and children's artistic representations*

An increasingly popular model of understanding children's artistic representations and art-making experiences is the Reggio Emilia approach (Gandini 2005; New 2007; Pelo 2016). A foundational part of this approach is the expressive languages of art, or hundred languages of expression (Gandini 2005). Art making in this approach is deeply connected to collaborative or co-constructed enquiries, research and exploration of learning through project-based work (Hewett 2001; Schwall 2005). Children access art materials within an *atelier*, or school art studio, to symbolically and aesthetically represent their ideas, knowledge and understanding from within an enquiry. As a generative space, the atelier 'has allowed rich combinations and creative possibilities among the different (symbolic) languages of children' (Malaguzzi 1998: 74). Further, the physical materials that are present in the environment play a crucial role in supporting children's learning (Pelo 2016) and creative expression of meaning. In this approach educators'/children's artistic representations are systematically documented and made visible to children, parents and educators to capture the life or memory of a project and act as a prompt to revisit, evaluate and expand on old ideas (Hewett 2001; see also Chapter 10).

## *Summary*

This chapter explored the processes by which children make meaning of the world around them and the modes of representation they use to represent their knowledge. Since meaning-making is inseparable from the symbolic systems utilized by the culture, the chapter considered cognitive constructivist and social constructivist theories of meaning-making, as well as current ideas about the development of theory of mind (ToM) in relation to symbolic meanings and to the cultural practices and values that help attribute meaning to them. Special attention was given to the role of language in children's meaning-making. Linguistic rights of Indigenous and minority-language children were discussed in relation to linguistically appropriate practice and translanguaging. New literacies and multiliteracies encompass multimodal forms that diversify the possibilities for constructing and expressing meanings. Art making was explored through a discussion of the practices of Reggio Emilia schools.

# CHAPTER SEVEN

# Childhoods and Play

***Proposition: Play is an integral part of childhood.***

While play is commonly viewed as inseparable from childhood, children's play and the role of play in their childhoods differ across and within cultures. Play is increasingly recognized as a complex, multifaceted phenomenon. This complexity is reflected in the array of meanings attached to the term 'play', as well as in the different approaches, functions and roles assigned to play within early childhood education. In addition to children's culture, gender and (dis)ability, global factors such as geo-political climate, socioeconomic status of the family, parents' level of education and their overall position in society, which can change with (im)migration, affect children's play. We explore the 'fundamentals of play' in relation to the following questions:

1 What is play?
2 How is play related to development?
3 How is play related to teaching and the curriculum?

For additional information, reflective questions and practical implications visit: https://www.bloomsbury.com/cw/learning-to-teach-young-children/chapter-7/

## What is play?

The idea of a universal childhood has been questioned and gradually replaced by another idea – that there are many childhoods (see also Chapter 1). The question here is, if many childhoods exist, is it possible to have a singular/universal understanding or definition of play? We take the view that while play is present in all cultures, the nature of children's play might vary widely depending on the values, beliefs, practices, institutions and tools of the culture in which the children live (Gaskins et al. 2007). The type of play and the materials children play with also vary across cultures (Tudge 2008). In the early childhood education (ECE) field, the lack of consensus about a specific definition of play or its outcomes results in two conflicting views currently affecting the field: play as a right, and play as an instrument of learning.

The first view is based on the 1989 United Nations Convention on the Rights of the Child, which identifies the right to play as a distinct component, though many scholars see it as fundamental to children's rights as a whole. The CRC defines, in some respects, the right to be a child (see also Chapter 2). Regarding the right to play, it states: 'States Parties recognise the right of the child to rest and leisure, to engage in play and recreational activities appropriate to the age of the child and to participate freely in cultural life and the arts' (Article 31).

This position has resulted in an increased reference to play globally, in both policies and early childhood curricula, and has similarly led to the promotion of play-based curricula and play-based or play pedagogy worldwide. More recently, the UN Committee on the Rights of the Child highlighted in General Comment No. 17 the role of play in providing opportunities for boys and girls to express their 'creativity, imagination, self-confidence, self-efficacy, and for the development of physical, social, cognitive and emotional strengths and skills' (2013: 4). The general comment also defined play as a 'key dimension of education, necessary to achieve the best possible health, integral to the child's optimum development, and a valuable route to recovery and reintegration after trauma, loss, neglect or violence' (Lansdown 2013: 2).

Positioning play as a 'key dimension of education' supports the second view of play as an 'instrument of learning future competencies' (Rogers 2011: 5). Due to the political pressure to raise standards and to prepare young children for the demands of schooling, in the last couple of decades teachers have felt forced to structure their delivery of the curriculum so that children meet rigid measurable learning outcomes (Fromberg 2002). Since play does not support linear step-by-step instruction/learning due to its unpredictable nature, it is often susceptible to increasing demands for educational accountability (Wood 2007). Consequently, there is little space for the unpredictability and messiness of play. This *pedagogization* of play means that play is increasingly used to fulfil academic goals. This tendency has received criticism, especially regarding the role of the adult in what is supposed to be children's 'free' play (Göncu and Gaskins 2011; Kuschner 2012). David Kuschner (2012) argues against classifying the various teacher-led interactive classroom activities as 'play'. Instead, he recommends that play should be part of the curriculum, that children be given adequate time to play and that play should not be used to achieve academic goals.

## *The challenge of defining play*

Play has been described and theorized in a variety of ways, including as an activity that is child initiated, as a personal experience and as a multifaceted, relative behaviour (Roopnarine and Johnson 1994). The broad scope of play behaviour described in the literature makes it difficult to provide a concise definition of play. In the 1980s, developmental psychologists achieved a partial consensus based on six common characteristics of play; it is:

- intrinsically motivated
- enjoyable
- without external rules, having only rules invented by the players
- goal-less, with its value in the process rather than its outcome
- engaging for the players
- nonliteral (e.g. the 'house' is just a corner of the room). (Rubin et al. 1983)

These characteristics remain at the core of some presently used definitions of play. For example, Doris Fromberg (2002) defines play as *voluntary* in relation to a specific context; having *meaningful* processes that connect with children's own experiences; *symbolic* of children's experiences; *rule-governed* by children; contributing to children's sense of *pleasure* and *episodic*, that is, focused on the activity, rather than the final outcome. Fromberg clarifies that the *context,* such as the physical and social environment, historical moment and cultural conditions, influence the *content* of children's play. The diversity of play contexts results in many ways of thinking about play and its related functions (Figure 7.1).

Some scholars have challenged the idealized view of play that is dominating the field of ECE. Jo Ailwood (2003) presents a critical analysis of the three dominant positions or discourses on play in ECE. In her analysis, the *romantic/nostalgic discourse of play* is based on the image of the child as innocent and pure (see also Chapter 1) and still dominates the majority-worldview of children. It presents play as being positive and *needed* by children if they are to develop 'normally'. Play is divided into different types largely based on the theories of Piaget and/or Vygotsky. The second dominant position, the *discourse of play characteristics*, is closely linked to the romantic or nostalgic understanding of play as 'free', 'intrinsic' or 'nonserious' and 'enjoyable' or 'fun'. Although freedom and intrinsic motivation are seen as key characteristics of play, this view of play is in contrast with most practices in ECE settings that are regulated by timetables and schedules, with materials presented to children that may not be of their choosing. As Gaile Cannella (1997) points out, 'choice for children is an illusion' (121). In addition, play may not necessarily be fun for all players (Sutton-Smith 1997). Play could be a means for children to exercise power and control over each other (MacNaughton 2006), reject each other based on race, gender, socioeconomic status or cultural or linguistic heritage (Grieshaber and McArdle 2010), or it could be a means for adults to enforce adult rules (Ailwood 2011) or serve as a tool for invisible coercion (Burman 2008). The

FIGURE 7.1 *Play varies across cultures*

third play discourse is the *developmental discourse on play* reinforced by the US-based approach of developmentally appropriate practice (DAP). In this discourse, the social and cultural aspects of life influencing play are simply 'added on' or considered in superficial ways. When play is seen to happen in a contextual (social, cultural and political) vacuum, it conceals Eurocentric/ ethnocentric understandings of play (Fleer 1998). For example, by setting up developmentally appropriate environments and materials that provide support for play, educators can advance the idea that whiteness is normal or desirable and consequently send negative messages to racially diverse children (Clarke and Watson 2014).

# How is play related to development?

## Play and development in ECE

While the idea of a universal childhood is becoming less prevalent, play is still often seen as having the same value for children of certain ages and stages of development across cultures, contexts and abilities. Therefore, play is viewed in relation to development. This thinking around play has largely favoured the dominant Eurocentric cultural practices (Fleer et al. 2009). Play features prominently in the ECE field, with much current practice informed by foundational research examining the role of play in child development.

Interpretations of play in early childhood education have been influenced by theoretical traditions that provided the background for the emergence of contemporary child development theories. These include, but are not limited to, the classical theories of play, such as surplus-energy theory (Friedrich Schiller), recreation theory (Moritz Lazarus), recapitulation theory (Stanley Hall) and practice theory (Karl Gross). Although these classical theories were limited in scope and explained a narrow range of play behaviours, they were crucial for understanding how play has been viewed from the perspective of multiple disciplines (see Table 7.1 in companion website). They also provided the basis for what is now referred to as 'modern' theories of play that expand on many of the ideas in the classical theories. The most influential modern theories include psychodynamic theory (e.g. Sigmund Freud, Erik Erikson) and constructivist/cognitive theories (e.g. Jean Piaget, Lev Vygotsky and Brian Sutton-Smith) (see Table 7.2 in companion website). A current critical view of the way in which many educational institutions introduce these modern theories to preservice teachers indicates that these theories are often presented without critique or debate, and thus are perceived as fact (Fleer et al. 2009).

To organize the various ways in which the 'modern' theorists have identified and explained the relationship between play and development, we find it useful to consider this relationship in the following ways: (a) play as a *reflection of* a child's current level of development, (b) play as a *source* of development, (c) play as *adaptive variability* and (d) play from *postdevelopmental perspectives*.

## Play reflects a child's current level of development

In his stage theory of children's intellectual development, the Swiss psychologist Jean Piaget (1962) proposed that the type of play in which children engage matches their level of cognitive development. For him, play has a mastery function: The child explores objects and either incorporates these experiences into existing schemas (*assimilation*) or modifies the schemas to fit the new experiences within them (*accommodation*) (see also Chapter 1). For example, two-year-old Ali enjoys banging on his family's pots and pans with a wooden spoon. The first time he plays with a drum, he is able to assimilate some aspects of the experience (e.g. the sounds, motion and reverberations) into the schemas he developed in his kitchen play. He may need to slightly modify his schemas to incorporate the less metallic sound the drum makes (accommodation). Changing those cognitive structures to match, imitate or conform with what is observed or experienced is at the core of this process. For Piaget, play was essentially assimilation, or assimilation dominating accommodation.

Piaget wondered why children, particularly those under seven years of age, use their imagination so much. Since he believed that young children do not engage in analytical or logical thought, he saw no reason for them to make a firm separation between 'the real' and 'the not real'. Through symbolic play, Piaget believed, children achieve satisfaction missing in their efforts to understand a complex and sometimes confusing world. Creating a special imagined world in play connects children with a world of desires that cannot be fulfilled in the real world through logical thinking (Figure 7.2). For Piaget, play emerges as a critical feature in early childhood, where it takes the form of sensory-motor/functional or practice play, symbolic or pretend play, and rule-governed play or games. (See Table 7.3 in companion website.)

According to Piaget, playing with other children is a way to learn about others' views and recognize they may be different from their own. That is, the child becomes less egocentric and focused on their own goals and desires. This process of 'decentring' also helps children build their own theory of mind (Piaget and Inhelder 1969/2000: 172; see also Chapter 6).

## Influences of Piaget's (constructivist) theory on practice

Within the Piagetian theoretical framework, the adult provides a variety of play objects for children to explore/manipulate individually or in groups,

FIGURE 7.2  *Do children play what they know or what they imagine?*

allowing the child to construct meaning through the 'discovery' of the play objects' properties in action. If Ali, in the earlier example, was attending preschool, upon observing his interest in making sounds by banging on different objects, his teacher might select a diverse range of materials and shapes to allow him to make different sounds. Ali would then be encouraged to play independently with these objects, with the expectation that he would learn about the acoustic properties of each preselected object, as well as their combinations, as he interacts with them. According to a Piagetian view of play, these materials need to match Ali's level of cognitive development and help him to incorporate these experiences into existing schemas about sounds (*assimilation*) and problem-solve independently, given sufficient time to do so. Providing stimulating play environments that include realistic or replica toys is understood to stimulate sociodramatic/symbolic play. The influence of the Piagetian view on play is still present in classroom practice. It is seen especially in the emphasis on children's choice, ownership and autonomy in play and the minimal involvement of adults.

## *Critique of Piaget's theory of play*

While Piaget's work has allowed scholars to argue for the importance of play in children's intellectual development, the idea of linking the types of play with corresponding developmental stages has been challenged. By connecting play to individual cognitive development, Piaget did not account for the social or group nature of play and the role of interactions with peers and others in fostering cognitive development (Frost et al. 2012). Sutton-Smith (1997) disputed the idea that children's imaginative play can be explained through links to their cognitive development because it is the foundation for playfulness in thought. Elkonin (2005b) critiqued Piaget's definition of play as assimilation – a process of converting the unknown to the known. Instead, Elkonin contended that play is a progressive revolutionary activity that changes the child's relationship to the world, including the transition from 'centred' to 'decentred' thinking. Play has a progressive role in the development of the child's whole personality, including the shift of thinking to a new, higher stage.

## *Play as a source of development*

Lev Vygotsky (1967) emphasized play as an activity essential for the development of a 'future child' and referred to play as the *leading activity* of a child's development. In other words, play does not show us what stage a child is at, as Piaget had suggested, but rather, play during the preschool and kindergarten years provides conditions for the developmental accomplishments expected at this age. More specifically, play helps preschool children to achieve several goals. First, they can overcome their impulsive, reactive behaviours (i.e. their immediate/reflexive responses to the environment) and behave in more intentional ways. For example, when four-year-old John is pretending to drive a truck, he is unlikely to leave the driver's seat to look at what Ana and Peter are doing in the play house because his role as a driver requires him to remain seated on the driver's seat. This accomplishment allows the child to develop higher mental functions: focused attention, deliberate memory and symbolic thought (see also Chapter 5). Second, young children have opportunities to use a variety of signs and symbol systems – from gestures and words to drawing and written marks – which prepares them for the increasingly complex symbol systems they will learn in school (Bodrova and Leong 2015). Vygotsky associated these accomplishments with sociodramatic or make-believe play. He identified three features of this type of play:

1. Children create an imaginary situation.
2. They take on and act out roles.
3. They follow a set of rules determined by those specific roles.

Each of these features plays an essential function in the development of higher mental functions. According to Vygotsky, the creation of pretend or imaginary play situations distinguishes play from other children's activities. He argued that the imaginary situation still has rules of behaviour (made by the children themselves), which a player is obligated to follow: 'The imaginary situation will always contain rules. In play, the child is free. But this is an illusory freedom' (1967: 10). While following these rules, children learn to act independently of what they see. Taking on the role of a truck driver, for example, means the child would hold a steering wheel while seated on a chair. If four-year-old John in the previous example were to take on this role, he would likely be looking for a steering wheel. He would scan the toys in the room to determine if anything could be used as a wheel. In spotting a plastic hoop, he would be likely to recognize its potential to become a steering wheel. In this case, his actions would have been determined not by the object – he did not first play with the hoop and then started pretending that it was a steering wheel. Rather, his 'selection' of a steering wheel was guided by his thought process which was motivated by the role he took – a truck driver – which was possible only because of the imaginary situation he created. The transition from object-governed to meaning-governed actions shows how play (through imagination) facilitates a shift between the two stages of human perception: being dominated first by object and then by meaning.

Therefore, through the creation of an imaginary situation, play provides a transitional stage from relating meaning with an object to the development of abstract thought. Abstract thinking is a developmental accomplishment typically expected between the ages of four and six (Bodrova and Leong 2007). Play as a leading activity in preschool facilitates the internalization process that moves development from visual thinking to internal (abstract) thinking through imagination. Generally, as Rogoff explains, Vygotskian theory asserts that 'in play, children enjoy ignoring the ordinary uses of objects and actions in order to subordinate them to imaginary meanings and situations' (Rogoff 2003: 298). In the example in Figure 7.3, the child imagines the broom (object) is a horse and creates an imaginary situation using this object.

For Vygotsky:

> Play is the source of development and creates the zone of proximal development. Action in the imaginative sphere, in an imaginary situation, the creation of voluntary intentions, and the formation of real-life plans and volitional motives – all appear in play and make it the highest level of preschool development. (1967: 16)

FIGURE 7.3 *Object/meaning inversion and the role of imagination*

Vygotsky made a distinction between play and similar activities that are beneficial for children's development, namely games with rules, and productive activities such as drama and storytelling. Although these kinds of activities may complement and enrich play, they are distinguished from pretend play because of their characteristics. For instance, Bodrova and Leong (2007) describe games with rules as different from play because there are explicit rules that are expected to be followed. Furthermore, while dramatic activities might involve 'acting out' roles in a way that may be similar to pretend play, the use of scripts (often written by adults) makes games very different from pretend play. Chess is an example of a game with explicit rules that the pieces (e.g. 'horse' or 'queen') must follow as they move on the board.

## *Post-Vygotskian theory of play*

Vygotsky's colleague Daniel Elkonin (2005a) also viewed play as the *leading activity*, one in which children master a variety of mental tools necessary for them to function successfully in society. However, Elkonin's theory of play differs from Vygotsky's (Figure 7.4). He believed the role a child acts out, not the imaginary situation, is at the centre of make-believe play. The role determines what pretend actions a child will take, what props they will use and how the relationships between play partners will be formed. Elkonin's (2005a) structural elements of play are as follows:

1 Roles
2 Pretend actions (these are more abbreviated and generalized than real actions)
3 The use of props (used to perform pretend actions)
4 The relationships children enter as they play, including play-specific communication, stepping into and out of the roles and setting the rules of communication to maintain the flow of play according to the roles

Play, according to Elkonin, develops in four levels. It starts with the 'object-centred' play of two- and three-year-old children (level 1) and develops to become the elaborate 'relationship-centred' play of kindergarten-aged children (level 4). Play is expected to develop to a mature or advanced level in order to lead to the expected achievement for preschool to kindergarten children (see Table 7.4 in companion website).

FIGURE 7.4 *Imaginary situation in play is not independent of cultural context*

## Influences of Vygotskian and post-Vygotskian (sociocultural/social constructivist) theories on classroom practice

According to Vygotskian and post-Vygotskian theoretical perspectives on play and development, 'play does not develop spontaneously in all children once they reach preschool age' (Bodrova and Leong 2015: 385). As Bodrova and Leong explain, 'mature play, the level necessary to be a principal activity for preschoolers, emerges only with adult mediation or as young children are assisted by older children who are acting as play mentors' (2015: 385). Children need exposure to play contexts where they can get support to gain the required play skills. Therefore, for play to realize its developmental benefits, teachers' meaningful participation with children is necessary.

The very nature of the sociocultural historical theory of learning requires teachers to examine the contexts in which today's children grow and develop to understand the role of play in their development. As Bodrova and Leong (2015) suggest, the changes in the culture of childhood in the Western/minority world over time has led more five- and six-year-old children, who according to Vygotsky's and Elkonin's theories should be at the peak of their play performance, to display signs of the immature play more typical of toddlers and younger preschoolers. They play only with realistic props, enact play scenarios that are stereotypical or lack imagination, and display a limited repertoire of themes and roles. This change can be attributed partly to the fact that fewer children in industrialized countries have an opportunity to learn how to play from their older siblings or friends because they attend early childhood programmes where they are typically placed in same-age groups. These programmes, delivered in institutionalized settings, may be the only place where they can learn how to play.

Yet learning how to play in the classroom is not the same as learning to play within the informal neighbourhood peer groups of the past. Teachers need to consider that 'the nature of play in the digital age is changing in terms of the resources available for play and the ways in which those resources are deployed in different types of play' (Marsh et al. 2016: 242). When adults scaffold play, they can ensure that children engage in mature forms of play. This, in turn, helps children to develop their play and enhances early academic skills (Bodrova and Leong 2007). For example, when children are assisted in developing play scenarios, they also develop narrative skills, such as understanding how stories are constructed with characters, settings, plot and so forth.

Fully understanding the implications of the sociocultural historical approach to learning means that child development is understood not only as dependent on the nature of the child's cultural context, but also on the culturally influenced choices made by the teachers in that setting, that is, the goals they expect the children to achieve and how they expect children to engage with adults and peers in this context (van Oers 2014).

## *Critique of Vygotskian and post-Vygotskian theory of play*

In the cultural-historical theory of Vygotsky, play is limited to the early stages of development, and the theory does not explain how play connects to school learning in children who are seven years of age and older. For example, both Vygotsky and post-Vygotskian scholars view play as children's way of gaining access to adult culture. However, they do not specify how older children or adolescents achieve such access. Although the cultural-historical theory of play accepts processes of spontaneous learning, including learning with and from peers, it overemphasizes play that is guided by others. Some scholars (e.g. Lambert 2000) call for using more current theories of play that reflect a concern for the rights of the individual, as well as contemporary pedagogical trends. Angeline Lillard and her colleagues (2013) analysed numerous research studies on the effects of pretend play in the development of cognition, social skills, language, narrative or storytelling skills and self regulation. They found 'little evidence' to support Vygotsky's belief that pretend play is a critical vehicle for children's development. In their view, what is needed is a theory of playful learning, which they view as the 'most positive means yet known to help young children's development' (28).

Suzanne Gaskins and her colleagues (2007) argue that pretend play appears to peak as an important kind of play at different ages in different cultures, and that 'it is unlikely to have the same developmental force at these different ages' (195). These authors note that cross-cultural variations are observed in how caregivers and children participate in, shape, and communicate within pretend play. For example, children's pretend play is highly supported by adults in Western/minority-world families, and while children and adults interact as peers in pretend play, adults are helping children to elaborate and expand their play themes over time. The themes are often fantasy themes and involve the use of toys. Drawing from the work of Mapopa Mtonga who explored Indigenous African (i.e. Chewa and Tumbuka) children's songs and games observed in rural and urban areas of Zambia, Serpell and Nsamenang (2014) discussed how games and play are a mean of socializing young children and they are able to rehearse adult roles and prepare for future responsibilities. In further reference to Mtonga's (2012) work, Serpell and Nsamenang (2014) state that the social organization of children's play and games in majority world emphasized inclusiveness and allowed for children's development into healthy adults. From a critical perspective then, Vygotskian and post-Vygotskian views of play and the role of pretend play in particular in development are seen to be based on minority-world cultural beliefs and practices.

## Play as adaptive variability

Brian Sutton-Smith's (1997) first theory of play falls into the category of a cognitive theory of play somewhat like Vygotsky's theory. In his retrospective review of his own theories of play, Sutton-Smith (2008) outlined his latest theory of play, which includes five adaptive layers (see Table 7.5 in companion website). This new theory of play as adaptive variability is based on brain-development research and evolutionary theory, as well as understandings of how animals play. In this theory Sutton-Smith draws a connection between play and evolution. Using biological evolution as a model for human development, he proposes the first principle of variation – flexibility, which is more important than precision and makes both play and learning possible. The second principle of variation is abundance – the body's ability to overproduce brain synapses also affords play and learning many different possibilities.

Not unlike Piaget's and Vygotsky's theories, symbolic play has a particular place in Sutton-Smith's theory of play. It is seen as a mutation, drawing together emotional expression and emotional regulation. He suggests that 'pretending or not pretending is an experiential duality' and that 'pretend play begins a child's training in the social duplicities' (2008: 119). He claims this playful duality, or 'ludic' duality in his terms, is involved in forming the minds and mental health of the very young.

Other scientific theories of animal play also advanced the concept of play as 'training for the unexpected' (Sharpe 2011; Spinka et al. 2001). From this perspective, development occurs as a process of growing complexity rather than a universal natural progression through stages. Larry Vandervert (2017) hypothesized that animals in play learn how to deal with the emotional aspect of being surprised or temporarily disoriented or disabled. He argued that human play evolved from animal play and that rule-governed imagination allowed play to help predict events through sequence detection. By testing this hypothesis, he concluded that 'the brain mechanisms of play have driven culture into existence and continue to drive its advancing forms. Play always leads culture' (222). Vandervert's research provides an explanation of Vygotsky's most compelling insights about play, including his conception of the ZPD in which children are a head taller than themselves (see also Chapter 5).

## Postdevelopmental perspectives on play

By taking a 'culture-free' approach to children's play (Kuschner 2007: 62), the field of early childhood education has reinforced, especially through DAP, the view of the universal child, suggesting that universal principles of child development apply to all children regardless of their backgrounds and experiences. Postdevelopmental perspectives reject the assumptions of developmentalism that have led to practices that used play as a way of reproducing dominant minority-world societal norms and values. These perspectives recognize diversity among children in terms of class, gender, race, sexuality, ethnicity, places of origin, abilities and other social factors (Pacini-Ketchabaw 2014). Therefore, they emphasize that the meanings of children's play cannot be fixed in any one context. Postdevelopmental perspectives point out that developmental approaches largely ignore power imbalances, how power operates and how it transforms social relations by creating categories such as race, citizenship and/or language/accent markers (see also Chapter 8).

Postdevelopmental perspectives also include postcolonial perspectives. These perspectives can help educators recognize that taken-for-granted understandings of play as a universal phenomenon consider those who cannot (or choose not to) play as 'abnormal' (Cannella and Viruru 2004). Early childhood scholars who apply postcolonial perspectives to the study of Indigenous knowledge have helped educators to question play pedagogies based on developmental minority-world standards and how these approaches might marginalize other ways of knowing and being in the world (Ritchie and Rau 2012). For example, a recent study with a Misak Indigenous community in Colombia found that the Misak do not even have a word for play in their language (Prochner et al. 2016). As in some other majority-world cultures, children are guided to participate in adult activities such as gardening and cooking and 'play through their work', but a minority-world concept of play does not exist.

Postdevelopmental perspectives also show how the power relationships between adults and children need to be challenged in early childhood education practices. These power relationships have led to silencing children's voices, not only in their play, and to taking away their right to make choices about 'their basic human necessities such as what and when they want to eat or when they go to the bathroom' (Ailwood 2011: 21).

## *Influences of postdevelopmental theories on classroom practice*

Postdevelopmental theories emphasize the need to develop a new language that actively works against the colonizing, racializing, heteronormative and racist discourses in the classroom. What is needed is the view that play is not necessarily 'innocent' and that it can be a place for 'political' conversations (Taylor 2007). The application of such frameworks to early childhood structures and practices sees play and learning through play as following 'regimes of truth' as discussed in the work of Michel Foucault (1980: 131). That is, developmental theories of play have authority and tell early childhood teachers 'what needs to be done in the field and how it should be done' (Rogers 2011: 10). From this perspective, the analysis of 'play as a significant tactic for the management of preschool childhoods' (Ailwood 2003: 287) is helpful in understanding how play came to be such a dominant pedagogical force in early childhood education (Figure 7.5).

FIGURE 7.5 *Controlling children through play*

Postdevelopmental theories call for educators' understanding of the complexity and diversity of play. These theories invite educators to question taken-for-granted notions of play, including its inherent 'goodness', and bring to the forefront the power dynamics underlying play experiences. For example, some classrooms may claim to be inclusive spaces where 'we are all friends', yet some children use play time to manoeuvre into positions of power. In her observation of children with developmental exceptionalities, Karen Watson (2018) describes that these children were excluded during play. These power dynamics also include adult–child relationships, the separation of childhood from adulthood and the idea that play is the 'work' of childhood. It ignores the role of play in shaping gender, (dis)ability and racial aspects of identity, as well as how these aspects of identity are affirmed or marginalized in play (see also Chapter 8).

## How is play related to learning, teaching and the curriculum?

The concepts of play and learning have long been the pillars on which discussions about ECE practices have been built. What does teaching mean in relation to the idea of learning through play? Sue Rogers (2011) calls it a conflict of interest. On one hand, the dominant view of play is that it is a free, child-initiated or at least child-led, spontaneous, intrinsically motivated activity. The idea of free play is based on a Piagetian view of the child as a young scientist (see also Chapter 5) who is expected to explore and discover the world without any adult intervention. On the other hand, learning implies teaching, which is often driven by a set of learning objectives and desired competencies, including a set of skills, attitudes and knowledge that the learner is expected to acquire. As has been persuasively argued by sociocultural theorists like Vygotsky (2004) as well as shown empirically by more recent scholars (Wallerstedt and Pramling 2012), play is dependent on previous experiences and the mastery of cultural tools (see also Chapters 4 and 5). These theories challenge the traditional view of free play. According to this latter view, it is vital that children have opportunities to play, but the teacher has an important role in introducing children to cultural tools and practices to extend this play.

More recently, the term playful pedagogy has attempted to resolve this 'conflict of interest'. It is defined as 'a systematic approach to the practice and study of playful learning and teaching in school that will help build a shared language and understanding of how to support learning through play' (Mardell et al. 2016). This approach asks teachers to 'be flexible, interactive, and relentlessly responsive, while engaging closely with the learners so they may guide learning while following play directed by the learners' (Goouch 2008: 94). This view adds to previous definitions of playfulness that may be manifested through children's and teachers' demonstrations of 'qualities of play namely *spontaneity, manifestation of joy*, and *sense of humor*' (Lieberman 1977: 23, italics in original).

Since pretend play consists mostly of enacted narratives (Nicolopoulou et al. 2014), pedagogy of play may also involve storytelling. Either alone or in the company of others, children create narratives for their own purposes. They do so without instruction, coercion or the conventional use of paper and pencil. The pedagogy is then organic, developing out of the moment in an intimate conversation between teacher and child, who share a relationship of trust (Goouch 2010). Songs, too, can be seen as playful behaviours. For many children in African societies, play through songs is an extension of 'songs for work' by adults (Finnegan 2014). Such play practices are also found in different life situations that children experience, like disaster and war. They demonstrate the recreation function as well as artistic creativity within such songs.

Mtonga's (2012) close analysis of specific examples of games in Zambian contexts illustrates how 'games help children to think, intellectualise or discuss their own activities, and explore the world around them' (quoted in Serpell and Nsamenang 2014: 20). Thus 'seeking and guessing games ... and riddle contests involve reasoning and understanding the psychology of other participants', and language games demonstrate 'playful and skillful manipulation of certain word-sounds in order to distort meaning, create new concepts, or paint a satirical caricature' (quoted in Serpell and Nsamenang 2014: 20).

## *Approaches to integrating play into the curriculum*

Although there is a long history of play as an integral part of early childhood curriculum and pedagogy, there is a new emphasis on teachers' own theories of play and how these theories impact aspects of their practice, including implementation of the curriculum, organization of the learning environment, planned learning outcomes and the pedagogical approaches used. The arguments in support of play in the early childhood curriculum seem to be based 'more on rhetoric than on sound pedagogical reasoning' (Bennett et al. 1997: 31). Neville Bennett and colleagues (1997) argue that there is a need for a focus on the reality of teachers' actual practices, asserting that knowledge of what teachers do in the classroom and why they do it is of utmost importance. Various researchers have explored the beliefs and practices of teachers with regard to play in an effort to tease out teachers' understandings of play, their approach to the integration of play into the curriculum and teacher roles assumed to promote learning in the play-based curriculum.

Joe Frost and colleagues (2012) describe three approaches for integrating play into the curriculum: trust-in-play approach, facilitate-play approach and learn-and-teach-through-play approach.

FIGURE 7.6 *Playful pedagogies*

In the trust-in-play approach, a teacher provides an environment and materials for self-guided and open-ended play. The assumption is that play leads to learning naturally without adult involvement. Based mostly on Freud's view of play as a way for children to express themselves, the overall goal for programmes adopting this approach is to enhance social development and mental health.

In the facilitate-play approach, the emphasis is on the guidance of the teacher in promoting play activities. The intention is to enhance the play abilities of children by emphasizing the kinds of play (e.g. pretend play and games) deemed particularly useful for achieving curriculum outcomes in school (Bodrova and Leong 2007). The teacher has the role of creating an environment for play, and also intervening and guiding by encouraging interaction.

The learn-and-teach-through-play approach is described as focusing not on play itself but rather on using play to meet learning outcomes. A teacher's role in programmes adopting this approach is to encourage play as a context for promoting concepts and skills in literacy, maths, language, social development and problem solving. However, these approaches are unclear about the role of children and whether or not they exercise agency through active participation (see also Chapter 2) in the construction of pedagogical approaches (Figure 7.6).

## *The construction of the playing-learning child*

Pramling Samuelsson and Carlsson (2008) introduced the concept of the playing-learning child who does not make a distinction between play and learning, although children separate them in their talk. The authors write: 'Some children who have been involved in a pedagogy where play and learning become integrated do not even make a distinction between play and learning when they are asked about it in primary school' (2008: 626). In their view, in early childhood children are too young to decipher what is play and what is to be considered learning. Considering this newly constructed image of the child, they propose a new pedagogy of early childhood with the following common dimensions of play and learning: creativity, mindfulness and possibility thinking.

Creativity is central to both play and learning. All learning is experiencing something in a different way or creating something new. Engaging in learning tasks that have an aspect of 'as if' – an aspect also central to pretend play – can lead to creativity. The very nature of play as an activity that allows us 'to see the world hypothetically' (Henricks 2008: 175) is comparable to research, not just learning, because it allows those involved in an activity to imagine both the processes involved and their possible outcomes. This 'as if' challenges children to go beyond their current level of thinking, or, in Vygotsky's words, to think within their ZPD.

Mindfulness – that is, the state of being aware, perceiving or being attentive towards something – is another dimension of play that is shared with learning. Ellen Langer (1997) identifies three characteristics of a mindful approach to any activity: 'the conscious creation of new categories; openness to new information; and an implicit awareness of more than one perspective' (4). In this sense, Vygotsky's (2004) famous example of a stick becoming a horse, provided earlier in this chapter, illustrates not only how reality and imagination are related to each other, but also how being attentive to the environment enhances the ability to work productively with problems, which is the very ability to generate new knowledge specific to the information and materials available in the context. This example also represents possibility thinking. The case of the stick (object)/horse (meaning) inversion (Figure 7.3) is an example of a child's creative 'solution' of the no-horse-problem; it represents their personal knowledge of horseback riding, the properties of the horse, as well as the properties of the stick and the essential commonalities between the two that allow the child to perform the role in play.

However, in many majority-world cultures, parents' priorities for their children are to learn to work and gradually take on responsibilities, first through observation, followed by imitation, then through regular participation in household work. In such cultures, adults tolerate a minimal amount of play, and pretend play in particular is of questionable appropriateness (Gaskins et al. 2007). Gaskins et al. (2007) identify four reasons why play, in some cultures, is less valued, less cultivated and less extensive: (a) children are engaged in meaningful everyday activities with adults which afford them many opportunities to learn and practice skills that are commonly attributed to play in minority-world cultures; (b) children are socialized to enter worlds that are less complex and less open-ended than typically required in post-industrial societies; (c) some parents deliberately curtail their children's play if they see it as endangering children, others or property; and (d) if play is a coping mechanism for children, children in some majority-world cultures may not need to play as much because they don't have to cope with as many or as high demands made on them. Nevertheless, even in these cultures, children are seen to benefit from play as an enjoyable activity.

## *Summary*

This chapter explored the difficulties associated with defining play and the main theories on the relationship between play and development that currently dominate the early childhood landscape. Play is framed in two conflicting ways: as a right affirmed by the UN Convention on the Rights of the Child, and as pedagogy that derives from pressures to prepare children for school. Particular attention was given to constructivist/cognitive theories of play in relation to development (Piaget), such as play as a leading activity (Vygotsky, Elkonin) or as adaptive variability (Sutton-Smith). The chapter critiqued these theories from a postdevelopmental perspective and discussed their application in early childhood practice. It also considered means of reconciling play, learning and teaching by describing approaches such as trust-in-play, facilitate-play, learn-and-teach-through-play, playful pedagogy and the notion of the playing-learning child.

# CHAPTER EIGHT

# Children, Difference and Diversity

***Proposition: Children have abilities, strengths and needs, as well as the right to be different.***

Although societies have always been characterized by differentiation – that is, they are made up of people of different genders, sexuality, age, abilities, race, ethnicity, religion and faith, socioeconomic status, power, etc. – there is a perception that today's societies are becoming increasingly diverse, due in part to the unprecedented influx of displaced people worldwide. Schools' potential to foster inclusion of different groups and to create a safe space for all students has been recognized. However, race, language, gender, ethnicity, ability and other markers of difference that position children socially in relation to the dominant group/norm have been used in practices of marginalization and exclusion in school. In this chapter we ask the following questions:

1. How is difference defined and how are difference and diversity related?
2. Where does 'difference as deficiency' come from and how can we interrupt the practice of pathologizing children?
3. What are the markers of difference and how are they related to children's developing sense of who they are in relation to others?
4. What does it mean to honour children's right to be different?

For additional information, reflective questions and practical implications visit: https://www.bloomsbury.com/cw/learning-to-teach-young-children/chapter-8/

## How is difference defined and how are difference and diversity related?

The *Merriam-Webster Dictionary* defines difference as:

a) the quality or state of being dissimilar or different
b) an instance of being unlike or distinct in nature, form or quality

The questions that are relevant to educators are these: If we think of or describe a child as 'different', in what way are they different? Who is the child different from? In other words, we need to critically examine how our views of difference came to be defined as such and what they represent. As anthropologist Norman Buchignani (1980) explains, difference as a concept 'operates on those who hold it, as a way of seeing part of the world around them; once formed, it provides the basis for action consistent with it' (80). In other words, not only seeing difference, but also acting on the way differences are perceived, is socially constructed.

Examples of difference as a social construct include binaries such as we/they, male/female, Black/White, and good/bad. When it comes to differences among human beings, these binary oppositions mask the complexities of the human condition. Any individual can be categorized by several characteristics at once that intersect in a unique way. Intersectionality, as a theoretical framework, explains 'how multiple social identities such as race, gender, sexual orientation, SES [socioeconomic status], and disability intersect at the micro level of individual experience to reflect interlocking systems of privilege and oppression (i.e. racism, sexism, heterosexism, classism) at the macro social-structural level' (Bowleg 2012: 1267). Intersectionality is therefore 'a way of understanding and analyzing the complexity in the world, in people, and in human experiences' (Collins and Bilge 2016: 2). It also helps us understand how the use of binaries masks the power related to characteristics such as class, sex, race/ethnicity/culture, dis/abilities, often leading to differential relationship between the groups. The actions of those in a position of power and privilege who see themselves as 'the norm' against which difference is defined can result in discrimination based on the perceived/identified differences.

Children's and their parents' rights based on both inherent characteristics (e.g. race, colour, sex, language, disability) and characteristics based on their external societal situation (e.g. language; religion; political or other opinion; national, ethnic or social origin; property or other status) seem to be protected by the 1989 United Nations Convention on the Rights of the Child (UNCRC): 'States Parties shall respect and ensure the rights set forth in the present Convention to each child within their jurisdiction without discrimination of any kind, irrespective of the child's or his or her parent's or legal guardian's race, colour, sex, language, religion, political or other opinion, national, ethnic or social origin, property, disability, birth or other status' (Article 2). However, these rights are often aspirational and are not universally enforced (see also Chapter 2). Drawing from the work of Kobayashi and Ray (2000), Robinson and Jones-Diaz (2005) explain that not all rights receive the same support, recognition or priority, indicating that political ideologies are situated along a spectrum, therefore the degree of commitment to equity fluctuates accordingly. The fact that the 2015 UNESCO *Incheon Declaration – Education 2030* states that it 'is inspired by a humanistic vision of education and development based on human rights and dignity; social justice; inclusion; protection; cultural, linguistic and ethnic diversity; and shared responsibility and accountability' is a recognition that after nearly thirty years since the declaration of UNCRC, children of the world are still faced with inequalities in educational opportunities, many of which are created by the ideologies of difference.

Martine Abdallah-Pretceille (2004) argues that the concept of difference itself serves as an instrument of power and domination because the focus of difference is always, as in the case of cultural difference, on a negative aspect of culture, which serves to legitimize a certain behaviour or a certain exercise of power. She indicates that 'diversity' is preferable to 'difference' because there is less stigma attached to the former. The search for differences, Abdallah-Pretceille concludes, should be replaced by an analysis of relationships where diversity and universality complement one another. Diversity can be associated with the notion of plurality, not difference.

## Where does 'difference as deficiency' come from and how can we interrupt the practice of pathologizing children?

The notion of difference as deficiency dates to the ancient Greek historian Herodotus, who, in his book *Histories*, written in 440 BC, called people who were different (from the Greeks) 'barbarians' (Cole and Gajdamaschko 2007: 195). Attempts to 'civilize' the 'barbarians' through education were formalized and spread throughout Europe with the publication of Comenius's *Orbis Sensualium Pictus* (the visible world in pictures) published in 1666 and translated shortly afterwards into all official European languages. Comenius's book established the 'civilizing' process of the modern individual through the creation of order in schooling and has since had an impact on pedagogical theory and practice in many ways, including generalizing the manners and customs of the higher medieval class (e.g. cleanliness and order) as a universal benchmark for a civilized modern individual. As a result, the everyday life of the underclass, unable to fit into the perfectly ordered (divine) structure of the world that was desired, was made invisible (Kirova and Prochner 2015). The underclass's way of living and being was thus excluded; it was seen as a 'type of "sickness" or "sinfulness" that can always be healed in the great beyond' (Lippitz 2007: 81).

Since the seventeenth century, education has played a central role in identifying, labelling and 'fixing' those deemed different and therefore deficient/other/abnormal. In Canada in 1879, for example, the journalist and newspaper publisher Nicolas Flood Davin (later the member of Parliament for Assiniboia West) proposed a residential school system for Indigenous children modelled on the Indian industrial schools in the United States and aimed at assimilating 'Indians' and 'half-breeds' into Canadian society (Prochner 2019). The premise of the residential school system was that 'the young children could be saved from their lifestyle and become productive citizens of the state and fully assimilate into the dominant society' (Nishnawbe Aski Nation n.d. quoted in Elementary Teachers' Federation of Ontario 2017: 49).

The processes by which people who belong to a particular group 'are seen by a more powerful group as abnormal' (Heydon and Iannacci 2009: 3) are now understood as *pathologizing*. Children from culturally and linguistically diverse backgrounds and those who are disabled are most commonly pathologized. However, it is important to understand, as Carolyn Shields and her colleagues (2005) point out, that although the processes of pathologizing affect individuals, the individuals themselves are not the targets of pathologizing; rather, the targets are the markers (e.g. race, language, gender, ethnicity, ability) that position the individual socially in relation to the dominant group/norm in any given society and in any given historical period of time. For example, using the markers 'ethnicity' and 'second language learners' for students from a particular group (e.g. Hispanic students in some areas of the United States) positions them as at risk 'minority' even when they are a numerical majority in a school. The students are labelled and treated as a minority within the larger societal and educational discourses and are expected to meet the expectations of the dominant (White, middle-class) group in terms of language proficiency, behaviours, etc. In these circumstances, it is appropriate to see such students as 'minoritized' rather than belonging to a minority group, because of how their knowledge, experiences, language and the cultural forms of mediation (see also Chapter 5) to which they are accustomed to in their families, or their 'funds of knowledge' (Moll et al. 1992), are devalued and excluded from the school curriculum and pedagogy. Prasanna Srinivasan (2009) puts forth how 'linguicism' is perpetuated by descriptions such as 'languages other than English' and 'culturally and linguistically diverse', which set the English majority culture as the norm against which all other groups are compared. It is important to recognize that such a categorization, based on group-based formulations, is limiting. As intersectionality research contends, 'no single social label – female, Black, bisexual, poor – can ever exhaust what it means for an individual to travel in the world'; therefore 'no analysis or label is ever complete' (Harris and Leonardo 2018: 5). However, by isolating the labels, we can interrupt and delegitimize the practices that continue to marginalize multiply minoritized individuals and communities (Artiles et al. 2016).

In their recent review of quality in early childhood education over the past thirty years, Mariana Souto-Manning and Ayesha Rabadi-Raol (2018) identified three assumptions about multiply minoritized and racialized children on which the discourse on ECE quality was constructed: inferiority, deficit and cultural difference:

- *Inferiority*: Children from multiply minoritized backgrounds have been seen as biologically inferior – as having smaller brains and lower IQs than White children, who have been seen as racially superior.

- *Deficit*: Children from multiply minoritized backgrounds have been seen as experiencing poor upbringings in their homes and communities and developing a deficit – whether linguistic or cultural – for example, having a word gap, being at risk, needing a head start to succeed in schools and schooling (grounded in the desirability of colonial monocultural, monolingual norms imposed ethnocentrically and violently onto them).

- *Cultural difference*: Children from multiply minoritized backgrounds have been seen as different from the colonial monocultural, White, monolingual norm. (205–6)

Although the assumption of biological inferiority of minoritized children is no longer prevalent, the dominant ECE discourses positioning minoritized and racialized students as being 'at risk for failure' (Swadener and Lubeck 1995: 2) are still evident in various ECE intervention programmes and services for 'at risk' families and children (e.g. HighScope/Head Start in the United States, Aboriginal Head Start in Canada). Such intervention programmes are built on the readiness discourses in ECE that position children from diverse backgrounds as ill-prepared for school and therefore in need of early educational interventions to compensate for their 'inadequate' or deficient home environments. The proliferation of such programmes today indicates that the discourses of school readiness, cultural and linguistic inferiority and developmental appropriateness according to White monolingual and monocultural norms still perpetuate the colonial values and beliefs firmly grounded in cultural and linguistic normativity. This 'at risk' discourse is paired with the discourse of 'accountability', which can be seen as a way of controlling the risk factors 'without giving up one's privilege; public education then becomes the repository for anxiety of risk' (Heydon and Iannacci 2009: 21).

## What are the markers of difference and how are they related to children's developing sense of who they are in relation to others?

### Markers of difference: Culture/cultural differences

The term 'culture' is found in many contemporary educational theories – cultural diversity, multicultural education, cultural sensitivity, cultural appropriateness, cultural sustainability, etc. To understand how 'cultural difference' has become one of the core markers of 'difference' in the process of pathologizing children, we need to begin by examining how the concept is defined in various theories. Anthropologists have criticized the tendency in both multicultural education and cultural sensitivity theories to view non-Western cultures as stable, tradition-bound, timeless entities. The underlying theme in these theories is that culture has existential autonomy and 'does things' to people (Hoffman 1996) which 'shifts us dangerously back toward viewing others as beings who are profoundly and inherently different from ourselves' (Perry 1992: 52). Thus, Dianne Hoffman continues, difference is made to 'support overarching frameworks of shared values or worldview firmly enshrined in that privileged existential space called *culture*' (550, italics in original). Such notion of culture(s) and cultural differences stresses that a romanticized notion of culture that 'fails to critically interrogate power', as George Dei asserts, 'is severely limited in the understanding of social reality' (1996: 27).

In reviewing the different definitions of the concept of culture in psychological research, Çiğdem Kâgitçibasi (2007) identifies two approaches to the study of cultural phenomena or concepts that can potentially lead to oversimplification of cultural differences and similarities: false uniqueness of each culture and false uniformity:

- *False uniqueness:* The study of culture *from within* emphasizes the uniqueness of concepts, as well as individual cases (a person, a culture, etc.) in each cultural context that require its study from within and in its own right, defying comparison. The danger of such an approach is that when differences are found in cross-cultural comparisons, they tend to be attributes of the (false) uniqueness of each culture.

- *False uniformity:* The study of culture *from without* emphasizes the 'typical', which can be compared across cultures using a common standard of measure. The emphasis on underlying similarities renders comparison possible. The danger of such an approach is that when similarities are found between or across cultures, they are attributed to either shared biology or social structure.

However, similarities across cultures do not imply genetic determination; they can be due to some universal (or commonly shared) psychological or social structural factors. For example, all societies have developed rules and social control mechanisms for maintaining intergroup harmony, care of the young and socialization of children. More specifically, similarities are found in child-rearing practices among societies with subsistent agricultural lifestyles, close-knit bonds in terms of dependency and conformity expectations from children (see also Chapter 3). Kağitçibaşi (2007) suggests that the solution to the dangers of either of these two approaches is to see them as complementary. She argues that all human psychology should be cultural psychology, because human phenomena always take place within culture.

Ratna Ghosh and Ali Abdi (2004) maintain that postmodern thought resists the idea of culture as an organizing principle because it creates borders around ethnicity, class and gender. Borders falsely homogenize cultures within a culture. Adopting a critical, nonessentialist approach to cultural difference means acknowledging that there is as much variation within groups as between them, which helps us to develop a more complex understanding of the interplay of cultural differences with other social statuses, such as ethnicity, class and sexual orientation. Such an approach also challenges discourses that construct exotic and stigmatized Others.

Vygotsky's cultural-historical theoretical framework has had a strong impact on the understanding of culture's profound and complex role (i.e. cultural signs, symbols and tools) in the development of psychological functioning (see also Chapter 5). It also had an impact on what is now called multicultural education. The application of Vygotsky's theory, however, presents a challenge to educators and educational researchers alike to answer the question related to uniqueness or universality of social interactions in the implications of these interactions for the education of children in pluralistic or diverse societies. For example, how does a newcomer child raised in a culture oriented towards the collective good adjust to a culture that is based on individual achievement, competition and personal success?

Schools are frequently the first major institutions that children of newcomer families encounter on their own and in which major socialization, outside of home, occurs (Garcia Coll and Markus 2009). For children, schooling is a process through which they must come to terms with host counties' societal expectations, while trying to remain connected to family and home culture. Immigrant children's school participation is often an experience of exclusion and marginalization. The ways in which newcomer children are classified and labelled at school could produce, reproduce and strengthen these children's social positions (see Chapter 6).

Influenced by three editions of DAP, the field of ECE has been dominated by a discourse of cultural differences that positioned newcomer children and their families, among other racialized and minoritized groups, as different from, meaning 'less than', the White, middle-class monolinguals whose values and practices have become the norm against which the 'others' were measured. When such families are included, they are described by their perceived deficits – for example, children who are developing multilingually and bilingually are positioned as not having language, which establishes their inferior position to their monolingual (English-speaking) peers. Their parents too are described as 'parents who do not speak English' (Copple and Bredekamp 2009: 183). Both the children and their families are sometimes referred to as 'having limited language proficiency' which puts them 'at risk' without acknowledging the multiple barriers to which such families have historically been subjected. As Souto-Manning and Rabadi-Raol assert, 'such descriptors signal the coloniality framing multiply minoritised children and their families' experiences, values, and voices in marginal and deficit-ridden ways' (2018: 207).

## Cultural identity

Essentialized definitions of culture lead to the understanding of self/cultural identity and self-esteem as fundamentally the same in all cultures and ethnic groups, while the differences in concepts of self are assumed to be among the most profound influences on cultural and social phenomena (see also Chapter 3). Hoffman (1996) believes that basing views of what constitutes healthy identity on Western norms of continuity, clarity, consistency, assertiveness, individuation and so forth is especially problematic. Instead, she argues, we need 'to be informed to a much greater extent by knowledge about and awareness of indigenous cultural psychologies that may or may not share the basic Western developmental paradigm' (Hoffman 1996: 557). Particularly problematic within the Western paradigm is the ownership formulation of identity as something one 'has' (i.e. 'all students have an ethnic identity' or 'every student has a culture'), which represents the relationship between person and culture as one of possession. This view reflects mainstream Western materialism and notions of property rights, making cultural identity compatible with the dominant economic structure of capitalist societies. Another related assumption is that of 'a one-to-one relationship between self and culture characterized by a clear, fixed commitment to a particular cultural or ethnic identity' (Hoffman 1996: 557). This assumption legitimizes the notion that there are already pre-given identities that can easily mask or even reiterate cultural hierarchies associated with Eurocentrism (Cornell and Murphy 2002).

## *Markers of difference: Race and ethnicity*

Race, according to Brigitte Vittrup (2016), 'is to a large extent a social construction of which only very little is rooted in genetics or biology. Nonetheless, race and ethnicity continue to serve as major organizing features of our society, and they play a big role in the development of one's social identity – especially for people whose racial or ethnic category is in a numerical minority' (549). However, it is important to make a distinction between race and ethnicity, which, although socially defined and constructed, are based on different characteristics. For example, 'race is *socially* defined but on the basis of *physical* criteria' (Van den Berghe 1967: 9, italics in original) while ethnicity 'is based on *cultural* criteria' (Van den Berghe 1967: 10, italics in original) such as religion, language, customs, institutions and history. However, the colour of one's skin cannot be separated from the historical practices that have constructed the understanding of races.

Critical race theory (CRT) makes visible how White supremacist ontologies disempower people of colour and advance the interests of White elites (Delgado and Stefancic 2017). With antiracist theorists, critical race theorists seek to combat racism as an intersection of classism, sexism and other forms of oppression (Solórzano and Yosso 2002). Critical race theorists see race as an analytic tool rather than socially constructed, and use it to compare and contrast social conditions (Sleeter and Bernal 2004). From a CRT perspective, Souto-Manning and Rabadi-Raol (2018) demonstrate how framing DAP neutrally reinforces the practices of White, middle-class, English-speaking families. The authors 'seek to disrupt the essentialism, the imposition of White ways of being, behaving, and communicating onto children of colour as if they applied to the entire universe of young children in today's (pre)school classrooms, thereby marginalizing and pathologizing those who are members of the global majority in early childhood education and beyond' (212).

## Racial identity

In reviewing the current literature of development of children's racial awareness, Vittrup (2016) indicates that around the age of three or four, children learn to recognize racial differences, label the differences and categorize themselves within a racial or ethnic group, typically based on physical criteria and labels that have been discussed in the contexts in which they live (i.e. home and preschool). It is between the ages of five and eight when children begin to show knowledge about the distinguishing characteristics of their racial or ethnic group and develop feelings about belonging to the group. During these early years they also start to absorb more complex information about racial and ethnic groups, including stereotypes and social status, from the adult world around them. They then apply these ideas to their specific situation to justify generalized identities, power and privilege.

Children who are biracial or multiracial may perceive their choice of identity as an imposition of racial identity – what others believe they *should* identify as. Since the mid-1980s (Rockquemore et al. 2009), mixed race is viewed as a valid racial identity where all the heritages of the person must be acknowledged (Edwards et al. 2010). Such individuals are believed to be capable of developing healthy biracial or multiracial identities. This post-race perspective aims to go beyond the notion of race and racial boundaries to encourage a 'sense of self beyond race' (Edwards et al. 2010: 951).

## Children's development of racial and ethnic concepts

The question of the timing of children's development of racial and/or ethnic distinctions and concepts is not new. The Piagetian tradition in psychology has shaped early childhood practitioners' beliefs that young children aged two to five, being in the 'egocentric stage' of cognitive development, are therefore 'incapable of meaningful understanding of major abstractions such as race, ethnicity, gender, or class' (Van Ausdale and Feagin 2001: 5). As discussed in Chapter 5, Piaget advanced the idea that a child's system of thought is fundamentally different from that of an adults, and therefore children's thinking remains incomplete until they begin to think like an adult. In other words, children need to overcome their egocentricity, which typically occurs at age seven or older, before they begin to grasp social abstractions. Following the same view of children's cognitive development, Lawrence Kohlberg (1966) postulated that children's level of moral reasoning before the age of seven is such that they cannot attend to or consider the views and concerns of others.

Debra Van Ausdale and Joe Feagin (2001) are critical of the Piagetian tradition in that its view of children as highly individual, internally oriented and incapable of understanding and employing abstract social concepts like gender, race and class has led both researchers and practitioners to believe that children's use of derogatory or racist comments is a function of the their mental functioning, naiveté or 'mere imitations of adult behaviours rather than reflections of the child's (or children's groups') significant interpretations of reality' (10). In their view, the main conceptual problem in research on children's development of racial and/or ethnic distinctions and concepts is grounded in the developmental picture created by Piaget's and Kohlberg's theories. The internal contradiction in this theoretical tradition can be summarized as follows: On one hand, developmentalists emphasize children's early experiences as foundational for later development and describe children as capable of developing their own hypotheses, not only about the physical world, but also about some complex social phenomena such as friendships and social status in a peer group. On the other hand, they view children's early experiences with racial distinctions and/or discrimination as either inconsequential or less so, and position young children as incapable of grasping racism and racist behaviours, which defines them as either blameless or ignorant.

These internal conceptual contradictions are addressed by researchers who work within the sociocultural-historical theory (e.g. Vygotsky, Rogoff) of development that emphasizes the role of adult members of society in children's cognitive development. From this theoretical perspective, children's everyday

# CHILDREN, DIFFERENCE AND DIVERSITY

FIGURE 8.1 *Does race have anything to do with who is 'right'?*

interactions with others and the language they use in these interactions, along with other culturally shaped symbols, help children learn about the world, which in turn influences their cognitive development (see also Chapter 5). Among these tools, Vygotsky puts a particular emphasis on language (see also Chapter 6) as a 'tool of the mind' that is used to manipulate and make sense of both the physical and the social worlds. Discriminatory practices and language in the environments in which children live affect how children adopt those to comprehend their own as well as others' race and ethnicity (Figure 8.1).

As children participate in shared activities with adult members of their social group and culture, they not only imitate what adults do, but also, as in play, make sense of the world through interactions with their peers (see also Chapter 7). In play, children interact with significant adults and peers in their social groups to creatively reconstruct and recreate their own observations of the world around them. In playing with their peers, children explore concepts, emotions and actions away from the watchful and often judgemental eye of the adult. In play, social roles (e.g. teacher, student, doctor, nurse, pilot, firefighter) are taken on and performed according to children's knowledge of these roles and their life experiences in different contexts involving encounters with adults who have such roles in the larger society. The performance of these roles depends on the duration of the play episode. However, other (ascribed) roles, such as racial and gender roles, though socially constructed, are carried from one situation to another, typically throughout one's entire lifetime, with the exception of transgender individuals. Between the ages of five and eight, Vittrup writes, 'children develop racial constancy, which means they understand that their race or ethnicity will not change' (2016: 450). Current scholarship indicates that identities are always in the making, and these elements intersect uniquely in an individual. Identity is plural and dynamic, not singular and static (Adballah-Pretceille 2004).

The use of the term 'role' is seen as misleading or incorrect when referring to children's race or gender because it does not reflect the deep significance the psychological meanings of these constructs. Rather, 'identity' should be used because children do not just perform racial and/or gender roles; these constructs are normalized in their meanings and contribute, consciously or subconsciously, to re-creating the structures of race, ethnicity and gender, not only in the child's mind, but also in the minds of their peer group and the society at large (Van Ausdale and Feagin 2001).

## *Markers of difference: Gender/gender identity and gender diversity*

Gender diversity encompasses experiences of gender within and beyond the gender binary, the idea that femininity and masculinity are two discrete categories aligned with two discrete sexes, female and male. Gender identity refers to 'one's internal sense of being a woman, a man, another gender, or no gender, while gender expression refers to one's external presentation of gender through, for example, behaviour and manner of dress' (Erickson-Schroth 2014: 614). Acquiring a gender identity is a complex process influenced by many factors, including the significant adults in children's lives, their culturally shaped behaviours towards each other as well as towards the children, and the media's representation of societal gender roles. Gender identity is also influenced by one's biology. However, while one's sex most often refers to biological differences, such as chromosomes, hormones and internal and external sex organs, gender is viewed as socially constructed; it 'describes the characteristics that a society or culture assigns to the categories of femininity and masculinity and what are considered to be appropriate feminine or masculine behaviours' (Jacobson 2016: 625).

The notion of the 'naturally developing' child has been reinforced through developmental psychology's emphasis on universal developmental stages through which 'normal' children pass. Within this view of development, Kohlberg's (1966) theory of gender identity formation claims that children achieve gender consistency at approximately six or seven years of age – that is, children know that superficial factors, such as the length of one's hair or the roles they play, do not alter one's gender (Browne 2004). Since the 1970s, social learning theory (Bandura 1962) based on observable behaviours has been typically used to explain children's development of gender roles. From this theoretical perspective, children acquire gender roles by watching others and then imitating models of gender behaviours that they see and value in their lives. Children's behaviours are then reinforced when people they trust and respect reprimand and reward their gendered behaviours. Based on this perspective of gender role development, there is a growing concern in the ECE field about the 'sexualization of childhood' (Derman-Sparks and Edwards 2010: 96) by media and popular culture through 'graphic sexual images' where 'girls learn that their value is determined by how "sexy" they look, rather than who they are and what they achieve' (96). Boys, on the other hand, learn to not only judge girls by these standards but to 'judge themselves and each other by how strong and independent they seem – and how ready they are to fight' (96; Figure 8.2).

Critics of developmentalism in general and social learning theory in particular point out that conventions about an absolute biological division between male and female are unquestioned, and therefore gender stereotypes are reinforced and perpetuated because the binary gender roles are presented as neutral and natural. However, as Mindy Blaise writes, 'this explanation of sex and gender is unable to explain why masculine gender roles are consistently privileged over female gender roles' (2016: 625). In addition, critics point out that social learning theory positions young children as passive reproducers of culture (see also Chapter 1), soaking up what they see and then simply imitating stereotypical gender-specific behaviours.

FIGURE 8.2 *Gendered role playing*

Early childhood educators who believe that gender is learned through observation have engaged in gender-equity strategies intended to encourage children to resist gender-stereotyped behaviours. Unfortunately, providing materials, including books and toys/dolls representing men and women in nontraditional gender roles, has not resulted in the anticipated outcome. Children continue to reproduce gender stereotypes in their play as well as in their daily interactions (Blaise and Taylor 2012). Research focusing on gender roles and children's play shows children as young as three years of age working hard to maintain female and male categories; Blaise writes that 'they perform stereotypical gender roles and gain pleasure from these gender performances' (2016: 625). When children's behaviours comply with the dominant gender discourse in society, the children see themselves as 'getting their gender "right" which gives a sense of satisfaction in succeeding' (Blaise and Taylor 2012: 90). Children's desire to be 'right' and 'successful' in the eyes of the important adults in their lives motivates them to repeat gender-predictable behaviours, thus reinforcing the 'truths' of the dominant gender discourse framed by heteronormativity. Formed by combining the words 'heterosexual' and 'normative', the term 'heteronormativity' deliberately names the assumption, dominating the Western political thought, that the heterosexual ideology represents the 'principle of social union itself' (Warner 1993: xxi). If children's gender performance falls outside of this heteronormative frame, as in boys' interest in the princess dress and role in make-believe play or girls volunteering to fix a 'broken car' on a play journey, the children risk being thought of or labelled as 'abnormal'. Although play has been recognized as a gendered activity among young children, recent studies suggest that boys often tend to be more actively engaged than girls in the (re)production of gendered play (Bryan 2018). Therefore, as Rita Chen points out, 'not only girls but boys themselves are the victims of this heterosexual hegemonic discourse in which what it means to be a "guy" and how to behave as a guy are strictly rule-governed' (2009: 150).

Feminist poststructuralist theorists help educators understand children as actively engaged in generating different kinds of gender roles in play: Young children are neither passive reproducers of gender roles, nor are they 'innocent' in playing them. Children take an active part in both maintaining and resisting gender roles, as well as in actively using the different kinds of power available to boys and girls through gender discourses operating in their contexts. Blaise and Taylor (2012) suggest that the use of queer theory that challenges the notions of gender as nature can help both researchers and teachers gain a new perspective – a 'queer eye' – on children's gender development that does not assume any kind of gender as normal but 'looks at the ways in which children's gender behaviour both reflects and reinforces the norms of heterosexuality' (89).

Recently in the social sciences, there has been a move away from understanding gender as difference or through roles, towards focusing on gender relations (Blaise 2016: 628). This shift makes it possible to consider that people may move in and out of diverse situations, which will allow for different kinds of gender relations. For example, gender relations may be mediated by technology, such as the internet, and they happen between females and between males. These new understandings of children's gender identity and gender performances invite educators to adopt a role of 'liberators' rather than 'punishers' when children transgress from what is perceived to be appropriate masculinity and femininity (Leiminer 2010).

## *Markers of difference (dis)ability*

Disability is now recognized as a political identity, socially constructed in tandem with race and class, rather than an objective medical condition. As such, it functions to 'other' students whose differences were envisaged through a deficit lens (Annamma et al. 2018). In tracing the notion of the 'normal' child, Naima Browne (2004) determined that the body of research based on Piaget's theory of learning and development as progressing through clearly defined universal stages. Within the normalizing discourse, children who do not fit the norm are seen as different, exceptional, usually deficient in some way or 'at risk' of failure in the school system. Both the differences evident in children's personal characteristics and the range of their experiences in the natural and social environments need to be taken into account when children are described as disabled.

According to the World Health Organisation's (2011) definition, 'disability arises from the interaction of health conditions with contextual factors – environmental and personal factors' (5). Postmodern theoretical perspective on disability, however, points that although this definition combines a medical model and a social model of understanding, it is still dichotomous; it 'does not account for the many types of differences experienced by the individual children and the influence of freedom on experience' (Wonderwood et al. 2012: 292). Acknowledgement of difference is the first principle of equality in inclusive education based on the capability approach in education, which emphasizes that 'each person has capabilities that are individually defined by that which they value' (Wonderwood et al. 2012: 291).

The capability approach, articulated by Amartya Sen (1999) and elaborated by Kathryn Wonderwood and colleagues (2012), emphasizes the acknowledgement of five kinds of differences in children: individual (e.g. biological or genetic); environmental (e.g. exposure to toxins in utero); social (e.g. access to social supports, programming; cultural differences); relational (e.g. language minority or economic status) and family (e.g. differential treatment by family members). These differences account for the freedom an individual has to achieve their capabilities – the actions or states of being that are valued by an individual (Wonderwood et al. 2012). Since most capabilities are not yet defined or realized in early childhood, a basic capability for this period of children's lives is the capability to be educated.

FIGURE 8.3 *Using technology to facilitate inclusion*

Because the main role of early childhood educators has traditionally been to prepare children for their later educational experiences, this expectation creates a tension between the goals of early intervention and those of inclusive programmes. Intervention programmes aim to improve specific functions (i.e. cognitive, emotional and/or physical), with the intention of preventing disability or ameliorating existing disabilities, while inclusive early childhood education for children with disabilities is an education alongside their abled peers. Early intervention programmes, operating from the position of 'difference as deficiency', have an overall goal, through the process of normalization, to 'change' the child with disability to be as close as possible to the 'normal' child of the same age.

An example of inclusive early childhood education is provided by the Reggio Emilia schools' philosophy and practice, which embraces the concept of difference among children and sees disability as just one of many possible differences a particular child could have. Seeing difference as a way of being promotes a close relationship between the educator and the child, as well as the child's family, in which the educator learns what it means for that child to approach life while overcoming some individual challenges (Figure 8.3). As Ivana Soncini explains, Malaguzzi strongly believed that 'differences could stimulate new thoughts and new ideas because when dealing with differences in all children, you cannot use homogeneous methods. The encounter with differences stimulates healthy uncertainty. It makes it necessary to interpret, understand, and observe more' (Soncini 2011: 190). This philosophy has led the educators in Reggio schools to replace the term *children with special needs or disabilities* with the term *children with 'special rights'*.

## What does it mean to honour children's right to be different?

In order to transform deficit-based practices based on the understanding of difference as a negative concept that continues to marginalize and oppress children from multiple minoritized communities, educators need to understand that children's right to be different is a question of social justice and equity. Typically, the first step in the process is acquiring knowledge of children's rights. However, knowing what these rights are does not mean that one has a sense of injustice when these rights are not enforced or are violated and thus feels compelled to act upon that feeling. The opposite can also be true: Having a sense of unfairness or injustice does not necessarily mean that one comprehends the rights and/or the historical and social contexts that are necessary to give meaning to these rights. In addition, the intersection of rights can lead to personal conflicts. For example, one may fully understand and support the right to religious freedom/expression but interprets the wearing of religious headgear (e.g. the hijab) as an expression or symbol of female subordination and therefore resents it on the grounds of sexual inequality. Other tensions can exist in the intersection of religious and privacy rights (sometimes related to sexual orientation) or disability and property rights. Kerry Robinson and Criss Jones-Diaz write that 'some early childhood educators, who have strong commitments to social justice and equity issues such as "race", ethnicity, gender or (dis)ability for example, can ironically uphold homophobic and heterosexist values and practices when it comes to dealing with sexuality. This slippage or contradiction around doing social justice work is not surprising when individuals are viewed as shifting subjects' (2005: 9).

The practice and expression of human rights in the twenty-first century have become increasingly complex. 'There are times when the claim to right of one individual or group directly affects the claim to the human rights of another group. Such competing rights claims can be played out in many places, from the classroom to workplaces, to the international stage, wherever individuals or groups actively claim the recognition of rights that may interfere with the access to rights of others' (Azmi et al. 2010: 5). However, instead of treating such rights as 'competing', educators would greatly benefit from embracing the theoretical lens offered by intersectionality to move towards intersectional justice for minoritized children. Such a transformation would require an acknowledgement that schools are poorly equipped to cope with increased diversity and that instead of playing a role in facilitating equity and belonging, schools often foster isolation and replicate racialized forms of injustice. It would also require teachers to critically examine some of the key assumptions underlying several constructs that have been used over the years within a framework of education for cultural diversity: multicultural education, antiracist education, social justice education, intercultural education, cultural sustainability, antibiased education, etc. For example, educators need to become aware that although the multicultural education movement has been educators' vehicle for advocating for the rights of all children, it has focused mainly on teaching students about cultural similarities and differences and on cultural celebrations, thus remaining at the superficial level of food, dance and music represented, for example, in the *piñata* curriculum' or the 'snowshoe curriculum' (Hoffman 1996: 550). Since the 1990s, multicultural education discourse has not only failed to make a clear distinction between race, ethnicity and culture, but has also 'renamed the difference from racial to cultural' (Willinsky 1999: 95). Therefore, there has been not only a lack of inherent understanding of the systemic nature of racism, but a reluctance to discuss racism of any kind (Dei 1996). In effect, multicultural discourse has allowed for the erasing of race from teachers' vocabulary, either by denying race matters or by using code words and phrases, like 'immigrant' or 'inner city', when referring to students of colour (Sleeter 1993). The common code for racial difference in Canada now is 'cultural difference' – a quality that racial minority children, especially Indigenous children, are said to have and which is given as the reason for any lack of school success (Schick and St. Denis 2005). The term 'cultural difference' connects education failure to the 'other' by de-emphasizing how dominant identities are implicated in the production of difference.

Intercultural and antiracist education emerged in opposition to this solidification of borders between majority and minority cultures. Antiracist education's aim is to increase cross-cultural understanding and appreciation of cultural diversity and to eliminate discrimination. Unlike multicultural education, which is concerned mainly with learning about other cultures, intercultural education aims to create a common space based on mutual understanding and recognition of similarities through dialogue (see also Chapter 3). Interculturalism ascribes to an understanding of culture as plural, dynamic and multifaceted, a frame influencing how people perceive and interact in the world while developing the ability to operate in multiple cultural settings.

Culturally relevant and sustaining pedagogies (e.g. Ladson-Billings 1995; Paris 2012; Paris and Alim 2017) focus on transforming oppressive practices by encouraging educators to develop critical consciousness – or what Souto-Manning and Rabadi-Raol call 'critical meta-awareness' – of oppressive conditions linked to White privilege and superiority. In addition, they assert, 'culturally relevant educators must have (a) high expectations for all children, believing in their infinite capacity and potential, and (b) a critical understanding of the monocultural nature of mainstream curricula, teaching, and assessments' (2018: 213). The authors elaborate that these approaches reject the language of academic, linguistic or developmental gaps that either blame the families and children from multiply minoritized backgrounds or present them as victims, using an 'at risk' discourse that positions them as needy and powerless. Gloria Ladson-Billings (2006) suggests that culturally relevant and sustaining pedagogies should adopt language that uncovers the education debt, which has historically, morally, economically and socio-politically disempowered individuals and communities of colour – and imposed multiple systems of overlapping oppressions.

Central to these transformative teaching and learning practices is the intentional integration and validation of the rich linguistic and cultural experiences and perspectives of children and families from diverse backgrounds who are seen as 'at promise' (Souto-Manning and Rabadi-Raol 2018: 217) rather than 'at risk'. Such practices will lead to recentring the Eurocentric positionings of these families established and perpetuated by ECE practices based on the principles of developmentalism, White superiority and middle-class values. Emphasis on pedagogical experiences centred on what is familiar to children and reflective of their cultures effectively meets the goals of education for intersectional justice, creating interest and leading children to learn about themselves and their peers in today's diverse classrooms. Culturally relevant and sustaining pedagogies should also acknowledge the normalization process that 'culturally different' teachers are subjected to as they too are expected to use and understand the normative 'professional' language of developmental appropriateness that still dominates the ECE field (Prochner et al. 2016).

## *Summary*

This chapter explored the complex issues of diversity and ideologies of difference as they relate to multiculturalism, inclusion and the right to be different through a variety of theoretical perspectives. It also investigated markers of difference and agentive possibilities for creating teaching and learning contexts that position concerns of social justice, care and equity as central to early childhood education. Challenging the notion of difference as deficiency, this chapter advanced the view that if society is to be enriched by diverse perspectives, experiences, ideas, knowledges and ways of being, education must actively confront racism, discrimination and prejudice against minoritized and/or racialized children and youth at both institutional and individual levels. In addition, it put forward the idea that children's right to be different must be understood and enacted in pedagogical practice if children are to achieve their full potential. Intercultural practice affirms children's funds of knowledge and multiple identities.

# CHAPTER NINE

# Teachers Are Researchers

***Proposition: Early childhood educators are (also) researchers.***

This chapter explores pedagogical documentation as a tool for creating reflective and democratic pedagogical practice. Pedagogical documentation is compared with child observation, which has been and is still used to assess children's psychological development in relation to normative categories produced from developmental psychology that define what the normal child should be doing at a particular age. The role of pedagogical documentation as a foundation of research in early childhood education is emphasized. Teachers have many responsibilities. The basic contractual duties of teachers are instruction and assessment. These duties can be undertaken in a technical way, using ready-made curricula and assessment checklists. However, we see teachers as researchers with a central role in making teaching and learning decisions. Chapter 9 explores the role of teachers as researchers in relation to three key questions:

1 How can pedagogical documentation be a learning process?
2 How do teachers learn to document, and what does pedagogical documentation look like in classrooms?
3 How does pedagogical documentation challenge the dominant discourse?

The chapter sets out documentation as part of a theory of teaching and as the basis for the discussion of assessment in Chapter 10.

For additional information, reflective questions and practical implications visit: https://www.bloomsbury.com/cw/learning-to-teach-young-children/chapter-9/

## How can pedagogical documentation be a learning process?

The pedagogical foundations of early childhood education are based in the disciplines of psychology and philosophy, with a bias towards a psychological grounding for teaching (Farquhar and White 2014). Moreover, different pedagogies have been associated with competing programme models in early childhood education (Goffin and Wilson 2001). Models of teaching reflect ideas about the design and arrangement of the teaching space, the type of materials and resources, the means of planning and assessment, and the manner of social relations amongst students and between children and teachers. In early childhood education, most models are based on child development theory and provide more or less prescriptive frameworks for practice. The models have been associated with individuals, such as Maria Montessori, Friedrich Froebel and Rudolf Steiner; training institutions such as Bank Street College; or local experiments such as in the city of Reggio Emilia, Italy (see Chapter 1). While the various models are characterized by distinctive expressions of teaching, there have been an interplay and exchange of ideas across the models, leading an Italian early childhood researcher to observe that 'early childhood pedagogy, is, in fact, both a very vivid expression of cultural niches and local particularities and the continuous contamination or *métissage* or crossfertilisation of paradigms and practices' (Bondioli 2007: 1116).

The Reggio Emilia approach is an excellent example of such crossfertilization: it draws upon elements of the ideas of psychologists Jean Piaget, Lev Vygotsky, John Dewey, Jerome Bruner and Howard Gardner; socialist-communist political ideology; and postmodern philosophy (Edwards et al. 2012; Hall et al. 2010; Smidt 2013). As a result, there are tensions in Reggio Emilia's mix of constructivist, social constructivist and progressive educational ideas about teaching and learning. The ideas of Dewey and Vygotsky, and of Vygotsky and Piaget, for example, differ on key points (Glassman 2001; Vianna and Stetsenko 2006; see Chapter 5). And Vygotskian theory is not entirely consistent with Reggio Emilia principles. Yet, as Stone (2012) points out, it coheres to the key ideas of the approach. For example, the Reggio Emilia idea of a child's self-discovery is possible in Vygotskian theory only after 'the child has already appropriated culturally constituted semantic structures and systems of meaning' (Stone 2012: 282). As described in Chapter 7, teachers' meaningful participation with children is necessary in order for play to realize its developmental benefits. Despite the emphasis on self-discovery in the Reggio Emilia approach, Malaguzzi designates a key role for adults in indirectly activating meaning.

However, Reggio Emilia is more than an eclectic mix of theories. One of its strengths is its essential open-mindedness, as opposed to approaches that have 'only a few curated ideas' (Higgins 2009: 54), such as the Montessori approach. Teaching in the Reggio Emilia approach requires open-mindedness to consider contrary views and evidence and the potential to revise opinions (Hare 1979), making it more like a philosophy of pedagogy than a method of teaching (Farquhar and White 2014).

In this view, teachers are not technicians – they need 'a basic flexibility of mind, a capacity to step outside their subject and consider it from without together with their student, a fundamental respect for their student's mind, and a willingness to encourage new ideas, doubts, questions and puzzlements' (Scheffler 1973: 61). In this way, teachers and researchers are similar: both value open-mindedness, have a focus on developing ethical and empathic relationships, and use diverse strategies and techniques in the course of 'doing research'. Indeed, the belief that teachers are intellectuals who are also researchers is a central idea in the Reggio Emilia approach. Moreover, identifying teachers as intellectuals 'positions them as professionals who produce knowledge about their practice' (Kincheloe 2003: 8) with the potential to bring about transformative learning. The notion of teachers as change agents is central to the perspective of teachers as intellectuals, which, for cultural theorist Henry Giroux (1988), meant they were transformative intellectuals. In this understanding, teachers along with students have agency, and a responsibility, to make change, and schools are political sites for 'emancipatory practice grounded in student empowerment' (Thompson 2010: 870).

The notion that teaching and research are connected activities is associated with John Dewey (1916), who believed that teachers required an 'intellectual thoroughness', by which he meant taking responsibility for thinking and actions. Dewey also identified 'flexible intellectual interest' (201–11) or open-mindedness as an essential quality for teachers, who, Doris Santoro explains, 'will look for examples of intelligence, thinking, and interest that may differ from their own or what they understand intelligence, thinking, and interest to be' (Santoro 2017: 122). Dewey wanted his laboratory school teachers to work as researchers in a way similar to scientists. He explained: 'Like any such laboratory it has two main purposes: (1) to exhibit, test, verify and criticize theoretical statements and principles; (2) to add to the sum of facts and principles in its special line' (Dewey 1896: 444). The main research question for Dewey was 'the proper organization of the subject-matter of the curriculum, and the relation of the subjects ... to other means of expression' (417). He was convinced that 'scientific recommendations could only be assessed by being applied in practice and [he] saw the teacher as a research worker testing out educational theory' (Hammersley 1993: 425). The current view of teacher as researcher includes a more expanded view of research and research methods. While the aim may still be to test educational theory, it can also be to enhance teaching and learning or assessment practices.

Teachers also actively construct theories about teaching and learning through a process of pedagogical documentation, which is the focus of this chapter. What is sometimes simply called 'documentation' can be viewed as a 'cycle of inquiry' serving as a framework for teachers' action research (Goldhaber 2007). Action research in an educational context is undertaken by teachers as a systematic enquiry into the teaching and learning process within their own classroom (Mills 2018). Pedagogical documentation is a reflective process supporting teachers' practice and decision making. As a reflective process, it requires that teachers move into a position of observation, pausing to wait before intervening.

The term 'pedagogical documentation' was popularized in the 1990s to refer to teaching in the mode of Reggio Emilia schools. Documentation is one of the teaching tools used by Reggio Emilia educators. It was initially described as a procedure involving the selection, discussion and display of symbolic representations, such as drawings or writings (Siraj-Blatchford 1999). However, establishing a single definition of pedagogical documentation has been described as a wicked problem (Fleet 2017), one that is enduring, complex and with unclear solutions with conflicting results (Rittel and Webber 1973). A further complicating factor is that terms used to describe a similar process across countries and contexts vary; it has been called pedagogical documentation, pedagogical narration, learning stories and action research. *Pedagogical narration* is a process of documenting and then sharing 'significant pedagogical occurrences' with children, teachers or families (Berger 2015: 131); *learning stories* are a form of documentation dictated by children and written by teachers for children and families (Carr and Lee 2012); *action research* is a teacher-led reflective process planned to learn about teaching. Documentation procedures have a common motivation to make learning 'visible', that is, ascribing meaning to and communicating ideas to be shared about actions and behaviours. Further, documentation of teaching is always done for a definite purpose, for example, to make a record of the instructional techniques used in a teaching situation and construct 'a narrative about the children and teacher's learning' (Wien et al. 2015: 104).

Thousands of teachers from more than eighty countries have learned about pedagogical documentation by attending study tours of the Reggio Emilia schools since 1994 (Hall et al. 2010). The idea has also been spread through travelling exhibitions of the work of teachers and children in Reggio preschools starting in 1981. The first exhibition was called *The Hundred Languages of Children*; the second was called *The Wonder of Learning*. The aim of the exhibitions was 'to affirm the vital right to education and learning, to recognize the "hundred languages" as extraordinary potentials of all children, and of human beings in general, and to promote the idea of participatory education' (Reggio Children n.d.: 4). A further aim was to serve as 'as an impetus toward the construction of a new idea and a new experience of citizenship' (Reggio Children n.d.: 5). The exhibitions were generally held alongside related professional development opportunities, special lectures, children's programmes, etc., helping to spread knowledge about pedagogical documentation, including the common element called documentation panels, use of daily logs, individual portfolios, photographs, recordings and transcriptions of conversations.

## *Documentation and democratic participation*

Chapter 2 described children's participation in their learning as a right of citizenship in which teachers are obligated to find ways for children to have their views heard and to participate in all aspects of their learning, including the assessment process. However, not all approaches to early childhood education are consistent with democratic principles, for example, behaviourally based teaching used in intervention programmes, or teaching focusing on transmitting information or using operant conditioning (Kaufman et al. 2015). Rights-based approaches require the consideration of a structure for participation, for example, routine opportunities for democratic dialogue, along with teaching strategies such as documentation (Knauf 2018). In early education within a rights-based framework, knowledge is constructed in meaningful relationships consistent with understandings of democracy.

There are, however, challenges to children's participation in pedagogical documentation, which occurs in the adult-defined contexts of preschool and theory and within unequal power relations between children and adults. As Dahlberg (2011) explains, 'what we make evident through our technologies and apparatus of documenting and experimenting does not exist outside of our theoretical and conceptual frameworks' (229). Further, documentation relies on listening to children's alternative languages, whereas there is a historical bias in schools towards visual and verbal instruction, even at the early childhood level. The hundred languages theory suggests potential for multiple expressive 'languages' for adults as well as children.

# How do teachers learn to document, and what does pedagogical documentation look like in classrooms?

Learning to document in the way inspired by Reggio Emilia is itself a process. It begins by learning to observe with a 'thinking lens' (Stacey 2015: 11) contributing to insights and interpretations about children's intentions. Documentation is part of a cyclical process: observation leads to reflection, documentation and decision making. In her study of teachers using pedagogical documentation, Laurie Kocher (2008) highlighted the importance of developing a 'disposition to document' and a 'heightened awareness' of learning situations (291), a commitment to building meaningful relationships, an identity as teacher/researcher, and a sense of being comfortable as a writer. Carol Anne Wien and her colleagues Guyevskey and Berdoussis (2011) describe learning to document as a progression rather than a series of stages or steps, by which they meant to emphasize the interrelated aspects of the process. The five 'progressions' are:

1. Developing habits of documenting
2. Becoming comfortable with going public with recounting of activities
3. Developing visual literacy skills
4. Conceptualizing a purpose of documentation as making learning visible
5. Sharing visible theories with others for interpretation and further design of curriculum

Project work in the Reggio Emilia approach is often described using the metaphor of a journey, one involving uncertainty and without a 'predefined progression, [with] no outcomes decided before the journey begins' (Rinaldi 2005: 19). The documentary journey is an integral part of the project work, 'which deepens the meanings of the work that was originally carried out' (Vecchi interviewed by Gandini 2011a: 313). In other words, documentation elaborates the learning for participants during and after the experience, as well as for those who were not present during the experience.

Importantly, documentation is not the aim of learning, but part of a process of teaching, which, in the Reggio Emilia approach, typically centres on intensive and prolonged projects. The topic for a project is used to pose problems and provoke thought. Children show what they know by talking about it, but also by using many different media, for example, models or drawings. Documentation panels record what children 'know' at all stages of the project, and the boards are used by children, teachers and parents to revisit learning as it progresses (Hendrick 2004).

Over the course of a school year, the physical space of the classroom shows traces of the teaching and learning that has occurred. However, while 'classrooms themselves are a form of documentation' (Stacey 2015: 8), it is not necessarily organized in the purposeful way that pedagogical documentation requires. As detailed in Chapter 2, classrooms are a resource as well as a space for learning. However, there are differences between displaying children's learning artefacts (e.g. their paintings or constructions) and documenting learning for a pedagogical purpose (Tolisano and Hale 2018). However, documentation can be used as a display, as in the example in Figure 9.1.

## How does pedagogical documentation challenge the dominant discourse?

In dominant ECE approaches, teachers use observation to make decisions about children's education and development, and documentation of learning is used for formative and summative assessment purposes (see Chapter 10). That humans learn from looking is a commonplace. How we interpret what we see, however, is endlessly complicated, influenced by the lens or image that is used, as discussed in Chapter 1. Our 'thinking lens', as described by Susan Stacey (2015), is informed by theories of how we learn by looking. Psychologist Albert Bandura identified observational learning as an essential element of social learning theory, involving cognitive processes such as attention, organization and memory. Bandura himself learned by looking at children's behaviour in his research as he tested his theory in his classic 'Bobo doll experiments' (Bandura et al. 1961). Bandura's lens, a modified behaviourist theory of child development, led him to postulate a relationship between children watching adults' aggressive behaviour and their own aggressive behaviour.

The idea that theory is a selective lens permitting us to see some things and not others is clear in historical examples, such as Sigmund Freud's diagnosis of hysteria in a patient, which current understandings suggest may have been due to a neurological disorder (Nicholson et al. 2016). Levenson (2005) drives this point home, writing: 'Nothing ... can be understood out of its time and place, its nexus of relationships. It is an epistemological fallacy to think that we can stand outside of what we observe, or observe, without distortion, what is alien to our own experience' (8).

Educational theorists and philosophers have long believed in the value of basing educational practice on observations of child development, which in earlier times was called child nature. Here, too, the question of lens is relevant: If precepts for teaching are to follow child nature, how was their nature understood? Lessons that Rousseau learned from his brief time as a tutor of two boys doubtless informed his depiction of his fictional tutor in his book *Emile, or On Education* (Strong 2002). Rousseau, reflecting eighteenth-century Enlightenment thought, encouraged parents and teachers to interpret information from observing children, but it was to be interpreted in a particular way. The aim was to develop a 'science of pedagogy that would enable teachers to discover rules of human nature by observing children and then to establish the goals of education based on their discoveries' (Gill 2016: 66). Observation was key to many of the theoretical positions discussed in Chapter 1. Nature theory, which is associated with Rousseau, along with unfoldment theory and genetic theory, were all developed alongside direct child observations, although using different lenses, which became a basis for educational goals and pedagogies when the theories were taken up for teaching. The emphasis on observation as a means of gathering information or creating knowledge logically privileged the sense of sight, and by the nineteenth century, the idea that the main pathway to learning was via observation was entrenched in educational theory.

Because learning through the eye was both a teaching and a learning strategy, the child's eye also needed to be trained. The nineteenth-century early education theorist William Wilderspin (1835) was certain that a child 'receives a great deal of knowledge from the eye' (16). While the Swiss pedagogue Johann Pestalozzi emphasized the development of all of the senses, his method of object lessons, in which children learned from physical objects, was popularized as pictures of objects called 'picture lessons'. For the lessons to be effective, teachers trained children to attend to visual detail and to make comparisons.

The French philosopher Michel Foucault (1975) described the interplay of language and 'the act of seeing' (ix) in *The Birth of the Clinic: An Archaeology of Medical Perception*. Foucault developed the notion of 'the medical gaze' as a metaphor of transparency in which the body is revealed through medical knowledge and technologies (Bleakley 2017), influencing not only medical practice but social life (Spitzack 1992). In theorizing child observation in a Foucauldian framework, not only children's actions but their intentions become knowable via the pedagogic gaze. From the perspective of gaze as surveillance, children are 'seen without seeing' and the teacher 'sees without being seen' (Sparrman and Lindgren 2010: 250), leading eventually to the child turning the gaze inward to scrutinize themselves.

Child observation, as a form of contemplation via the senses (Sullivan 2017), is a central aspect of the teacher as researcher. A report by an American visitor to Maria Montessori's school in Rome entitled *DON'T TOUCH! BE STILL!* (uppercase used in the original) described how, as the children explored shapes blindfolded, 'they are learning to recognise through the "eyes of their fingers" … to see the beauty of our world' (Bailey 1913: 14). In her emphasis on learning via touch, Montessori followed in the tradition of eighteenth-century sensationalist philosophers such as Jean-Barnard Mérian, who believed that if children were 'disencumbered of sight' their 'touch would acquire the most exquisite finesse … their fingers would be like microscopes' (Mérian 1984: 185–6 quoted in Purnell 2017: 71). Mérian's plan, which was never put into action, was to raise a group of children from birth in complete darkness in an experiment to support his theory.

The maxim 'Look but don't touch' was both an approach to learning by observation and a classroom management strategy used by Montessori. Of course, the children did touch – it is how they were meant to learn – but only when told to do so. The teachers' observations had a dual role as a means to both learn about and manage children's behaviour. In Foucauldian terms, the children, as they observed their teacher watching them, were meant to learn to manage their own behaviour. Observational learning is also an aspect of Bandura's social learning theory, reviewed in Chapter 2, in which children learn from observing the behaviour of others, peers or adults, through a process of vicarious reinforcement. In a related process, children who observe others being punished learn to avoid the behaviour through the effect of vicarious punishment (Seligman and Baldacci 2005).

## *Recording and reporting child observations*

Baby biographies were a popular genre of scientific literature in the nineteenth and early twentieth centuries. They were a biographical method in which regular observations were conducted on babies, who were often the researchers' own children. The researchers' aim was both to understand child development and gain insights into adult development through the study of what was considered to be evidence of dormant behaviour from the evolutionary past (Smuts 2006), reviewed as recapitulation theory in Chapter 1.

But researchers observed children for many reasons. The scientist Charles Darwin (1877) observed his infant son William in the context of his scientific investigations as he was building his theory of emotions (Hellal and Lorch 2010). Of course, teachers observe children as a way to gather information to make good teaching decisions, not to learn about child development as an evolutionary psychologist. But how can teachers observe children appropriately in the midst of classroom action? How can they use observation to plan curriculum for individual children as well as groups of children? Indeed, the goals of observation are broad to the point of being unrealizable. Ulich and Mayr (1999), for example, identify six wide-ranging aims for observation:

1 Identifying at-risk children
2 Becoming aware of individual differences
3 Monitoring children's development and progress with a predetermined curriculum
4 Developing a child-centred perspective and curriculum
5 Assessing and developing quality
6 Professionalizing and empowering teachers. (26)

Some of the commonly used tools for conducting observations in ECE settings are anecdotal records, checklists, running records, time or event samples and developmental checklists (Beaty 2014). Running records are meant to be brief, text-based recordings, and, along with anecdotal records, are popular and quick methods for classroom use. Observation is sometimes used for more clinical purposes, for example, to understand the dynamics of separation (Adamo and Rustin 2014) in accordance with psychoanalytic theory (see Chapter 1). For many years, early childhood education was influenced by the clinical methods of Susan Isaacs, with her legacy being that 'deep observation was the key to understanding the complex and unique

FIGURE 9.1 *Documentation as display*

realities of individual children' (Willan 2009: 151). This notion was similar to Anna Freud's idea, in which detailed and ongoing child observations added to 'the reconstructed image of children obtained during the course of the analysis of adults', which was based on memory (Sandler 2012: 50). The teachers at Freud's childcare centre in Vienna carried a pad and pencil at all times, with instructions to write down anything that interested them. Freud used their notes for daily discussions with the teachers or to add to insights into child development in a reciprocal process of observation of children and reconstruction of the image of the child (Woods and Pretorius 2016). While the image was not stable, new information was made to fit the old frame, one bounded by psychoanalytic concepts of the ego, defence mechanisms, regression and so forth (Holder 1995).

As Christiane Thompson (2015) points out, while observations conducted by teachers can be used for diagnostic purposes, they are frequently treated as an 'open procedure' in which 'it is not clear beforehand what there is to be seen or what should be seen' (6). She therefore asks, 'How does the practice of observation form the educational subject?' (6). For Anna Freud, the observations contributed to understandings of child development within the frame of the loss of innocence perspective on childhood. In relation to pedagogical documentation, we can ask how the subjectivity of our 'thinking lens' shapes our ideas about children and educational goals.

While observation 'is conceived as one of the most important activities for educators in the area of early education' (Thompson 2015: 6), very little attention is given to the observation practices of children in preschool contexts. Lindgren and Grunditz (2017) used the phrase 'children's looking practices' to refer to children's observations in preschool. In their historical study of a preschool in Sweden, they argued that just as teachers' observations shape the relations, space and environment of preschool (i.e. have material effects), so too do children's looking practices. In their study, children were found to attend to, or even perform, teachers' observation practices. In one example, children were observed 'playing preschool', which involved some children directing others in activities and observing them while taking notes.

## *Technologies for making learning visible*

Cameras have been a prominent technology for scientific observations for over a century, used, for example, in the 1880s by Charles Darwin in his study of the emotions (Prodger 2009). In the twentieth century, psychologist Arnold Gesell (see Chapter 1) used photography for his child observations in the framework of genetic theory and in 1934 published a series of photographic frames in *An Atlas of Infant Behaviour*. The Yale child psychology lab used a specially constructed photographic dome to restrict external environmental exposure and support the still and motion-picture cameras which were placed on tracks (Curtis 2011). Gesell believed motion pictures were superior to the human eye as a means of gathering information for the purpose of analysis. By using film, he could conduct a frame-by-frame analysis of behaviour that was isolated and taken out of time and context, which he called *cinemanalysis*. The camera in this instance aided 'psychology's bid for scientific legitimacy' (Curtis 2011: 438), which, as Scott Curtis writes, 'has always required [psychology] to make intangibles such as "mind" or "growth" visible and tangible' (2011: 438). And, in Gesell's (1935) view, the camera promised to reveal 'the developmental epoch' (549) preset in a child's genes.

Laboratory preschools, which developed for research or teacher education in many universities starting in the 1920s, followed Gesell's observational principle to restrict children's external environmental exposure, including exposure to the observer. The preschools were often equipped with darkened galleries or booths with mesh screens or one-way mirrors for observers to remain unseen (Figure 9.2). A more common situation today is for researchers or students to observe from a remote classroom using video streamed from cameras in the preschool. Where observation booths are used, observers are typically asked not to engage with the children as they sit in semi-darkness watching them. In cases where classrooms are not equipped with cameras, mirrors may be specially placed in order to observe children in 'hard-to-see corners of the room' (CDL, 'Observation Rules': 4), reducing the chance for any aspect of children's behaviour to go unnoticed.

Observation used in the process of pedagogical documentation is based on theories and methodologies that are distinct from the child-development-based observation techniques. It also involves a different ethic of observation. The observing teacher is not an objective onlooker, as explained by Dahlberg and her colleagues: 'Pedagogical documentation is a process of visualisation, but what we document does not represent a true reality any more than claims about the social and natural world represent a true reality – it is a social construction, where pedagogues, through what they select as valuable to document are also participative co-constructors' (Dahlberg et al. 2013: 147).

Lasse Lipponen and his colleagues (2016) drew upon a set of three theories to explain the nature and function of using visual artefacts to represent children's learning experiences. Etienne Wenger's (1998) idea of reifying experiences explains how children and teachers give a material form and meaning to an immaterial learning process, using tools, symbols, stories and so on. 'Reification' is a term used to explain 'the process of capturing and materializing one's experiences into "thingness"' (Lipponen et al. 2016: 940). Whereas taking a photograph is part of the reification process, so too is the photo itself, as is its later use as an element in a documentation panel or display (Figure 9.1). Vygotsky explained how our thinking is mediated through symbols, social mediators and artefacts, including photographs. As mediating artefacts, photographs can help to mediate memories, experiences and communication, creating meanings that are

FIGURE 9.2 *Observation booth: Surveying children in the name of educational research*

FIGURE 9.3 *A documentation dilemma (C. Thompson 2015)*

'negotiated, renegotiated and contested' (Lipponen et al. 2016: 941). Marx Wartofsky (1979) identified three levels of artefacts: primary artefacts used in production, which in the process of documentation can be a camera or photograph; secondary artefacts that are representations of primary objects (e.g. a story about a photograph or a photograph of another artefact); and tertiary or imaginary artefacts that are representations of secondary artefacts (using the photograph as a mediator to imagine different possibilities).

Lenz Taguchi (2010) refers to the actual documentation as 'a material-discursive apparatus' (63). While a professional photographer took photographs of the children's routines in the historical example of the Swedish preschool, the main technologies teachers used for their documentation were a notepad and pencils. The activity of documenting contributed to shaping the preschool space and relations, with a silent teacher detached from the scene sitting in a chair by the side of the action. In current practice, photography by teachers and children and the displays called documentation panels are part of the 'apparatus of pedagogical documentation', which 'is in itself an active agent in generating discursive knowledge' (Lenz Taguchi 2010: 63). Using photography in this way is not a matter of teaching with images or developing children's visual literacy. Rather, it 'is part of the process of constructing meaning about children's learning, as it generates a material observation as a note, photography, video-film, etc.' (Lenz Taguchi 2010: 63). The camera in particular operates 'as a second-order observer'; it 'emphasizes the activity of observation and confirms that there is something to see' (Thompson 2015: 8) (Figure 9.3).

## *Criticism of pedagogical documentation*

The main criticisms of pedagogical documentation are that (1) it is hard to learn and implement, (2) it can be a form of monitoring children and teachers, and (3) it assumes children's agreement to participate. Making the change from traditional teaching practices to pedagogical documentation procedures is difficult for many teachers (Kroeger and Cardy 2006). This is partly due to the complex processes of learning to document. While documentation needs to become a habit (Wien et al. 2015), it is more successful when teachers have particular qualities, for example, a disposition to document and highly developed written communication skills (Felstiner et al. 2006). And, while a disposition and writing skills can be learned, influencing teaching belief systems underlying dispositions is recognized as being difficult (Ashton 2014). There are also practice-oriented challenges. In their study of preschool teachers in Sweden, Emilson and Pramling Samuelsson (2014) found that documentation is time-consuming and can conflict with other teaching activities. They also flagged the potential for generating too much documentation, and noted that teachers can have limited objectivity in its interpretation.

The second criticism concerns the increased scrutiny of children and teachers through the documenting procedure, and, in particular, the prominent role given to photography and the display of visual and textual evidence on documentation panels as an expression of the ethos to make teaching and learning visible. The use of photographs in pedagogical documentation is pervasive. As Anna Sparrman and Anne-Li Lindgren (2010) point out, the development of widely accessible and simple-to-use digital photographic technologies occurred in parallel with the popularity of pedagogical documentation. The complicated system of Gesell's photographic dome, which was needed to support bulky motion picture cameras, has been replaced by the small, simple and ubiquitous cell phone camera.

This trend follows other twenty-first-century patterns in which video and photographic recording of children's growth and behaviour starts before birth for many Western families, creating a type of visual biography (Sparrman and Lindgren 2010). The documentation extends from home to public spaces through surveillance by on-street cameras, to school, where learning behaviours are chronicled by teachers and perhaps other students. Sparrman and Lindgren (2010) ask, what does it mean for children 'to be brought up in an environment where being repeatedly looked at and monitored by video lenses is regarded as normal?' (248). The third criticism challenges the assumption that children 'want to participate in visual documentation' (249) in classrooms. And it may be so, that children's exposure to cameras at home and in their communities makes them 'accepting of surveillance' (260). The argument can also be made that documentation allows for child participation and for children's perspectives to be shared, as required by the United Nations Convention on the Rights of the Child (see Chapter 2). However, in most situations, children, along with their teachers, are only assumed to consent to the strategies used in documentation (Tarr 2011). Other critics argue that documentation is not necessarily a democratic process. Eugene Matusov, Ana Marjanovic-Shane and Sohyun Meacham (2016) maintain that documentation is another form of assessment in the neoliberal tradition which essentializes student learning. Furthermore, Melinda Miller (2014) claims that there can be a mismatch between the evidence of teaching and learning selected for documentation and what occurred in practice. In this way, she argues, pedagogical documentation is reduced to an 'institutional performance' (156) with the potential to conceal undemocratic and racialized practices.

## *Summary*

This chapter identified research as a central activity of early childhood teaching, undertaken through pedagogical documentation. Documentation, described as based on an eclectic mix of compatible theories and exemplified in the Reggio Emilia approach, was contrasted with conventional child observation strategies based in developmentalist ideas and used as a diagnostic tool or means to construct curriculum. Documentation relies on listening to children's alternative languages and is consistent with rights-based early childhood education. Learning to document was explained as a progression from developing documenting as a habit, to making learning visible by sharing interpretations and theories. Some technologies associated with observation and documentation, including cameras and observation booths, were reviewed and their limitations discussed. Criticisms of pedagogical documentation were also identified, including its association with child surveillance and its potential to unwittingly reify traditional teaching practices and understandings of student learning.

# CHAPTER TEN

# Children Are Collaborators in Assessment

***Proposition: Children are active collaborators in and users of assessment.***

Chapter 10 focuses on understanding how children's learning is enabled by an ongoing process of gathering information about what is being learned and reflecting on its meaning. This is a cyclical process that allows connections, relationships and new questions to emerge. As the ultimate users of assessment information, children must be aware of their own ways of constructing and representing knowledge. The chapter provides examples of how pedagogical documentation could serve as the means for pedagogues and other researchers to engage in dialogue and negotiation about pedagogical work that leads to the production of new knowledge. In this chapter we consider the assessment process with a focus on formative assessment in relation to two key questions:

1 What is assessment for?
2 How does assessment support all learners?

For additional information, reflective questions and practical implications visit: https://www.bloomsbury.com/cw/learning-to-teach-young-children/chapter-10/

## What is assessment for?

Assessment of learning is a core act of teaching (Alexander 2008). Its purpose is to enhance learning by improving teaching. Since the 1970s, educational assessment has been distinguished as either formative or summative. Although these concepts are long-standing in education, the terminology is relatively recent, drawn from the field of programme evaluation in social research in the 1960s (Cizek 2010). In social research, evaluation is called formative when it provides information for improvement in a programme's early stages (Rossi et al. 2004). In educational contexts, formative assessment refers to the in-progress evaluation of learning, providing information for changes to instruction or curriculum. In social research, summative evaluations are undertaken to determine if programme expectations have been met as part of an accountability process. In educational contexts, summative assessment occurs at the end of a unit or a lesson and is similarly used for accountability as well as improving instruction.

As part of instruction, assessment is often associated with the organization and enactment of curriculum, involving setting aims, planning activities, undertaking interactions, reviewing learning and summing up (Black 2013). Although the latter two steps are generally associated with formative and summative assessments, cyclical interactions occur across all steps of the teaching and learning process. For example, formative assessment can arise from dialogue between students and teachers in step two as part of planning activities and in the course of activities in step three.

As discussed in Chapter 9, observation-based assessment has been the main approach to assessment used in preschool classrooms. Observations are typically undertaken by teachers in the course of children's activities. They may also include use of observation 'tools', such as the systems developed by companies like HighScope (2018) or Teaching Strategies (2018), to assess children's learning and development in classroom contexts. Whether teachers use proprietary systems or create their own informal but systematic methods, such as portfolios, they are undertaking formative assessment leading to decisions about teaching.

Because achievement is 'an intrinsically embedded phenomenon, assessment of achievement is also an embedded activity, that is to say an activity embedded in the real-time dynamics of teaching and learning and student-teacher interaction' (Steenbeek and van Geert 2018: 1282). As such, 'the meaning of embeddedness goes beyond the existing and usual distinction between formative and summative assessment' (1282). This is particularly true for early childhood contexts, in which teachers undertake assessments to plan and evaluate the curriculum and their teaching and 'to understand what children learn' (Drummond 2003: 13). Such assessment is based on the presupposition that learning is more purposeful when children are involved in planning and assessing their own learning. Moreover, because learning is more effective when done for what children see as genuine reasons, assessment is best done in authentic learning contexts resembling real-world experiences. The concept of authentic learning is similar to Dewey's (1938) idea of learning through experience and Vygotsky's notion of social context of learning.

For Dewey, all genuine learning is based on experience, but not all experience is educational – some experiences are interesting but disconnected, while Dewey deemed others, such as drill and practice teaching methods, to be

FIGURE 10.1 *Authentic assessment*

'mis-educative' (1938: 13). Educational experiences were those which instilled learning, were interactive and oriented towards growth, had continuity and were facilitated by an adult using child-centred teaching strategies. Thus, Dewey-inspired teachers have historically provided children with opportunities to engage in useful 'industries', such as cooking, carpentry and gardening, rather than the spelling bees of traditional education (Clifford 1975). For Vygotsky, teachers or more experienced peers played key roles as mentors in guiding children's learning in relation to experience (Glassman 2001).

The idea of authentic learning has become synonymous with the notion of real-world experiences, which can occur in school classrooms or in children's homes or communities, as discussed in Chapter 4. It therefore follows that authentic assessment of students (Figure 10.1) takes place in contexts of real-world learning and is based on teachers' understandings of children's unique abilities and cultures (Soderman 2016).

## *School readiness*

Authentic assessment differs from approaches that start from an assumption that children have social skills or learning deficits, or one based on a concept of readiness. In the *ages of man view* based on maturationist theory (see Chapter 1) children's learning is supported, or not supported, by their environment. In maturationist theory, learning is optimized when it is adjusted to the level of a child's maturity and is based on individual and developmental readiness. In this case, the teacher's role is restricted to assessing what is missing and filling in the developmental gaps, as Elizabeth Graue (1993: 7) described using a metaphor of a puzzle:

> The ready child is a puzzle with all the pieces in place. If skills are seen as the pieces of the puzzle, the key to fixing the readiness problem is to (1) identify the missing pieces and then (2) provide instruction to generate their placement.

Many commonly used early childhood assessments are based on maturationist theory. Some are designed to check that children are ready for school, such as the Gesell school readiness tests, which continue to be widely employed despite their low predictive validity for grade-one performance (Gullo 2015). Other assessments of school readiness measure approaches to learning based on sociocultural theory, or learning behaviours based on social learning theory (Barbu et al. 2015).

Some preschool programmes are designed with built-in school-readiness aims, for example, preschool programmes found in many countries around the world in which children are afforded extra time to get ready for school. Whereas education experts in the 1950s emphasized the value of preschool for children's social adjustment, by the 1960s preparation for academic activities (school readiness) was considered imperative. This was particularly so for children considered to be at risk of school failure due to environmental factors, such as poverty and home cultures that were judged inadequate in relation to parental attitudes, child-rearing practices and language development, explained in terms of the cultural deprivation theory popular at the time (Bloom et al. 1967). In the twenty-first century, kindergarten especially, but also other preschool programmes, have increasingly adopted school readiness as a goal. Graue (2009) observed that as a result, preschool and kindergarten programmes have been 'calibrated' such that 'increasing numbers of teachers say their students are not prepared for the rigors of kindergarten's new structure' (2). This trend has the potential to increase the gap between privileged and poor students, with elite private preschools and kindergartens focusing on academic preparation and poverty-track preschools offering skill-based programmes (Lubeck 1985). Moreover, participating in a low-quality early childhood programme can widen the gap further (Magnuson and Waldfogel 2005).

Because school readiness is a socially constructed concept and not an objective measure, views differ on what counts as readiness. In a 1990s study, Eugene Lewit and Linda Schuurmann Baker (1995) looked at the issue with teachers and parents, asking both groups for their views on eleven common indicators of readiness. They found that teachers were far more likely than parents to place importance on behaviours such as 'is not disruptive in class', 'takes turns and shares' and 'sits still and pays attention'. Parents were more likely to highlight items reflecting what they considered to be skills needed for academics, such as 'can count to 20 or more', 'knows the letters of the alphabet' and is 'able to use pencils or paint brushes'. A more recent study based on data from 1998 to 2010 reported that teachers' beliefs have changed; they now agree with parents on the importance of knowing the alphabet and believe parents should teach it to their children prior to starting kindergarten. Moreover, while teachers continued to rate social regulation and social skills highly, 80 per cent of teachers believed children should learn to read in kindergarten, compared with 31 per cent in 1998 (Bassok et al. 2016), marking a move away from the historical bias against teaching reading in kindergarten (Prochner and Robertson 2012).

Emer Ring and her colleagues (2016) analysed children's perceptions of school in their study of school readiness in Ireland. Children's ideas of what they called Big School focused on the lack of play at school and the schools' physical size, but the children also expected to have agency and ability to make choices in their activities. Some children relayed information told to them by their parents that they must behave and listen to the teacher. However, the children did not give any sense that they believed themselves unready for school.

## *Assessment of learning*

How and why are children assessed once at school? An emphasis on academic readiness can lead to a 'schoolification' of early childhood that includes the standardized testing practices that are tools of summative assessment.

Standardized test results can be used to compare student performance with other students within a classroom, but also between classrooms, amongst schools or across nations. The logic of standardized testing is that the tests provide an objective measure of achievement that can be used for accountability purposes and to improve instruction (Kempf 2016). What has been called the testing movement (Reese 2013) has influenced formal teaching approaches, such as whole class lessons and direct instruction 'migrating down to the preschools as the demand for children's learning to be measured and scored increases' (Gunnarsdottir 2014: 243). This is sometimes called a 'push-down effect' in which the teaching practices and curriculum for one grade are brought down to an earlier grade. In these cases, when preschool children become 'miniature students' (Lee and Yelland 2017), their one hundred languages are narrowed to only a few, as was described by Loris Malaguzzi as part of Reggio Emilia theory (see Chapter 2). Being classified as miniature students changes both the image and experience of childhood. Lee and Yelland (2017) consider the situation in their Foucauldian analysis of governance in which '"miniature students" are deemed to be school subjects suitable for "rigorous" and "objective" assessments to identify their potential for learning, which includes defining particular learning outcomes and overt behaviours' (49).

There has been a similar critique of the Organisation for Economic Cooperation and Development's International Early Learning Study (OECD IELS), launched in 2016. The study, known as 'Baby PISA' for its relationship to the long-standing OECD Program for International Student Assessment, aims to test children's learning in early childhood centres in select OECD member states across four domains (emergent literacy, emergent mathematics, self-regulation, social and emotional skills) to improve curriculum and teaching (OECD 2017). As one outcome, IELS will use 'a common language and framework' to share best practices across diverse contexts. IELS has attracted substantial criticism from early childhood scholars who have expressed concerns over the technical aspect of the study, its universalizing approach to early education and narrow view of culture and context, and its usage of soft power as in a Foucauldian argument (de Vocht et al. 2017; Moss et al. 2017; Moss and Urban 2017). A country-level critique by scholars in New Zealand highlighted the study's possible negative impact on the early childhood curriculum framework *Te Whāriki*. Margaret Carr and her colleagues (2016) contended that IELS use of standardized tests to measure learning outcomes is incompatible with *Te Whāriki*'s grounding in a sociocultural perspective and emphasis on formative assessment.

In England, criticism of requirements for baseline assessments for four-year-olds entering reception classes (preschools) has focused on the assessment's contribution to the data-based governance of teachers as well as children (Bradbury and Roberts-Holmes 2017). In Guy Roberts-Holmes and Alice Bradbury's (2016) Foucauldian analysis, comparative data within and across countries 'are the "technologies of governing" and key to the "governance turn"' (120). While student performance has been linked to teacher performance in higher grades from the 1980s and to the development of TIMSS (Trends in International Mathematics and Science Study) and PISA (Gurl et al. 2016), it is a relatively new development for teachers in early years classrooms.

Historically, practices of assessment in early childhood education have reflected the aims and purposes of the programmes. Student learning in infant schools, the name for preschools in the early nineteenth century, was individually evaluated according to procedures of the monitorial system (May et al. 2014). In infant schools, children were placed in ability groups led by slightly older, more experienced pupils, called monitors, in the method of mutual instruction, meaning 'I teach you and you teach me'. As historian Carl Kaestle (1973) noted, learning in a monitorial system 'was like a spelling bee all day long' (6–7). However, when this individualized system proved problematic due to a lack of experienced peers and a surplus of pupils, there was a shift to simultaneous instruction. In simultaneous instruction children were placed in age-graded groupings under the instruction of a single, trained teacher. This shift was accomplished by the massing of children in the newly invented educational technology of tiered structures called galleries (Figure 10.2), with the youngest children seated in the bottom rows, allowing lessons for children 'of nearly one age, learning one thing' (Sengupta 2011: 84). Children answered their teacher's questions using a choral response, which continues to be used as a behaviourally based teaching technique (Hagan-Burke 2005). Small groups of children, classed by ability, were provided with additional instruction in mathematics, reading and other subjects. Memorization was a main learning

FIGURE 10.2 *Gallery teaching, Wilderspin, 1840*

strategy, and oral recitation by individuals or groups – for example, of the alphabet or multiplication tables – continued to be the dominant form of assessment throughout the nineteenth century (Giordano 2005).

However, teachers' assessments of learning based on student recitations were highly subjective – more like 'personal opinion' or 'guesswork' (Cubberley 1934, quoted in Giordano 2005: 23) – and by the early twentieth century, educators were inspired by psychology and 'mental testing' to seek a more scientific and systematic approach. With the rise of public education and the common school in the nineteenth century, there was also a drive for efficiency to serve the greater number of children in schools, particularly in larger urban centres, and pupils were grouped in age-graded classrooms in a system that continues today. Assessment was used to increase the efficiency of the classrooms, in which the majority of students in each grade were close in age, while a minority were routed to special schools or classes based on intelligence testing and educational assessment (Kelly and Surbeck 2007). Students were also streamed to vocational programmes or special education classrooms based on their racial backgrounds or social class, which is also a situation that continues today (Galabuzi 2014).

In an education context, developmental, behavioural and intelligence testing can contribute to meaningful decisions about learning objectives. However, such measures are not necessarily useful for assessing whether learning objectives have been met, which is the purpose of summative assessment, for example, through standardized examinations. The value of summative assessment is frequently disparaged, as shown in critiques of IELS, PISA and state-wide or provincial grade-level achievement tests (Lenkeit et al. 2016). Yet, in education systems around the world, the measure of student success is determined through testing, which is both extolled as a key to education reform and criticized as being driven by big business (Reimann 2015): Student testing is a billion-dollar industry (Chingos 2015). And, as Gita Steiner-Khamsi (2018) and her colleagues point out, international testing is also a 'travelling policy tool' (192) used to shape educational policies worldwide.

## *Assessment for learning*

Summative assessment is criterion referenced, meaning that the same criteria are used for all students in order for an individual student's achievement to be compared with the achievement of others. Formative assessment refers to strategies used by teachers or students in the process of learning to provide feedback 'to modify teaching and learning activities' (Black and Wiliam 1998: 140). The most effective formative feedback is provided to children during their activities (Siraj-Blatchford 2010) and focuses on 'self-regulation, metacognition, attribution, self-efficacy, and goal orientation' (Ruiz-Primo and Li 2013: 7). Feedback can be from teachers, peers or via self-assessment. Summative assessment can be used as formative assessment, where students can use feedback from tests to modify their learning strategies and objectives. Children receive formative feedback from teachers or peers in the process of scaffolding (see Chapter 5), for example, through additional questions aimed at asking for clarification or justification of responses (Faltis and Valdés 2016). This is a particularly helpful type of formative assessment for children who are multilingual learners. And evidence from formative assessment can become part of summative assessment 'provided that a distinction is made between the evidence and the interpretation of the evidence' (Harlen 2012: 8), which is to say that summative evaluations are not merely a collection of evidence gathered during the course of teaching.

Dylan Wiliam (2018) identified five general teaching strategies for creating contexts for formative assessment that is embedded (i.e. integrated) in classrooms: (1) sharing their learning intentions with students as a way to support their self-regulation; (2) finding out what students know by using questioning or discussion to check for understanding; (3) giving feedback oriented to the future while involving students in reflecting on their own learning; (4) creating conditions for students to help one another learn, for example, through negotiations or problem solving; and (5) engaging students as activators of their own learning. The success of using embedded formative assessment as a pedagogy relies on the skills and experience of individual teachers to recognize 'teachable moments' in which to utilize 'on-the-fly formative assessment' (Shavelson et al. 2008). Teachable moments are defined by a teacher's identification of a child's readiness to learn based on their observation of a child's interest and their understanding of development (Hyun 2006). Curriculum that has formal formative assessment built in by design is termed curriculum-embedded formative assessment (Shavelson et al. 2008). The assessments are developed by teachers or curriculum makers and embedded into units or lessons to 'inform the teacher about what students currently know, and what they still need to learn (i.e., "the gap") so that teachers can provide timely feedback' (Shavelson et al. 2008: 301). Montessori's self-correcting didactic material reflects principles of curriculum-embedded formative assessment. An example is Montessori's material called cylinder blocks, consisting of ten wooden cylinders of graduated size fitting into corresponding holes cut into a long wooden block. A child successfully completes the task by matching the cylinders to the holes through a process of self-correction, an element of what Montessori (2004) called auto-education.

## How does assessment support all learners?

Teachers undertake assessments using information from observations of children's everyday language, daily living skills, behaviour and play, collaborative discussion with children and dialogue with parents and professionals. Assessment supports the learning of all children in the classroom: those with typical and atypical development, English-language learners and learners of diverse cultural backgrounds. Moreover, because teachers are also researchers and consequently learners, early childhood classrooms are learning spaces for everyone. In the following section we address the question, 'How does assessment support all learners in early childhood classrooms?' Our focus is on formative assessment, which William Penuel and Lorrie Shepard (2016) describe as 'assessment that is part of teaching' (787), rather than on summative assessment. As discussed in relation to the OECD's International Early Learning Study, standardized tests should be used with caution with young children. However, information from standardized assessments is generally required to access special services for children. In these circumstances, we note that effective and fair summative assessment, screening and testing of young children follows six principles: (1) it should be used for appropriate purposes; (2) it should be linguistically and culturally appropriate; (3) it should have the primary purpose of improving teaching; (4) it should be developed and interpreted with caution; (5) it should be administered by individuals with cultural and linguistic competence; and (6) it should involve families (Snow and Van Hemel 2008). Because summative assessment is used to report children's progress and performance and for accountability purposes, the focus of the principles is on the test makers' and test administrators' attention to reducing test bias and ensuring reliability (i.e. that measures are consistent) and validity (i.e. that measures test what is intended).

In the child-centred view of education common to Western schooling contexts, children are considered to be individuals, which applies to their learning goals. In a child-centred view of assessment, the adult's role 'is to try to understand what the child wants from an activity and, if necessary, provide ways to extend the learning' (Sharman et al. 2015: 5). However, because child-centred teaching does not mean just one thing (Chung and Walsh 2010), the 'pedagogical implications' of this idea 'are not always as clearly drawn as they might be' (Entwistle 2012: 22). Moreover, the notion of 'child as individual' is out of step with the idea of a child developing within an ecological system, as described by Bronfenbrenner (1979a, 1979b), or as interconnected with family, kin and community, as described in Kağitçibaşi's (2007) interdependence model of child socialization (see Chapter 3). While children are individuals insofar as 'each child is unique in the complex of ability, aptitude, interest, experience and cultural capital which they bring to school' (Entwistle 2012: 22), children also live in relationship with others and have a sense of belonging to many communities. Formative assessment therefore acknowledges the complexity of children's relationships and involves culturally relevant and sustaining pedagogies (see Chapters 3 and 8), for example, by attending to the ways children are 'engaged in community contexts outside the school context' (Ramirez 2017: 260).

Jan Dubiel (2016) identified eight principles of formative assessment for young children: (1) it is accurate and authentic; (2) it reflects understandings of how children develop and learn; (3) it reflects the values of the teacher;

(4) it is driven by the professional; (5) it has a clear purpose to support provision and pedagogy; (6) it is manageable; (7) it incorporates a means for accountability and (8) it takes account of ethical considerations. Because formative assessment is a teaching activity, the focus of the principles is on teachers' attention to undertaking assessment in real-world contexts.

## *Pedagogical documentation*

An example of formative evaluation in early education is pedagogical documentation (see Chapter 9). In the vivid words of Wien and colleagues (2011), the process of documentation 'stops the train of standardized expectations and slows down our thinking processes to consider some topic with exquisite care' (154). Teachers in Reggio Emilia schools employ documentation as a 'democratic alternative' to standardized assessment (Roberts-Holmes 2017: 159). The aim is to make teaching and learning visible for 'democratic deliberation' (160) by drawing upon the collaborative reflection and input of children, teachers, parents and community members. This participatory approach to assessment is contrasted with the audit-style approach to testing, which can contribute to governance of children, teachers and parents and is cited as a barrier to the wider use of Reggio-style documentation in public schools in North America (Gandini 2011b). Although pedagogical documentation may not always be manageable for teachers with reference to Dubiel's principles – it can be difficult to employ in some contexts (Emilson and Pramling Samuelsson 2014; MacDonald 2007) – it can nevertheless provide 'additional observational evidence' for formative assessments of learning (MacDonald 2007: 241).

The learning stories approach is a type of pedagogical documentation that is dictated by children, written by teachers and created for the child and family (Carr and Lee 2012). Teachers use this narrative approach to profile children's learning dispositions rather than what children can do or what they know. The five domains of learning dispositions are drawn from New Zealand's curriculum framework *Te Whāriki* and are also regarded as outcomes for education, namely, taking an interest, being involved, persisting with difficulty or uncertainty, communicating with others and taking responsibility (Carr 2001).

Learning stories serve as a 'framework for assessment interactions' (Cowie and Carr 2009: 107), bringing children, teachers and families together to share ideas about common goals. Cowie and Carr call this a sociocultural based assessment, meaning assessment of learning and development that is 'distributed across people, places, and things' (105). Learning stories are closely associated with the early childhood services in New Zealand and were developed in relation to *Te Whāriki*, which considered assessment to be embedded and continuous in all activities and interactions. As Sonja Arndt and Marek Tesar (2015) describe, 'learning stories perform *Te Whāriki's* framework and guiding principles' (77).

Indeed, although learning stories are not an officially required assessment in New Zealand, they have become linked with *Te Whāriki* and are the major assessment used in early childhood classrooms in the country.

In common with other types of pedagogical documentation, learning stories can be hard to learn and implement (Knauf 2018). Moreover, the construct of learning dispositions, which is key to the approach, is ambiguous and can have different meanings in different cultural contexts (Li and Grieshaber 2018). Learning stories have also been criticized as an assessment for being influenced by the developmental tradition and for being overly individualistic. Indeed, with reference to the New Zealand framework, Qilong Zhang (2017) notes that *Te Whāriki* 'prohibits "making comparisons between children"' (256). There is a tension between sociocultural assessment and other types of formative assessment, as shown in Ken Blaiklock's (2010) critique of learning stories, which points to their lack of validity, limited use for planning future learning, and the difficulty of showing changes over time. The learning story approach, as with the general approach of pedagogical documentation, is a social construction with potential to be transformative and a way of resisting traditional assessments, but it is also a 'risky method' that may not be consistent with expectations of the curriculum or culture in contexts outside New Zealand (Alasuutari et al. 2014; Li and Grieshaber 2018).

There are also tensions over claims for children's democratic participation in assessments such as learning stories and pedagogical documentation. Pedagogical documentation, like learning stories, creates contexts for dialogue, drawing children, teachers and parents together for conversations about teaching and learning. But Tim Waller and Angeliki Bitou (2011) raise concerns about the unequal nature of adult/child participation, for example, the limited ability of adults to become members of children's groups to understand their experiences; the influence of the adult agenda on children's experiences, including the choice of technologies such as cameras to document experiences; and the potential for the assessment process to intrude on children's privacy, as discussed in Chapter 9.

## *Dynamic assessment*

Another example of formative assessment in early education is dynamic assessment (Figure 10.3). Dynamic assessment is based on Vygotsky's ideas of mediated learning (see Chapters 5 and 6) and those of researchers who elaborated on his theory after his death, and on Reuven Feuerstein's (1980) like-minded idea of mediated learning experience (Stringer 2018). Dynamic assessment is distinct from assessments which 'theorise a lag of learning behind development as in the case of Piaget or which theorise learning as developing as in the case of Skinner' (Daniels 2011: 683), or those which theorize a gap in development, as with Gesell.

FIGURE 10.3 *Dynamic assessment*

Vygotsky developed his learning concept of the zone of proximal development (ZPD) in response to formal testing of students, believing that 'tests should measure not what children already know and can do by themselves but what they can do with the assistance of a more knowledgeable partner' (Berk and Harris 2006: 2). The focus of dynamic assessment is on children's potential, where teachers use 'purposeful teaching ... to see what the child can attain with social support' (Berk and Harris 2006: 3). It is the interactive nature of the assessment that makes it dynamic (Gipps and Stobart 2003: 554). The aim is not only to discover what a child knows, but also their ability to use the knowledge in new situations, making assessment a teaching and learning experience. Dynamic assessment is compatible with teaching approaches implied by Dewey's idea of psychologizing the subject matter. As explained by Penuel and Shepard (2016), Dewey's idea involved the teacher 'seeing on the horizon the full mastery of disciplinary knowledge and practices and translating that into intermediate understandings and ways of participating connected to the experience of the individual learner' (787). Vygotsky's concern, however, and the significance of the ZPD, was the relation between instruction and development (Chaiklin 2003); for Dewey, the central relation was instruction and curriculum.

In dynamic assessment, teachers identify and then support a child's emerging knowledge or skill that is in their ZPD in a tutoring process called scaffolding (Wood et al. 1976). Scaffolded interactions are temporary supports in which the aim is for the child to use the skills and knowledge independently (Bodrova and Leong 2018). Scaffolding can take several forms: the teacher and child can work on a task together, the teacher can offer a tool or strategy to the child to mediate their learning, or the teacher can establish a context for support from peers (Bodrova and Leong 2018). An example of a tool for young children is private speech (see Chapter 6), which can be used as a form of self-instruction or self-guidance for complex tasks (Berk 1992).

Feuerstein identified characteristics of mediated learning that highlight the importance of the quality and the future orientation of the interaction between the teacher and child. Mediation is defined as 'any interaction in which an adult *intends* to convey a particular *meaning* or skill *and* encourages the child to *transcend*, that is, to relate the meaning to some other thought or experience' (Feuerstein and Lewin-Benham 2012: 19, emphasis in original). For Feuerstein, mediation changes a child's cognitive structure in a dynamic interplay between the child and the environment, as explained by his theory of structural cognitive modifiability. Feuerstein gives adults the main role as mediators: Teachers are positioned to strategically use graduated prompts to encourage the child to transcend the immediate meaning of an experience. Prompts are contingent on the previous response, and they 'are graduated so that each subsequent prompt provides more explicit information about how to reformulate a response, giving the learner increasingly explicit forms of regulation and providing multiple opportunities for reformulation' (Davin et al. 2017: 633).

Mediated learning can use 'focused conversation' as a mediation strategy – helping children learn to focus – along with asking good questions, listening acutely and keeping records of what children say (Lewin-Benham 2011). In an example in the context of preschool math learning, a teacher engaged children in mathematical conversations in different learning contexts, asked general questions to draw out the children's understanding of concepts, listened carefully to adjust to individual learning needs and recorded children's understanding using checklists (Kirova and Bhargava 2002).

Criticisms of dynamic assessment include the difficulty for teachers of 'mediating learning through whole class interaction' (Davin et al. 2017: 633). However, teachers can use mediation strategies in the context of a class discussion or formal lesson, such as questioning, naming the thinking skills used by children and encouraging children to make comparisons (Feuerstein and Lewin-Benham 2012). Another criticism of dynamic assessment is its heavy reliance on language and verbal mediation. Language-based mediation reflects a Western bias, whereas many cultures, including Indigenous cultures, prefer learning through observation and teaching through demonstration (Berk and Harris 2006). However, in cases where language is the focus, for Indigenous children who are English-language learners, dynamic assessment that avoids the bias of Western-style direct questioning can be a contextually relevant approach (Banks and Neisworth 1995; Ukrainetz et al. 2000).

## *Summary*

This chapter considered how children's learning is enabled by the process of gathering information about what is being learned and reflecting on its meaning. Children were described as active collaborators in and users of assessment, making learning more purposeful and effective. Formative and summative assessments were reviewed, along with the concepts of authentic learning, learning through experience and social learning. The concept of school readiness was explained as having its basis in deficit ideas of child development, and practices of the global testing movement are described as inconsistent with assessment for learning that takes place in contexts similar to real-world experiences. Three formative assessment procedures as teaching activities supporting all learners were presented: pedagogical documentation, learning stories and dynamic assessment.

FIGURE 10.4 *Emma and Luka say goodbye*

# REFERENCES

Abdallah-Pretceille, M. (2004), *L'éducation interculturelle*, 2nd edn, Paris: Presses Universitaires de France.

Adamo, S. M. G. and M. Rustin (2014), 'Introduction', in S. M. G. Adamo and M. Rustin (eds), *Young Child Observation: A Development of the Theory and Method of Infant Observation*, London: Karnac.

Adams, M., and M. Fleer (2017), 'International Transactions: Generating Subjective Sense and Subjective Configuration in Relation to the Development of Identity', *Mind, Culture and Activity*. doi:10.1080/10749039.2017.1346686

Adolph, K. E., and S. E. Berger (2006), 'Motor Development', in D. Kuhn and R. Siegler (eds), *Handbook of Child Psychology*, 161–212, Hoboken, NJ: John Wiley and Sons.

Ailwood, J. (2003), 'Governing Early Childhood through Play', *Contemporary Issues in Early Childhood*, 4 (3): 286–99.

Ailwood, J. (2011), 'It's about Power: Researching Play, Pedagogy and Participation in the Early Years of School', in S. Rogers (ed), *Rethinking Play and Pedagogy*, 19–32, London: Routledge.

Akerman, J. (2010), 'The Image of the Child from the Perspective of Plains Cree Elders and +Plains Cree Early Childhood Teachers', Master's thesis, University of Alberta.

Alasuutari, M., A.-M. Markström and A.-C. Vallberg-Roth (2014), *Assessment and Documentation in Early Childhood Education*, New York: Routledge.

Alberta Education (2008), *Kindergarten Program Statement*. Available online: https://education.alberta.ca/media/563583/kindprogstate2008.pdf (accessed 25 November 2018).

Albon, D., and A. Hellman (2018), 'Of Routine Consideration: "Civilizing" Children's Bodies Via Food Events in Swedish and English Early Childhood Settings', *Ethnography and Education*. doi:10.1080/17457823.2017.1422985

Alexander, R. (2008), *Essays in Pedagogy*, Abingdon, UK: Routledge.

Allen, A. T. (2000), 'Children between Public and Private Worlds: The Kindergarten and Public Policy in Germany', in R. Wollons (ed), *Kindergartens and Cultures: The Global Diffusion of an Idea*, 16–41, New Haven, CT: Yale University Press.

Altenbaugh, R. J. (1999), *Historical Dictionary of American Education*, Westport, CT: Greenwood.

Ames, D. R., E. D. Knowles, M. W. Morris, C. W. Kalish, A. D. Rosati and A. Gopnik (2001), 'The Social Folk Theorist: Insights from Social and Cultural Psychology on the Contents and Contexts of Folk Theorizing', in D. A. Baldwin, B. F. Malle and L. J. Moses (eds), *Intentions and Intentionality: Foundations of Social Cognition*, 307–29, Cambridge, MA: MIT Press.

Ames, R. T. (2015), 'The Great Commentary (Dazhuan) and Chinese Natural Cosmology', *International Communication of Chinese Culture*, 2: 1–18.

Annamma, S. A., B. A. Ferri and D. J. Connor (2018), 'Disability Critical Race Theory: Exploring the Intersectional Lineage, Emergence and Potential Futures of DisCrit in Education', *Review of Research in Education*, 42, 46–71.

Arndt, S., and M. Tesar (2015), 'Early Childhood Assessment in Aotearoa New Zealand: Critical Perspectives and Fresh Openings', *Journal of Pedagogy*, 6 (2): 71–86.

Artiles, A., S. Dorn and A. Bal (2016), 'Objects of Protection, Enduring Nodes of Difference: Disability Intersections with "Other" Differences, 1916–2016', *Review of Research in Education*, 40, 777–820.

Ashton, P. T. (2014), 'Historical Overview and Theoretical Perspectives of Research on Teachers' Beliefs', in H. Fives and M. G. Gill (eds), *International Handbook on Teachers' Beliefs*, 31–47. New York: Routledge.

Azmi, S., L. Foster and L. Jacobs (2010), 'Editors Introduction', *Canadian Diversity*, 8 (3): 1. Available online: http://www.ohrc.on.ca/ (accessed 25 November 2018).

Bae, B. (2010), 'Realizing Children's Right to Participation in Early Childhood Settings: Some Critical Issues in a Norwegian Context', *Early Years: An International Journal of Research and Development*, 30 (3): 205–18.

Bailey, C. S. (1913), '"Don't Touch!" "Be Still!"' *The Delineator*, 83: 14, 71–2. Available online: https://hdl.handle.net/2027/iau.31858046092197?urlappend=%3Bseq=148 (accessed 25 November 2018).

Bailie, P. E. (2016), 'Best Practices in Nature-based Early Childhood Education', in D. Sobel, P. E. Bailie, P. Finch, E. K. Kenny and A. Stires (eds), *Nature Preschools and Forest Kindergartens: The Handbook for Outdoor Learning*, 211–28, St. Paul, MN: Redleaf.

Bandura, A. (1962), *Social Learning through Imitation*, Lincoln: University of Nebraska Press.

Bandura, A. (1997), *Self-efficacy: The Exercise of Control*, New York: W. H. Freeman.

Bandura, A., D. Ross and S. Ross (1961), 'Transmission of Aggression through Imitation of Aggressive Models', *The Journal of Abnormal and Social Psychology*, 63 (3): 575–82.

Banks, J. A. (2008), *An Introduction to Multicultural Education*, 4th edn, Boston, MA: Pearson.

Banks, J. A. (2015), *Cultural Diversity and Education: Foundations, Curriculum and Teaching*, 6th edn, New York: Routledge.

Banks, S. R., and J. T. Neisworth (1995), 'Dynamic Assessment in Early Intervention: Implications for Serving American Indian/Alaska Native Families', *Journal of American Indian Education*, 34 (2): 27–43.

Baraldi, C. (2014), 'Children's Participation in Communication Systems: A Theoretical Perspective to Shape Research', in M. N. Warehime (ed), *Soul of Society: A Focus on the Lives of Children and Youth*, 63–92, Bingley, UK: Emerald.

Barbu, O. T., D. B. Yaden, D. Levine-Donnerstein and R. W. Marx (2015), 'Assessing Approaches to Learning in School Readiness: Comparing the Devereux Early Childhood Assessment to an Early Learning Standards-based Measure', *AERA Open*, 1 (3): 1–15. doi:10.1177/2332858415593923

Bashford, A., and P. Levine (2010), *The Oxford Handbook of the History of Eugenics*, Oxford: Oxford University Press.
Bassok, D., S. Latham and A. Rorem (2016), 'Is Kindergarten the New First Grade?' *AERA Open*, 1 (4): 1–31. doi:10.1177/2332858415616358
Bateson, P. (2015), 'Ethology and Human Development', in R. M. Lerner (ed), *Handbook of Child Psychology And Developmental Science*, 7th edn, Hoboken, NJ: Wiley.
Bateson, P., and P. Gluckman (2011), *Plasticity, Robustness, Development and Evolution*, Cambridge, UK: Cambridge University Press.
Battiste, M. (2005), 'Indigenous Knowledge: Foundations for First Nations', *World Indigenous Nations Higher Education Consortium Journal*. Available online: https://www2.viu.ca/integratedplanning/documents/IndegenousKnowledgePaperbyMarieBattistecopy.pdf (accessed 25 November 2018).
Bauman, Z. (1991), *Modernity and Ambivalence*, Cambridge, UK: Polity Press.
Baumrind, D. (1966), 'Effects of Authoritative Parental Control on Child Behavior', *Child Development*, 37 (4): 887–907.
Beatty, B. (2009), 'Transitory Connections: The Reception and Rejection of Jean Piaget's Psychology in the Nursery School Movement in the 1920s and 1930s', *History of Education Quarterly*, 49 (4): 442–64.
Beatty, B. (2017), 'John Dewey's High Hopes for Play: Democracy and Education and Progressive Era Controversies Over Play in Kindergarten and Preschool Education', *The Journal of the Gilded Age and Progressive Era*, 16: 424–37.
Beaty, J. J. (2014), *Observing Development of the Young Child*, 8th edn, Boston: Pearson.
Beckstead, Z. (2015), 'Cultural Objects in a Transforming World', *Culture and Psychology*, 21 (3): 380–91.
Bennett, N., E. Wood and S. Rogers (1997), *Teaching Through Play: Teachers' Thinking and Classroom Practice*, Buckingham: Open University Press.
Berger, I. (2015), 'Pedagogical Narrations and Leadership in Early Childhood Education as Thinking in Moments of Not Knowing', *Canadian Children*, 40 (1): 130–47.
Berk, L. (1992), 'Children's Private Speech: An Overview of Theory and the Status of the Research', in R. M. Diaz and L. E. Berk (eds), *Private Speech: From Social Interaction to Self-regulation*, 17–55, New York: Psychology Press.
Berk, L., and S. Harris (2006), 'Lev Vygotsky', *Encyclopedia of Cognitive Science*, New York: Wiley InterScience.
Bernstein, B. B., and A. Morais (2001), *Towards a Sociology of Pedagogy: The Contribution of Basil Bernstein to Research*, New York: Peter Lang.
Berry, J. W. (2007), 'Conceptual Approaches to Acculturation', in K. Chun, P. B. Organista and G. Marin (eds), *Acculturation: Advances in Theory, Measurement and Applied Research*, 17–33, Washington, DC: American Psychological Association.
Berzoff, J., L. M. Flanagan and P. Hertz (2016), *Inside Out and Outside In: Psychodynamic Clinical Theory and Psychopathology in Contemporary Multicultural Contexts*, 4th edn, Lanham, MD: Rowman and Littlefield.
Bhabha, H. K. (1994), *The Location of Culture*, London: Routledge.
Biesta, G., and C. Bingham (2010), *Jacques Rancière: Education, Truth, Emancipation*, London: Continuum.

Black, P. (2013), 'Formative and Summative Aspects of Assessment: Theoretical and Research Foundations in the Context of Pedagogy', in J. H. McMillan (ed), *SAGE Handbook of Research on Classroom Assessment*, 167–78, Los Angeles, CA: SAGE.

Black, P., and D. Wiliam (1998), 'Assessment and Classroom Learning', *Assessment in Education*, 5 (1): 7–73.

Blaiklock, K. E. (2010), 'Assessment in New Zealand Early Childhood Settings: A Proposal to Change from Learning Stories to Learning Notes', *Early Education*, 48 (2): 5–10.

Blaise, M. (2016), 'Gender Roles', in D. Couchenour and J. K. Chrisman (eds), *The SAGE Encyclopedia of Contemporary Early Childhood Education*, 624–27, Thousand Oaks, CA: SAGE.

Blaise, M., and A. Taylor (2012), 'Using Queer Theory to Rethink Gender Equity in Early Childhood Education', *Young Children*, January, 88–98.

Bleakley, A. (2017), *Thinking with Metaphors in Medicine: The State of the Art*, New York: Routledge.

Bloch, M. (1992), 'Critical Perspectives on the Historical Relationship between Child Development and Early Childhood Education Research', in S. Kessler and B. Swadener (eds), *Reconceptualizing the Early Childhood Curriculum*, 3–20, New York: Teachers College Press.

Bloch, M. N., B. B. Swadener and G. S. Cannella (2014), *Reconceptualizing Early Childhood Care and Education: A Reader*, New York: Peter Lang.

Bloom, B., A. Davis and R. D. Hess (1967), *Compensatory Education for Cultural Deprivation: A Report Based on Working Papers Contributed by Participants in the Research Conference on Educational and Cultural Deprivation*, New York: Holt, Rinehart and Winston.

Boddice, R. (2011), 'The End of Anthropocentrism', in R. Boddice (ed), *Anthropocentrism: Humans, Animals, Environments*, 1–18, Leiden, the Netherlands: Brill.

Bodrova, E. (2008), 'Make-Believe Play versus Academic Skills: A Vygotskian Approach to Today's Dilemma of Early Childhood Education', *European Early Childhood Education Research Journal*, 16 (3): 357–69.

Bodrova, E., and D. J. Leong (2007), *Tools of the Mind: The Vygotskian Approach to Early Childhood Education*, 2nd edn, Upper Saddle River, NJ: Pearson Education.

Bodrova, E., and D. J. Leong (2013), 'Play and Self-regulation: Lessons from Vygotsky', *American Journal of Play*, 6 (1): 111–23.

Bodrova, E., and D. J. Leong (2015), 'Vygotskian and Post-Vygotskian Views on Children's Play', *American Journal of Play*, 7 (3): 371–88.

Bodrova, E., and D. J. Leong (2018), 'Tools of the Mind: A Vygotskian Early Childhood Curriculum', in M. Fleer and B. van Oers (eds), *International Handbook of Early Childhood Education*, 1095–111, Dordrecht, Netherlands: Springer.

Bogin, B., J. Bragg, and C. Kuzawa (2015), 'Childhood, Biocultural Reproduction and Human Lifetime Reproductive Effort', in C. L. Meehan and A. N. Crittenden (eds), *Childhood: Origins, Evolution and Implications*, 45–74, Albuquerque: University of New Mexico Press.

Bondioli, A. (2007), 'Italy', in R. S. New and M. Cochran (eds), *Early Childhood Education: An International Encyclopedia*, Volume 4, 1110–54, Westport, CT: Praeger.

Bone, J. (2013), 'The Animal as Fourth Educator: A Literature Review of Animals and Young Children in Pedagogical Relationships', *Australasian Journal of Early Childhood*, 38 (2): 57–64.

Bornstein, M. H., and T. Leventhal (2015), 'Children in Bioecological Landscapes of Development', in R. M. Lerner (ed), *Handbook of Child Psychology and Developmental Science*, 7th edn, Hoboken, NJ: Wiley.

Bourdieu, P. (1986), 'The Forms of Capital', in J. G. Richardson (ed), *Handbook of Theory and Research for the Sociology of Education*, 241–59, New York: Greenwood.

Bowleg, L. (2012), 'The Problem with the Phrase Women and Minorities: Intersectionality – An Important Theoretical Framework for Public Health', *American Journal of Public Health*, 102: 1267–73.

Bradbury, A., and G. Roberts-Holmes (2017), *The Datafication of Primary and Early Years Education: Playing with Numbers*, New York: Routledge.

Braidotti, R. (2016), 'Posthuman Critical Theory', in D. Benerji and M. R. Paranjape (eds), *Critical Postmodernism and Planetary Futures*, 13–32, New York: Springer.

Branscombe, N. A., K. Castle, A. G. Dorsey, E. Surbeck and J. B. Taylor (2003), *Early Childhood Curriculum: A Constructivist Perspective*, Boston: Houghton Mifflin.

Braun, S. J., and E. P. Edwards (1972), *History and Theory of Early Childhood Education*, Worthington, OH: C. A. Jones.

Brison, K. J. (2011), 'Producing "Confident" Children: Negotiating Childhood in Fijian Kindergartens', *Anthropology and Education Quarterly*, 42 (3): 230–44.

Britzman, D. P. (2003), *After-education: Anna Freud, Melanie Klein and Psychoanalytic Histories of Learning*, Albany: SUNY Press.

Bronfenbrenner, U. (1979a), 'Contexts of Child Rearing: Problems and Prospects', *American Psychologist*, 34 (10): 844–50.

Bronfenbrenner, U. (1979b), *The Ecology of Human Development*, Cambridge, MA: Harvard University Press.

Bronfenbrenner, U., and P. A. Morris (2006), 'The Ecology of Developmental Processes', in W. Damon and R. M. Lerner (eds), *Handbook of Child Psychology*, Volume 1, 5th edn, 993–1028, New York: Wiley.

Brooks, M. (2009), 'Drawing to Learn', in M. Narey (ed), *Meaning Making: Constructing Multimodal Perspectives of Language, Literacy and Learning through Arts-based Early Childhood Education*, 9–29, Pittsburgh: Springer.

Browne, N. (2004), *Gender Equity in the Early Years*, Buckingham: Open University Press.

Bruner, J. (1966), *Towards a Theory of Instruction*, Cambridge, MA: Harvard University Press.

Bruner, J. (1985), 'Vygotsky: A Historical and Conceptual Perspective', in J. V. Wertsch (ed), Culture, Communication and Cognition: Vygotskian Perspectives, 21–34, Cambridge, UK: Cambridge University Press.

Bruner, J. (1991), 'The Narrative Construction of Reality', *Critical Inquiry*, 18: 1–21.

Bruner, J. (1993), *Acts of Meaning*, Cambridge, MA: Harvard University Press.

Bruner, J. (1996), *The Culture of Education*, Cambridge, MA: Harvard University Press.

Bryan, B. (2018), 'Playing with or Like the Girls: Advancing the Performance of "Multiple Masculinities in Black Boys' Childhood Play" in U.S. Early Childhood Classrooms', *Gender and Education*. https://doi.org/10.1080/09540253.2018.1447091

Buchanan, E. (2015), 'Economistic Subjects: Questioning Early Childhood Pedagogies of Learning, Participation, Voice', in T. Lightfoot-Rueda and R. L. Peach (eds), *Global Perspectives on Human Capital in Early Childhood Education: Reconceptualizing Theory, Policy and Practice*, 199–213, New York: Palgrave Macmillan.

Buchanan, E. (2017), 'From Developing Child to Competent Learner: A Genealogical Study of the Kindergarten Child and Progressive Reform in Aotearoa New Zealand', Doctoral diss., Melbourne Graduate School of Education, Australia.

Buchignani, N. (1980), 'Culture or Identity: Addressing Ethnicity in Canadian Education', *McGill Journal of Education*, 15 (1): 79–93.

Burman, E. (1996), 'Local, Global or Globalized? Child Development and International Child Rights Legislation', *Childhood*, 3 (1): 45–66.

Burman, E. (2008), *Deconstructing Developmental Psychology*, 2nd edn, London: Routledge.

Burman, E. (2013), 'Conceptual Resources for Questioning "Child as Educator"', *Studies in Philosophy and Education*, 32 (3): 229–43.

Buti, A. (2002), 'The Removal of Aboriginal Children: Canada and Australia Compared', *University of Western Sydney Law Review*, 2. Available online: http://www.austlii.edu.au/au/journals/UWSLRev/2002/2.html (accessed 25 November 2018).

Cagliari, P., M. Castagnetti, C. Giudici, C. Rinaldi, V. Vecchi and P. Moss (2016), *Loris Malaguzzi and the Schools of Reggio Emilia: A Selection of His Writings and Speeches, 1945–1993*, trans., J. McCall, New York: Routledge.

Cannella, G. S. (1997), *Deconstructing Early Childhood Education: Social Justice and Revolution*, New York: Peter Lang.

Cannella, G. S., and R. Viruru (2004), *Childhood and Postcolonization: Power, Education and Contemporary Practice*, New York: Routledge Falmer.

Carr, M. (2001), *Assessment in Early Childhood Settings: Learning Stories*, London: Paul Chapman.

Carr, M., L. Mitchell and L. Rameka (2016), 'Some Thoughts about the Value of an OECD International Assessment Framework for Early Childhood Services in Aotearoa New Zealand', *Contemporary Issues in Early Childhood*, 17 (4): 450–54.

Carr, M., and W. Lee (2012), *Learning Stories: Constructing Learner Identities in Early Education*, London: SAGE.

Castellano, M. B. (2000), 'Updating Aboriginal Traditions of Knowledge', in G. S. Dei, B. L. Hall and D. G. Rosenberg (eds), *Indigenous Knowledges in Global Contexts*, 21–36, Toronto: University of Toronto Press.

Chaiklin, S. (2003), 'The Zone of Proximal Development in Vygotsky's Analysis of Learning and Instruction', in A. Kozulin, B. Gindis and S. M. Miller (eds), *Vygotsky's Educational Theory in Cultural Context*, 39–64, Cambridge, UK: Cambridge University Press.

Chang, N. (2012), 'What Are the Roles that Children's Drawings Play in Inquiry of Science Concepts?' *Early Child Development and Care*, 182 (5): 621–37. https://doi.org/10.1080/03004430.2011.569542

Cheah, C. S. L., and V. Chirkov (2008), 'Parents' Personal and Cultural Beliefs Regarding Young Children: A Cross-cultural Study of Aboriginal and Euro-Canadian Mothers', *Journal of Cross-Cultural Psychology*, 39 (4): 402–23.

Chen, R. (2009), *Early Childhood Identity Construction, Culture and the Self*, New York: Peter Lang.

Chingos, M. M. (2015, February 2), 'Testing Costs a Drop in the Bucket' [blog post], Brookings Institute. Available online: https://www.brookings.edu/blog/up-front/2015/02/02/testing-costs-a-drop-in-the-bucket/ (accessed 25 November 2018).

Choi, Y., M. Park, J. Park Lee, T. Y. Kim and K. Tan (2017), 'Culture and Family Process: Examination of Culture-Specific Family Process via Development of New Parenting Measures among Filipino and Korean American Families with Adolescents', in Y. Choi and H. C. Ham (eds), *Asian American Parenting: Family Process and Intervention*, 37–86, New York: Springer.

Chumak-Horbatsch, R. (2012), *Linguistically Appropriate Practices: A Guide for Working with Young Immigrant Children*, Toronto: University of Toronto Press.

Chung, S., and D. J. Walsh (2010), 'Unpacking Child-centeredness: A History of Meanings', *Journal of Curriculum Studies*, 32 (2): 215–34.

Cizek, G. J. (2010), 'An Introduction to Formative Assessment: History, Characteristics, and Challenges', in H. Andrade and G. J. Cizek (eds), *Handbook of Formative Assessment*, 3–17, New York: Routledge.

Clark, J., and S. Richards (2017), 'The Cherished Conceits of Research with Children: Does Seeking the Agentic Voice of the Child through Participatory Methods Deliver What It Promises?' in I. E. Castro, M. Swauger and B. Harger (eds), *Researching Children and Youth: Methodological Issues, Strategies and Innovations*, 127–47, Bingley, UK: Emerald.

Clarke, V., and D. Watson (2014), 'Examining Whiteness in a Children's Centre', *Contemporary Issues in Early Childhood*, 15 (1): 69–80.

Cleverley, J. F., and D. C. Phillips (1986), *Visions of Childhood: Influential Models from Locke to Spock*, revised edn, New York: Teachers College Press.

Cliff, K., and Z. Millei (2011), 'Biopower and the "Civilization" of Children's Bodies in a Preschool Bathroom: An Australian Case Study', *International Social Science Journal*, 62: 351–62.

Clifford, G. J. (1975), *The Shape of American Education*, Englewood Cliffs, NJ: Prentice-Hall.

Cochelin, I. (2000), 'Besides the Book: Using the Body to Mould the Mind – Cluny in the Tenth and Eleventh Centuries', in G. Ferzoco and C. Muessig (eds), *Medieval Monastic Education*, 21–34, London: Leicester University Press.

Cochran, M. M., and J. A. Brassard (1979), 'Child Development and Personal Networks', *Child Development*, 50 (3): 601–16.

Coe, H. A. (2017), 'Embracing Risk in the Canadian Woodlands: Four Children's Risky Play and Risk-taking Experiences in a Canadian Forest Kindergarten', *Journal of Early Childhood Research*, 15 (4): 374–88.

Cole, M. (1996), *Cultural Psychology: A Once and Future Discipline*, Cambridge, MA: Harvard University Press.

Cole, M. (2005), 'Cultural-Historical Activity Theory in the Family of Sociocultural Approaches', *International Society for the Study of Behavioral Development Newsletter*, 47 (1): 1–4.

Cole, M., and N. Gajdamaschko (2007), 'Vygotsky and Culture', in H. Daniels, J. Wertsch and M. Cole (eds), *The Cambridge Companion to Vygotsky*, Cambridge, UK: Cambridge University Press.

Cole, M., and K. Stewart (2014), *Our Children and Other Animals: The Cultural Construction of Human-Animal Relations in Childhood*, Farnham, UK: Ashgate.

Collins, A., J. S. Brown and S. E. Newman (1989), 'Cognitive Apprenticeship: Teaching the Crafts of Reading, Writing, and Mathematics', in L. B. Resnick (ed), *Knowing, Learning and Instruction: Essays in Honor of Robert Glaser*, 453–94, Hillsdale, NJ: Lawrence Erlbaum.

Collins, P. H., and S. Bilge (2016), *Intersectionality*, Cambridge, UK: Polity Press.

Comrie, B. (2012), 'Language and Thought'. Available online: https://www.linguisticsociety.org/resource/language-and-thought (accessed 25 November 2018),

Connolly, P. (2004), *Boys and Schooling in the Early Years*, London: RoutledgeFalmer.

Copple, C., and S. Bredekamp (2009), *Developmentally Appropriate Practice in Early Childhood Programs Serving Children from Birth through Age 8*, 3rd edn, Washington, DC: National Association for the Education of Young Children.

Cornell, D., and S. Murphy (2002), 'Anti-racism, Multiculturalism and the Ethics of Identification', *Philosophy and Social Criticism*, 28 (4): 419–49.

Cornett, C. E., and K. L. Smithrim (2000), *The Arts as Meaning-makers: Integrating Literature and the Arts throughout the Curriculum*, Canadian edn, Toronto, ON: Prentice Hall.

Côté, J. (1996), 'Sociological Perspectives on Identity Formation: The Culture-Identity Link and Identity Capital', *Journal of Adolescence*, 19 (5): 417–28.

Cowie, B., and Carr, M. (2009), 'Consequences of Sociocultural Assessment', in A. Anning, J. Cullen and M. Fleer (eds), *Early Childhood Education: Society and Culture*, 2nd edn, 105–29, Los Angeles: SAGE.

Crain, W. (2016), *Theories of Development: Concepts and Applications*, New York: Routledge.

Cubberly, E. P. (1934), *Public Education in the United States: A Study and Interpretation of American Educational History*, Boston: Houghton Mifflin.

Cudworth, E. (2014), 'Beyond Speciesism: Intersectionality, Critical Sociology and the Human Domination of Other Animals', in N. Taylor and R. Twine (eds), *The Rise of Critical Animal Studies: From the Margins to the Centre*, 19–25, New York: Routledge.

Cummins, J. (2012), 'Foreword', in *Linguistically Appropriate Practices: A Guide for Working with Young Immigrant Children*, ix–xiv, Toronto, ON: University of Toronto Press.

Curtis, S. (2011), 'Tangible as Tissue: Arnold Gesell, Infant Behavior, and Film Analysis', *Science in Context*, 24 (3): 417–42.

Dahlberg, G. (2011), 'Pedagogical Documentation: A Practice for Negotiation and Democracy', in C. Edwards, L. Gandini and G. Forman (eds), *The Hundred Languages of Children: The Reggio Emilia Experience in Transformation*, 3rd edn, 225–31, Santa Barbara, CA: Praeger.

Dahlberg, G., P. Moss and A. Pence (2013), *Beyond Quality in Early Childhood Education and Care: Languages of Evaluation*, 3rd edn, New York: Routledge.

Dang, G., and L. S. Pheng (2015), 'Theories of Economic Development', in G. Dang and L. S. Pheng (eds), *Infrastructure Investments in Developing Economies*, 11–26, Singapore: Springer.

Dangel, J. R., E. Guyton and C. B. McIntyre (2004), 'Constructivist Pedagoy in Primary Classrooms: Learning from Teachers and Their Classrooms', *Journal of Early Childhood Teacher Education*, 24: 237–45.

Daniels, H. (2011), 'Vygotsky and Psychology', in U. Goswami (ed), *The Wiley-Blackwell Handbook of Childhood Cognitive Development*, 2nd edn, 673–96. Malden, MA: Wiley-Blackwell.

Darwin, C. (1877), 'A Biographical Sketch of an Infant', *Mind*, 2 (7): 285–94.

Davin, K. J., J. D. Herazo and S. Sagre (2017), 'Learning to Mediate: Teacher Appropriation of Dynamic Assessment', *Language Teaching Research*, 21 (5): 632–51.

Davis, B. (2004), *Inventions of Teaching: A Genealogy*, Mahwah, NJ: Lawrence Erlbaum.

Davis, B., D. Sumara and R. Luce-Kapler (2008), *Engaging Mind: Changing Teaching in Complex Times*, 2nd edn, New York: Routledge.

Davis, R., H. Shrobe and P. Szolovits (1993), 'What Is a Knowledge Representation?' *AI Magazine*, 14 (1): 17–33. Available online: http://groups.csail.mit.edu/medg/ftp/psz/k-rep.html#role2MIT (accessed 26 November 2018).

De Graeve, K. (2016), 'Theorizing Identities in Early Childhood', in A. Farrell, S. L. Kagan and K. M. Tisdall (eds), *The SAGE Handbook of Early Childhood Research*, London: SAGE.

Dei, G. S. (1996), *Anti-racism Education: Theory and Practice*, Halifax, NS: Fernwood.

Delgado, R., and J. Stefancic (2017), *Critical Race Theory: An Introduction*, 3rd edn, New York: New York University Press.

Derman-Sparks, L., and J. O. Edwards, eds. (2010), *Anti-bias Education for Young Children and Ourselves*, Washington, DC: National Association for the Education of Young Children.

de Vocht, L., G. Mackey and D. Hill (2017), 'PISA' for Five-Year-Olds? A Position Paper on OECD Plans for a Global Testing Tool', *Early Education*, 61: 27–28.

Dewey, J. (1896), 'The University School', *The University Record*, 1 (32).

Dewey, J. (1899), *The School and Society*, Chicago: University of Chicago Press. Available online: https://archive.org/details/schoolandsociet03dewegoog (accessed 26 November 2018).

Dewey, J. (1916), *Democracy and Education: An Introduction to the Philosophy of Education*, New York: Macmillan. Available online: https://archive.org/details/democracyandedu00dewegoog (accessed 23 November 2018),

Dewey, J. (1938), *Experience and Education*, New York: Macmillan.

Drummond, M. J. (2003), *Assessing Children's Learning*, 2nd edn, London: David Fulton.

Dubiel, J. (2016), *Effective Assessment in the Early Years Foundation Stage*, 2nd edn, Los Angeles: SAGE.

Duckworth, E. (1987), *The Having of Wonderful Ideas and Other Essays on Teaching and Learning*, New York: Teachers College Press.

Edwards, C., L. Gandini and G. Forman (2012), 'Introduction: Background and Starting Points', in C. Edwards, L. Gandini and G. Forman (eds), *The Hundred*

*Languages of Children: The Reggio Emilia Experience in Transformation*, 3rd edn, Santa Barbara, CA: Praeger.

Edwards, R., C. Caballero and S. Puthussery (2010), 'Parenting Children from "Mixed" Racial, Ethnic and Faith Backgrounds: Typifications of Difference and Belonging', *Ethnic and Racial Studies*, 33 (6): 949–67.

Edwards, S., and A. Cutter-Mackenzie (2013), 'Next Time We Can Be Penguins: Expanding the Concept of Learning Play to Support Learning and Teaching about Sustainability in Early Childhood Education', in O. Lillemyr, S. Dockett and B. Perry (eds), *Varied Perspectives on Play and Learning: Theory and Research on Early Childhood Education*, 55–74, Charlotte, NC: Information Age.

Elementary Teachers' Federation of Ontario (2017), *First Nations, Métis and Inuit Education Resource: Engaging Learners through Play*, Toronto: Elementary Teachers' Federation of Ontario.

Elkonin, D. (2005a), 'Chapter 1: The Subject of Our Research: The Developed Form of Play', *Journal of Russian and East European Psychology*, 43 (1): 22–48.

Elkonin, D. (2005b), 'Chapter 3: Theories of Play', *Journal of Russian and East European Psychology*, 43 (2): 3–89.

Emilson, A., and I. Pramling Samuelsson (2014), 'Documentation and Communication in Swedish Preschools', *Early Years*, 34 (2): 175–87.

Entwistle, H. (2012), *Child-centred Education*, Milton Park, UK: Routledge. (Original work published in 1970)

Epstein, J. L. (2011), *School, Family and Community Partnerships: Preparing Educators and Improving Schools*, Boulder, CO: Routledge.

Erickson-Schroth, L., ed (2014), *Trans Bodies, Trans Selves: A Resource for the Transgender Community*, New York: Oxford University Press.

Erikson, E. (1968), *Identity: Youth and Crisis*, New York: Norton.

Erstad, O., Ø. Gilje, J. Sefton-Green and H. C. Arnseth (2016), *Learning Identities, Education and Community: Young Lives in the Cosmopolitan City*, Cambridge, UK: Cambridge University Press.

Esser, F., M. S. Baader, T. Betz and B. Hungerland (2016), *Reconceptualizing Agency and Childhood: New Perspectives in Childhood Studies*, New York: Routledge.

Esteban-Guitart, M., and L. C. Moll (2014), 'Funds of Identity: A New Concept Based on the Funds of Knowledge Approach', *Culture and Psychology*, 20 (1): 31–48.

Ezell, M. J. M. (1983), 'John Locke's Images of Childhood: Early Eighteenth-Century Responses to Some Thoughts Concerning Education', *Eighteenth Century Studies*, 17 (2): 139–55.

Fallace, T. (2012), 'Recapitulation Theory and the New Education: Race, Culture, Imperialism, and Pedagogy, 1894–1916', *Curriculum Inquiry*, 42 (4): 510–33.

Fallace, T. (2015), 'The Savage Origins of Child-centered Pedagogy, 1871–1913', *American Educational Research Journal*, 52 (1): 73–103.

Faltis, C. J., and G. Valdés (2016), 'Preparing Teachers for Teaching and Advocating in Linguistically Diverse Classrooms: A Vade Mecum for Teacher Educators', in D. H. Gitomer and C. A. Bell (eds), *Handbook of Research on Teaching*, 549–92, Washington, DC: American Educational Research Association.

Farquhar, S., and E. J. White (2014), 'Philosophy and Pedagogy of Early Childhood', *Educational Philosophy and Theory*, 46 (8): 821–32.
Felstiner, S., L. Kocher and A. Pelo (2006), 'The Disposition to Document', in A. Fleet, C. Patterson and J. Robertson (eds), *Insights: Behind Early Childhood Pedagogical Documentation*, 55–76, Castle Hill, Australia: Pademelon Press.
Fernyhough, C. (2008), *The Baby in the Mirror*, London: Granta.
Feuerstein, R. (1980), *Instrumental Enrichment: An Intervention Program for Cognitive Modifiability*, Baltimore: University Park Press.
Feuerstein, R., and A. Lewin-Benham (2012), *What Learning Looks Like: Mediated Learning in Theory and Practice, K–6*, New York: Teachers College Press.
Finnegan, R. (2014), 'Child Play Is Serious: Children's Games, Verbal Art and Survival in Africa', *International Journal of Play*, 3: 293–315.
Flax, J. (1990), *Thinking Fragments: Psychoanalysis, Feminism and Postmodernism in the Contemporary West*, Berkeley: University of California Press.
Fleer, M. (1998), 'Universal Fantasy: The Domination of Western Theories of Play', in E. Dau (ed), *Children's Play: Revisiting Play in Early Childhood Education Settings*, 67–80, Sydney: MacLennan and Petty.
Fleer, M. (2003), 'Early Childhood Education as an Evolving "Community of Practice" or as Lived "Social Reproduction": Researching the "Taken-for-Granted"', *Contemporary Issues in Early Childhood*, 4 (1): 64–79.
Fleer, M. (2010), *Early Learning and Development: Cultural Historical Concepts of Play*, Melbourne: Cambridge University Press.
Fleer, M. (2017), 'Scientific Playworlds: A Model of Teaching Science in Play-based Settings', *Research in Science Education*, 1–22. https://doi.org/10.1007/s11165-017-9653-z
Fleer, M., M. Hedegaard and J. Tudge (2009), 'A Cultural-Historical Analysis of Play as an Activity Setting in Early Childhood Education: Views from Research and from Teachers', in M. Fleer, J. Tudge and M. Hedegaard (eds), *Childhood Studies and the Impact of Globalization: Policies and Practices at Global and Local Levels*, 292–312, New York: Routledge.
Fleet, A. (2017), 'The Landscape of Pedagogical Documentation', in A. Fleet, C. Patterson and J. Robertson (eds), *Pedagogical Documentation in Early Years Practice: Seeing through Multiple Perspectives*, Los Angeles: SAGE.
Flynn, J. R., and C. Blair (2013), 'The History of Intelligence: New Spectacles for Developmental Psychology', in P. D. Zelazo (ed), *The Oxford Handbook of Developmental Psychology*, Volume 1, 765–90, New York: Oxford University Press.
Foucault, M. (1975), *The Birth of the Clinic: An Archaeology of Medical Perception*, New York: Vintage.
Foucault, M. (1980), *Power/Knowledge: Selected Interviews and Other Writings 1972–1977*, ed. C. Gordon, London: Harvester Wheatsheaf.
Fraser, S. (2012), *Authentic Childhood; Experiencing Reggio Emilia in the Classroom*, 3rd edn, Toronto: Nelson.
Frideres, J. (2008), 'Aboriginal Identity in the Canadian Context', *Canadian Journal of Native Studies*, 28 (2): 313–42.
Friesen, J. W. (2013), 'They Had What the World Has Lost: Traditional Native American Child-raising Practices', *Early Childhood Education*, 41 (1): 4–13.
Froebel, F. (1904), *Pedagogics of the Kindergarten or, His Ideas Concerning the Play and Playthings of the Child*, trans. J. Jarvis, New York: D. Appleton.

Original work published 1861. Available online: https://archive.org/stream/friedrichfroebel03fr#page/n9 (accessed 26 November 2018).

Fromberg, D. P. (2002), *Play and Meaning in Early Childhood Education*, Boston: Allyn and Bacon.

Frost, J. L., S. C. Wortham and S. Reifel (2012), *Play and Child Development*, 4th edn, Upper Saddle River, NJ: Pearson Education.

Galabuzi, G.-E. (2014), 'Race and the Streaming of Ontario's Children and Youth: Restacking the Deck – Streaming by Class, Race and Gender in Ontario Schools', *Our Schools/Our Selves*, 23 (2): 185–226.

Gandini, L. (2005), 'From the Beginning of the *Atelier* to Materials as Languages: Conversations from Reggio Emilia', in L. Gandini, L. Hill, L. Cadwell and C. Schwall (eds), *In the Spirit of the Studio*, 6–15, New York: Teachers College Press.

Gandini, L. (2011a), 'The Atelier: A Conversation with Vea Vecchi', in C. Edwards, L. Gandini and G. Forman (eds), *The Hundred Languages of Children: The Reggio Emilia Experience in Transformation*, 3rd edn, 303–16, Santa Barbara, CA: Praeger.

Gandini, L. (2011b), 'The Challenge of Assessment: Scaling Up the Reggio Emilia Approach in the USA', *Early Childhood Matters*, 117: 78–82. Available online: http://earlychildhoodmagazine.org/wp-content/uploads/2012/01/ECM117_The-challenge-of-assessment-scaling-up-the-Reggio_15.pdf (accessed 26 November 2018).

García, O., and L. Wei (2014), *Translanguaging: Language, Bilingualism and Education*, New York: Palgrave Macmillan.

Garcia Coll, C., and A. K. Marks (2009), *Immigrant Stories: Ethnicity and Academics in Middle Childhood*, Oxford: Oxford University Press.

Gardner, H. (1999), *Intelligence Reframed: Multiple Intelligences for the 21st Century*, New York: Basic Books.

Garrison, J. W., S. Neubert and K. Reich (2016), *Democracy and Education Reconsidered: Dewey after One Hundred Years*, London: Routledge.

Gaskins, S., W. Haight and D. F. Lancy (2007), 'The Cultural Construction of Play', in A. Göncü and S. Gaskins (eds), *Play and Development: Evolutionary, Sociocultural and Functional Perspectives*, 179–202, Mahwah, NJ: Lawrence Erlbaum.

Gauvain, M. (2005), 'Sociocultural Contexts of Learning', in A. E. Maynard, and M. I. Martini (eds), *Learning in Cultural Context: Family, Peers and School*, 11–40, New York: Kluwer.

Gauvain, M., and R. D. Parke (2010), 'Socialization', in M. H. Bornstein (ed), *Handbook of Cultural Developmental Science*, 239–58, New York: Psychology Press.

Georgis, R., L. Brosinsky, T. Mejia, A. Kirova, R. Gokiert and Knowledge Exchange Advisory (2017), *RAISED between Cultures: A Knowledge and Reflection Guidebook for Intercultural Practice in the Early Years*, Edmonton, AB: Community-University Partnership, University of Alberta.

Gesell, A. (1935), 'Cinemanalysis: A Method of Behavior Study', *The Journal of Genetic Psychology*, 152 (4): 549–62.

Ghosh, R., and A. Abdi (2004), *Education and the Politics of Difference: Canadian Perspectives*, Toronto: Canadian Scholars' Press.

Gidley, J. (2016), *Postformal Education: A Philosophy for Complex Futures*, Switzerland: Springer.

Gill, N. (2016), *Educational Philosophy in the French Enlightenment: From Nature to Second Nature*, New York: Routledge.
Gillis, J. (1992), 'Views of Native Parents about Early Childhood Education', *Canadian Journal of Native Education*, 19 (1): 73–81.
Giordano, G. (2005), *How Testing Came to Dominate American Schools: The History of Educational Assessment*, New York: Peter Lang.
Giordano, P. J. (2017), 'Individual Personality Is Best Understood as Process, Not Structure: A Confucian-inspired Perspective', *Culture and Psychology*, 23 (4): 502–18.
Gipps, C., and G. Stobart (2003), 'Alternative Assessment', in T. Kellaghan, D. L. Stufflebeam and L. A. Wingae (eds), *International Handbook of Educational Evaluation*, 549–76, London: Kluwer Academic.
Giroux, H. A. (1988), *Teachers as Intellectuals: Toward a Critical Pedagogy of Learning*, Westport, CT: Bergin and Garvey.
Glassman, M. (2001), 'Dewey and Vygotsky: Society, Experience, and Inquiry in Educational Practice', *Educational Researcher*, 30 (4): 3–14.
Goffin, S., and C. S. Wilson (2001), *Curriculum Models and Early Childhood Education: Appraising the Relationship*, Upper Saddle River, NJ: Prentice Hall.
Goldhaber, J. (2007), 'The Development of an Early Childhood Teacher Research Collaborative', *Theory into Practice*, 46 (1): 74–80.
Göncu, A. and S. Gaskins (2011), 'Comparing and Extending Piaget's and Vygotsky's Understanding of Play: Symbolic Play as Individual, Sociocultural and Educational Interpretation', in A. D. Pellegrini (ed), *Oxford Handbook of the Development of Play*, 48–53, New York: Oxford University Press.
Goouch, K. (2008), 'Understanding Playful Pedagogies, Play Narratives and Play Spaces', *Early Years: An International Journal of Research and Development*, 28 (1): 93–102.
Goouch, K. (2010), *Towards Excellence in Early Years Education: Exploring Narratives of Experience*, London: Routledge.
Gordon, A. M., and K. W. Browne (2014), *Beginnings and Beyond: Foundations of Early Childhood Education*, 9th edn, Belmont, CA: Wadsworth Cengage.
Gounari, P. (2006), 'How to Tame a Wild Tongue: Language Rights in the United States', *Human Architecture: Journal of the Sociology of Self-knowledge*, 4 (3): 71–77. Available online: http://scholarworks.umb.edu/humanarchitecture/vol4/iss3/9 (accessed 26 November 2018).
Graham, P. (2008), 'Susan Isaacs and the Malting House School', *Journal of Child Psychotherapy*, 34 (1): 5–22.
Graham, P. (2009), *Susan Isaacs: A Life of Freeing the Minds of Children*, London: Karnac.
Graue, E. (1993), *Ready for What? Constructing Meanings of Readiness for Kindergarten*, Albany: SUNY Press.
Graue, E. (2009), 'Reimagining Kindergarten', *The School Administrator*, 66 (1): 10–15.
Graveline, F. (1998), *Circle Works*, Halifax, NS: Fernwood.
Gredler, M. E. (1997), *Learning and Instruction: Theory into Practice*, 3rd edn, Upper Saddle River, NJ: Prentice-Hall.
Gredler, M. E. (2009a), 'Hiding in Plain Sight: The Stages of Master/Self-regulation in Vygotsky's Cultural-historical Theory', *Educational Psychologist*, 44 (1): 1–19. https://doi.org/10.1080/00461520802616259

Gredler, M. E. (2009b), *Learning and Instruction: Theory into Practice*, 6th edn, Upper Saddle River, NJ: Pearson.

Gredler, M. E., and C. C. Shields (2008), *Vygotsky's Legacy: A Foundation for Research and Practice*, New York: Guilford Press.

Greenwood, M. (2009), 'Places for the Good Care of Children: A Discussion of Indigenous Cultural Considerations and Early Childhood in Canada and New Zealand', Doctoral diss., University of British Columbia, Vancouver, Canada.

Grieshaber, S., and F. McArdle (2010), *The Trouble with Play*, Maidenhead, UK: Open University Press.

Gullo, D. F. (2015), 'Assessment and School Readiness: Implications for Children, Implications for Schools', in O. Saracho (ed), *Contemporary Perspectives on Research in Assessment and Evaluation in Early Childhood Education*, Charlotte, NC: Information Age.

Gunnarsdottir, B. (2014), 'From Play to School: Are Core Values of ECEC in Iceland Being Undermined by 'Schoolification?' *International Journal of Early Years Education*, 22 (3): 242–50.

Gupta, A. (2015), 'Using Postcolonial Theory to Critically Re-frame the Child Developmental Narrative', in T. David, K. Goouch and S. Powell (eds), *The Routledge International Handbook of Philosophies and Theories of Early Childhood Education and Care*, London: Routledge. Available online: https://www.routledgehandbooks.com/doi/10.4324/9781315678979.ch16 (accessed 26 November 2018).

Gurl, T. J., L. Caraballo, L. Grey, J. H. Gunn, D. Gerwin and H. Bembenutty (2016), *Policy, Professionalization, Privatization and Performance Assessment: Affordances and Constraints for Teacher Education Programs*, New York: Springer.

Gutek, G. (1997), *Philosophical and Ideological Perspectives in Education*, London: Allyn and Bacon.

Hagan-Burke, S. (2005), 'Choral Responding', in M. Hersen, J. Rosqvist, A. M. Gross, R. S. Drabman, G. Sugai and R. Horner (eds), *Encyclopedia of Behavior Modification and Cognitive Behavior Therapy*, London: SAGE. http://dx.doi.org/10.4135/9781412950534.n3033

Hakkarainen, K. (2010), 'Communities of Learning in the Classroom', in K. Littleton, C. Wood and J. K. Staarman (eds), *International Handbook of Psychology in Education*, 177–225, Bingley, UK: Emerald.

Hall, G. S. (1904), *Adolescence: Its Psychology and Its Relations to Physiology, Anthropology, Sociology, Sex, Crime, Religion and Education*, New York: D. Appleton.

Hall, K., M. Horgan, A. Ridgway, R. Murphy, M. Cunneen and D. Cunningham (2010), *Loris Malaguzzi and the Reggio Emilia Experience*, London: Continuum.

Hall, S. (1990), 'Cultural Identity and Diaspora', in J. Rutherford (ed), *Identity: Community, Culture, Difference*, 222–37. London: Lawrence and Wishart.

Hall, S. (1991), 'Ethnicity: Identity and Difference', *Radical America*, 23 (4): 9–20.

Hall, S. (1997), *Representation: Cultural Representations and Signifying Practices*, Thousand Oaks, CA: SAGE and Open University.

Hallam, J., H. Lee and M. Das Gupta (2014), 'Collaborative Cognition: Co-creating Children's Artwork in an Educational Context', *Theory and Psychology*, 24 (2): 166–85.

Hallpike, C. R. (1979), *The Foundations of Primitive Thought*, Oxford: Clarendon Press.
Hamm, J. V., and L. Zhang (2010), 'School Contexts and the Development of Adolescents' Peer Relations', in J. L. Meece and J. S. Eccles (eds), *Handbook of Research on Schools, Schooling and Human Development*, 128–45, New York: Routledge.
Hammersley, M. (1993), 'On the Teacher as Researcher', *Educational Action Research*, 1 (3): 425–45. https://doi.org/10.1080/0965079930010308
Hansen, D. T., and C. James (2016), 'The Importance of Cultivating Democratic Habits in Schools: Enduring Lessons from Democracy and Education', *Journal of Curriculum Studies*, 48 (1): 94–112.
Hare, W. (1979), *Open-mindedness and Education*, Montreal: McGill-Queen's University Press.
Harkness, S., C. M. Super, C. J. Mavridis, O. Barry and M. Zeitlin (2013), 'Culture and Early Childhood Development: Implications for Policy and Programs', in P. Rebello Britto, P. L. Engle and C. M. Super (eds), *Handbook of Early Childhood Development Research and its Impact on Global Policy*, 142–60, New York: Oxford University Press.
Harkness, S., C. M. Super, M. A. Sutherland, M. Blom, U. Moscardino, C. J. Mavridis and G. Blom (2007), 'Culture and the Construction of Habits in Daily Life: Implications for the Successful Development of Children with Disabilities', *OTJR: Occupation, Participation and Health*, 27: 33S–40S.
Harlen, W. (2012), 'On the Relationship between Assessment for Formative and Summative Purposes', in J. Gardner (ed), *Assessment and Learning*, 87–102, Thousand Oaks, CA: SAGE.
Harris, A., and Z. Leonardo (2018), 'Intersectionality, Race-Gender Subordination and Education', *Review of Research in Education*, 42: 1–27.
Harris, J. R. (1998), *The Nurture Assumption: Why Children Turn Out the Way They Do*, New York: Touchstone.
Hart, M. A. (2010), 'Indigenous Worldviews, Knowledge, and Research: The Development of an Indigenous Research Paradigm', *Journal of Indigenous Voices in Social Work*, 1 (1): 1–16.
Hawkins, C. (2017), 'Planning for Risky Possibilities in Play' in A. Woods (ed), *Child-initiated Play and Learning: Planning for Possibilities in the Early Years*, 2nd edn, 77–94, London: Routledge.
Hayashi, A., and J. Tobin (2015), *Teaching Embodied: Cultural Practice in Japanese Preschools*, Chicago: University of Chicago Press.
Hedegaard, M. (2007), 'The Development of Children's Conceptual Relation to the World, with a Focus on Concept Formation in Preschool Children's Activity', in H. Daniels, M. Cole and J. Wertsch (eds), *The Cambridge Companion to Vygotsky*, 246–76, Cambridge, UK: Cambridge University Press.
Hedegaard, M., and S. Chaiklin (2005), *Radical-local Teaching and Learning: A Cultural-historical Approach*, Aarhus, Denmark: Aarhus University Press.
Hellal, P., and M. Lorch (2010), 'Darwin's Contribution to the Study of Child Development and Language Acquisition', *Language & History*, 53 (1): 1–14.
Hendrick, J. (2004), *Next Steps towards Teaching the Reggio Way: Accepting the Challenge to Change*, 2nd edn, Upper Saddle River, NJ: Pearson/Merrill Prentice Hall.

Hennig, K., and A. Kirova (2012), 'The Role of Cultural Artifacts in Play as Tools to Mediate Learning in an Intercultural Preschool Program', *Contemporary Issues in Early Childhood*, 13 (3): 226–41.

Henricks, T. (2008), 'The Nature of Play: An Overview', *American Journal of Play*, 1 (2): 157–80. Available online: http://www.journalofplay.org/issues/1/2/article/nature-play-overview (accessed 26 November 2018).

Hewett, V. M. (2001), 'Examining the Reggio Emilia Approach to Early Childhood Education', *Early Childhood Education Journal*, 29 (2): 95–100.

Heydon, R. M., and L. Iannacci (2009), *Early Childhood Curricula and the De-pathologizing of Childhood*, Toronto: University of Toronto Press.

Higgins, C. (2009), 'Open-mindedness in Three Dimensions', *Paidensis*, 18 (1): 44–59.

HighScope Educational Research Foundation (2018), 'Welcome to COR Advantage'. Available online: https://coradvantage.com/ (accessed 26 November 2018).

Hoffman, D. M. (1996), 'Culture and Self in Multicultural Education: Reflections on Discourse, Text and Practice', *American Educational Research Journal*, 33 (3): 545–69.

Hoffman, D. M. (2003), 'Childhood Ideology in the United States: A Comparative Cultural View', *International Review of Education*, 49 (1–2): 191–211.

Hofstede, G. (1997), *Cultures and Organizations: Software of the Mind*, London: McGraw-Hill.

Hohmann, M., B. Banet and D. P. Weikart (1979), *Young Children in Action: A Manual for Preschool Educators*, Ypsilanti, MI: High/Scope Educational Research Foundation.

Holder, A. (1995), 'Anna Freud's Contribution to the Psychoanalytic Theory of Development', *Journal of Child Psychotherapy*, 21 (3): 326–46.

Hookimaw-Witt, J. (1998), 'Any Changes since Residential School?' *Canadian Journal of Native Education*, 22 (2): 159–70.

Howe, B. (2005), 'Citizenship Education for Child Citizens', *Canadian and International Education*, 34 (1): 42–9. Available online: http://ir.lib.uwo.ca/cgi/viewcontent.cgi?article=1031andcontext=cie-eci (accessed 26 November 2018).

Hunter, I. (1994), *Rethinking the School: Subjectivity, Bureaucracy, Criticism*, New York: St. Martin's Press.

Hyman, J. (2015), *Action, Knowledge, and Will*, Oxford: Oxford University Press.

Hyun, E. (2006), *Teachable Moments: Re-conceptualizing Curricula Understandings*, New York: Peter Lang.

I'Anson, J. (2013), 'Beyond the Child's Voice: Towards an Ethics for Children's Participation Rights', *Global Studies of Childhood*, 3 (2): 104–14.

Ignelzi, M. (2000), 'Meaning-making in the Learning and Teaching Process', *New Directions for Student Services*, 82: 5–14.

Illeris, K. (2007), *How We Learn: Learning and Non-learning in Schools and Beyond*, New York: Routledge.

Isaacs, S. (1933), *Social Development in Young Children: A Study of Beginnings*, London: George Routledge and Sons.

Ishay, M. (2008), *The History of Human Rights: From Ancient Times to the Globalization Era*, Los Angeles: University of California Press.

Jackson, P. W. (1998), 'Child-centered Education for Pacific Rim Cultures?' *Early Child Development and Care*, 143: 47–57.

Jacobson, T. (2016), 'Gender Diversity', in D. Couchenour and J. K. Chrisman (eds), *The SAGE Encyclopedia of Contemporary Early Childhood Education*, 621–23, Thousand Oaks, CA: SAGE.

James, A. (2009), 'Agency', in J. Qvortrup, W. Corsaro and M. Honig (eds), *The Palgrave Handbook of Childhood Studies*, 34–45, Basingstoke, UK: Palgrave Macmillan.

James, A., C. Jenks and A. P. Prout (1998), *Theorizing Childhood*, New York: Teachers College Press.

Jarvis, P. (2009), *Learning to Be a Person in Society*, London: Routledge.

Jenkins, H. (1998), 'Introduction: Childhood Innocence and Other Modern Myths', in H. Jenkins (ed), *The Children's Culture Reader*, 1–39, New York: New York University Press.

Jensen, A. R. (1969), 'How Much Can We Boost IQ and Scholastic Achievement?' *Harvard Educational Review*, 39: 1–123.

Jerome, L. (2016), 'Interpreting Children's Rights Education: Three Perspectives and Three Roles for Teachers', *Citizenship, Social and Economics Education*, 15 (2): 143–56.

Jewitt, C. (2008), 'Multimodality and Literacy in School Classrooms', *Review of Research in Education*, 32: 241–67.

Johnson, A. (1995), 'Constructing the Child in Psychology: The Child-as-Primitive in Hall and Piaget', *Journal of Phenomenological Psychology*, 26 (2): 35–57. doi:10.1163/156916295X00088

Johnson, R. (2000), 'Colonialism and Cargo Cults in Early Childhood Education: Does Reggio Emilia Really Exist?' *Contemporary Issues in Early Childhood*, 1 (1): 61–78.

Jones, J., and P. Cloke (2008), 'Nonhuman Agencies: Trees in Place and Time', in C. Knappett and L. Malafouris (eds), *Towards a Non-anthropocentric Approach*, 79–96, New York: Springer.

Jones, P., and S. Welch (2010), *Rethinking Children's Rights: Attitudes in Contemporary Society*, London: Continuum.

Kaestle, C. F., ed. (1973), *Joseph Lancaster and the Monitorial School Movement. A Documentary History*, New York: Teachers College Press.

Kağitçibaşi, Ç. (2007), *Family, Self and Human Development across Cultures: Theory and Applications*, 2nd edn, Mahwah, NJ: Lawrence Erlbaum.

Kamii, C., and R. DeVries (1973), *Piaget-based Curriculum for Early Childhood Education: The Kamii-Devries Approach*, ERIC Document No. ED 080 192.

Kangas, J., M. Ojala and T. Venninen (2015), 'Children's Self-regulation in the Context of Participatory Pedagogy in Early Childhood Education', *Early Education and Development*, 26: 847–70. https://doi.org/10.1080/10409289.2015.1039434

Kaufman, M. J., S. R. Kaufman and E. C. Nelson (2015), *Learning Together: The Law, Politics, Economics, Pedagogy and Neuroscience of Early Childhood Education*, Lanham, MD: Rowman and Littlefield.

Kegan, R. (1982), *The Evolving Self: Problem and Process in Human Development*, Cambridge, MA: Harvard University Press.

Kegan, R. (1994), *In Over Our Heads: The Mental Demands of Modern Life*, Cambridge, MA: Harvard University Press.

Keller, E. F. (2010), *The Mirage of a Space between Nature and Nurture*, Durham, NC: Duke University Press.

Kelly, M. F., and E. Surbeck (2007), 'History of Preschool Assessment', in B. A. Bracken and R. J. Nagle (eds), *Psychoeducational Assessment of Preschool Children*, 4th edn, 1–19, New York: Routledge.

Kempf, A. (2016), *The Pedagogy of Standardized Testing: The Radical Impacts of Educational Standardization in the US and Canada*, New York: Palgrave Macmillan.

Kendrick, M. E., and R. A. McKay (2009), 'Researching Literacy with Young Children's Drawings', in M. Narey (ed), *Meaning Making: Constructing Multimodal Perspectives of Language, Literacy and Learning through Arts-based Early Childhood Education*, 53–70, Pittsburgh: Springer.

Kerr, M., H. Stattin, G. Biesecker and L. Ferrer-Wreder (2003), 'Relationship with Parents and Peers in Adolescence', in R. M. Lerner, M. A. Easterbrooks and J. Mistry (eds), *Handbook of Psychology, Volume 6, Developmental Psychology*, 395–422, New York: Wiley.

Kilderry, A. (2015), 'Repositioning Developmentalism', in M. Reed and R. Walker (eds), *A Critical Companion to Early Childhood*, 116–26. Los Angeles: SAGE.

Kincheloe, J. (2003), *Teachers as Researchers: Qualitative Inquiry as a Path to Empowerment*, 2nd edn, New York: RoutledgeFalmer.

Kind, S. (2005), 'Windows to a Child's World: Perspectives on Children's Art Making', in R. L. Irwin and K. Grauer (eds), *StARTing with…*, 2nd edn, 9–18, Toronto: Canadian Society for Education Through Art.

Kindler, A., and B. Darras (1997), 'Map of Artistic Development', in A. M. Kindler (ed), *Child Development in Art*, 17–42, Reston, VA: National Arts Education Association.

Kirova, A. (2008), 'Critical and Emerging Discourses in Multicultural Education Literature: A Review', *Canadian Ethnic Studies Special Issue: Multiculturalism Discourses in Canada*, 40 (1): 102–24.

Kirova, A. (2010), 'Children's Representations of Cultural Scripts in Play: Facilitating Transition from Home to Preschool in an Intercultural Early Learning Program for Refugee Children', *Diaspora, Indigenous and Minority Education: An International Journal*, 4: 74–91.

Kirova, A. (2012), 'Creating Shared Learning Spaces: An Intercultural, Multilingual Early Learning Program for Preschool Children from Refugee Families', in F. McCarthy and M. Vickers (eds), *Refugee and Immigrant Student: Achieving Equity in Education*, 23–44, Charlotte, NC: Information Age.

Kirova, A., and A. Bhargava (2002), 'Learning to Guide Preschool Children's Mathematical Understanding: A Teacher's Professional Growth', *Early Childhood Research and Practice*, 4 (1). Available online: https://eric.ed.gov/?id=ED464764 (accessed 26 November 2018).

Kirova, A., and L. Prochner (2015), 'The Issue of Other-ness in Pedagogical Theory and Practice: The Case of Roma', *Alberta Journal of Educational Research*, 61 (4): 381–98.

Knauf, H. (2018), 'Learning Stories as a Narrative Assessment in Elementary Education: An Empirical Study of the Concept on German Daycare Centers', *Journal of Educational Science*, 21 (3): 424–39.

Kocher, L. M. (2008), *The Disposition to Document: The Lived Experience of Teachers Who Practice Pedagogical Documentation – A Case Study*. Doctoral diss., University of South Queensland, Toowoomba, Australia. Available online: https://eprints.usq.edu.au/6223/2/Kocher_2008_whole.pdf (accessed 26 November 2018).

Kohlberg, L. (1966), 'A Cognitive Developmental Analysis of Children's Sex-role Concepts and Attitudes', in E. E. Maccoby (ed), *The Development of Sex Differences*, Stanford, CA: Stanford University Press.

Kohlberg, L., and R. Mayer (1972), 'Development as the Aim of Education', *Harvard Educational Review*, 42 (4): 449–96.

Konstantoni, K., and A. Emejulu (2016), 'When Intersectionality Met Childhood Studies: The Dilemmas of a Travelling Concept', *Children's Geographies*, 15 (1): 6–22.

Kosher, H. (2016), 'The History of Children's Rights', in H. Kosher, A. Ben-Arieh and Y. Hendelsman (eds), *Children's Rights and Social Work*, 9–18, New York: Springer.

Kobayashi, A., and B. Ray (2000), 'Civil risk and Landscapes of Marginality in Canada: A Pluralist Approach to Social Justice', *Canadian Geographer*, 44 (4): 401–17.

Kozulin, A. (2003), 'Psychological Tools and Mediated Learning', in A. Kozulin, B. Gindis and S. M. Miller (eds), *Vygotsky's Educational Theory in Cultural Context*, 15–39, Cambridge, UK: Cambridge University Press.

Kramer, M. (1988), *Maria Montessori: A Biography*, Reading, MA: Addison-Wesley.

Kress, G. (1997), *Before Writing: Rethinking the Paths to Literacy*, London: Routledge.

Kroeger, J., and T. Cardy (2006), 'Documentation: A Hard Place to Reach', *Early Childhood Education Journal*, 33 (6): 389–98.

Kuschner, D. (2007), 'Children's Play in the Journal *Young Children*: An Analysis of How It Is Portrayed and Why It Is Valued', in D. J. Sluss and O. S. Jarrett (eds), *Play and Culture Studies*, Volume 7, Investigating Play in the 21st Century, 55–73, Lanham, MD: University Press of America.

Kuschner, D. (2012), 'Play Is Natural to Childhood but School Is Not: The Problem of Integrating Play into Curriculum', *International Journal of Play*, 1 (3): 242–49. http://dx.doi.org/10.1080/21594937.2012.735803

Ladson-Billings, G. (1995), 'But That's Just Good Teaching! The Case for Culturally Relevant Pedagogy', *Theory into Practice*, 34: 159–65.

Ladson-Billings, G. (1998), 'Just What Is Critical Race Theory and What's It Doing in a Nice Field Like Education?' *International Journal of Qualitative Studies in Education*, 11 (1): 7–24. doi:10.1080/095183998236863

Ladson-Billings, G. (2006), 'From the Achievement Gap to the Education Debt: Understanding Achievement in U.S. Schools', *Educational Researcher*, 35 (7): 3–12.

Lall, M. (2011), 'Pushing the Child Centered Approach in Myanmar: The Role of Cross National Policy Networks and the Effects on the Classroom', *Critical Studies in Education*, 52 (3): 219–33.

Lam, C. (2012), 'The Disablement and Enablement of Childhood', *International Studies in Sociology of Education*, 22 (2): 147–67.

Lambert, E. B. (2000), 'Questioning Vygotsky's "Theory" of Play', *Early Child Development and Care*, 160: 25–31.

Lambert, W. E. (1990), 'Persistent Issues in Bilingualism', in B. Harley, P. Allen, J. Cummins and M. Swain (eds), *The Development of Second Language*

*Proficiency* (Cambridge Applied Linguistics), 201–18, Cambridge, UK: Cambridge University Press. doi:10.1017/CBO9781139524568

Lancy, D. F. (2010), 'When Nurture Becomes Nature: Ethnocentrism in Studies of Human Development', *Behavioral and Brain Sciences*, 33: 99–100.

Lancy, D. F. (2014), '"Babies Aren't Persons": A Survey of Delayed Personhood', in H. Otto and H. Keller (eds), *Different Faces of Attachment: Cultural Variations on a Universal Human Need*, 66–109, Cambridge, UK: Cambridge University Press.

Landry, P. L. (2018), 'Re-imagining "Indigeneity": From Dichotomous toward Intrinsic Based Understanding of Indigenous Philosophy and Pedagogy', in P. E. Petrovic and R. M. Mitchell (eds), *Indigenous Philosophies of Education Around the World*, 17–39, London: Routledge/Taylor and Francis.

Langer, E. J. (1997), *The Power of Mindful Learning*, Harlow, UK: Addison-Wesley.

Lankshear, C., and M. Knobel (2003), 'New Technologies in Early Childhood Literacy Research: A Review of Research', *Journal of Early Childhood Literacy*, 3: 59–82. doi:10.1177/14687984030031003

Lansdown, G. (2013), 'Children's Right to Play', in L. Brooker and M. Woodhead (series eds), *Early Childhood in Focus 9, The Right to Play: 2*, Milton Keynes, UK: Open University Press.

Lather, P. (1991), *Getting Smart: Feminist Research and Pedagogy with/in the Postmodern*, London: Routledge.

Lave, J., and E. Wenger, (1991), *Situated Learning: Legitimate Peripheral Participation*, Cambridge, UK: Cambridge University Press.

Lee, I.-F., and N. J. Yelland (2017), 'Crafting Miniature Students in the Early Years: Schooling for Desirable Childhoods in East Asia', *International Journal of Early Childhood*, 49 (1): 36–56.

Leiminer, M. (2010), '"Like a Wilde Thing": Analysing the "Deviant Competence" of Girls in Home-preschool Communications', in N. Yelland (ed), *Contemporary Perspectives on Early Childhood Education*, 192–210, Maidenhead, UK: Open University Press.

Lenkeit, J., Y. El Masri, K. Cantrell, J. Ryan and J.-A. Baird (2016), 'Lessons Learned from PISA: A Systematic Review of Peer-reviewed Articles on the Programme for International Student Assessment', *Scandinavian Journal of Educational Research*, 62 (3): 333–53.

Lenz Taguchi, H. (2010), *Going beyond the Theory/Practice Divide in Early Childhood Education: Introducing an Intra-active Pedagogy*, New York: Routledge.

Leonard, M. (2016), *The Sociology of Children, Childhood and Generation*, London: SAGE.

Leontiev, A. N. (1932), 'Studies in the Cultural Development of the Child: III. The Development of Voluntary Attention in the Child', *The Pedagogical Seminary and Journal of Genetic Psychology*, 40: 52–83.

Lerner, R. M. (1979), 'A Dynamic Interactional Concept of Individual and Social Relationship Development', in R. L. Burgess and T. L. Huston (eds), *Social Exchange in Developing Relationships*, 271–306, New York: Academic Press.

Lerner, R. M. (2018), *Concepts and Theories of Human Development*, 4th edn, New York: Routledge.

Levenson, E. A. (2005), *The Fallacy of Understanding: An Inquiry into the Changing Structure of Psychoanalysis*, Hillsdale, NJ: Analytic Press.

LeVine, R. A., S. Dixon, S. LeVine, A. Richman, P. H. Liederman, C. H. Keefer and T. B. Brazelton (1994), *Child Care and Culture: Lessons from Africa*, Cambridge, UK: Cambridge University Press.

Lewin-Benham, A. (2011), *Twelve Best Practices for Early Childhood Education: Integrating Reggio and Other Inspired Approaches*, New York: Teachers College Press.

Lewis, M. (2015), 'Emotional Development and Consciousness', in R. M. Lerner (ed), *Handbook of Child Psychology and Developmental Science*, Hoboken, New Jersey: John Wiley and Sons.

Lewit, E. M., and L. S. Baker (1995), 'School Readiness', *Critical Issues for Children and Youths*, 5 (2): 128–39.

Li, M., and S. Grieshaber (2018), 'Learning Stories as Cross-national Policy Borrowing: The Interplay of Globalization and Localization in Preprimary Education in Contemporary China', *Educational Philosophy and Theory*, 50 (12): 1124–32. doi.org/10.1080/00131857.2018.1434073

Lieberman, J. N. (1977), *Playfulness: Its Relationship to Imagination and Creativity*, New York: Academic Press.

Lillard, A. S., M. D. Lerner, E. J. Hopkins, R. A. Dore, E. D. Smith and C. M. Palmquist (2013), 'The Impact of Play on Children's Development: A Review of the Evidence', *Psychological Bulletin*, 139 (1): 1–34.

Limnatis, N. G. (2008), *German Idealism and the Problem of Knowledge: Kant, Fichte, Schelling and Hegel*, Dordrecht, the Netherlands: Springer.

Lindgren, A.-L., and S. Grunditz (2017), *Seeing Children's Looking Practices: Children's Embodied Gazes as Creators of Time and Place in Preschool in Historical Time – A Re-analysis of Observations from the 1930s*. Paper presented at the conference of the Society for the History of Children and Youth, Rutgers University, Camden, New Jersey, June 21–23.

Lindsay, G. (2015), 'Reflections in the Mirror of Reggio Emilia's Soul: John Dewey's Foundational Influence on Pedagogy in the Italian Educational Project', *Early Childhood Education Journal*, 43 (6): 447–57.

Lippitz, W. (2007), 'Foreignness and Otherness in Pedagogical Contexts', *Phenomenology and Practice*, 1 (1): 76–96.

Lipponen, L., A. Rajala, J. Hilppö and M. Paananen (2016), 'Exploring the Foundations of Visual Methods Used in Research with Children', *European Early Childhood Education Research Journal*, 24 (6): 936–46.

Lo Bianco, J. (2012), 'National Language Revival Movements: Reflections from India, Israel, Indonesia and Ireland', in B. Spolsky (ed), *The Cambridge Handbook of Language Policy*, 501–22. Cambridge, UK: Cambridge University Press.

Loring, D., and D. Ashini (2000), 'Past and Future Pathways: Innu Cultural Heritage in the Twenty-first Century', in C. Smith and G. Ward (eds), *Indigenous Cultures in an Interconnected World*, 167–89, Vancouver: UBC Press.

Louv, R. (2010), *Last Child in the Woods: Saving Our Children from Nature-deficit Disorder*, New York: Atlantic Books.

Lubeck, S. (1985), *Sandbox Society: Early Childhood Education in Black and White America*, Philadelphia: Falmer.

Lysklett, O. B. (2017), 'Nature Preschools of Denmark, Sweden, German and Norway: Characteristics and Differences', in T. Waller et al. (eds), *The SAGE Handbook of Outdoor Play and Learning*, 242–50, London: SAGE.

MacBlain, S. (2014), *How Children Learn*, Thousand Oaks, CA: SAGE.
MacDonald, M. (2007), 'Toward Formative Assessment: The Use of Pedagogical Documentation in Early Elementary Classrooms', *Early Childhood Research Quarterly*, 22 (2): 232–42.
MacNaughton, G. (2003), *Shaping Early Childhood: Learners, Curriculum and Contexts*, London: McGraw-Hill.
MacNaughton, G. (2006), 'Constructing Gender in Early-years Education', in C. Skelton, B. Francis and L. Smulyan (eds), *The SAGE Handbook of Gender and Education*, 127–38, London: SAGE.
MacVannel, J. A. (1905), *The Educational Theories of Herbart and Froebel*, New York: Teachers College Press. Available online: https://archive.org/stream/educationaltheor00macvuoft#page/n9/mode/2up (accessed 26 November 2018).
Magnuson, K., and J. Waldfolgel (2005), 'Early Childhood Care and Education: Effects on Ethnic and Racial Gaps in School Readiness', *The Future of Children*, 15 (1): 169–96. Available online: https://futureofchildren.princeton.edu/sites/futureofchildren/files/media/school_readiness_15_01_fulljournal.pdf (accessed 26 November 2018).
Mahn, H. (2003), 'Periods in Child Development: Vygotsky's Perspective', in A. Kozulin, B. Gindis and S. M. Miller (eds), *Vygotsky's Educational Theory in Cultural Context*, 119–38, Cambridge, UK: Cambridge University Press.
Malaguzzi, L. (1994), 'Your Image of the Child: Where Teaching Begins', *Child Care Information Exchange*, 3: 52–61. Available online: https://www.reggioalliance.org/downloads/malaguzzi:ccie:1994.pdf (accessed 26 November 2018).
Malaguzzi, L. (1998), 'History, Ideas and Basic Philosophy: An Interview with Lella Gandini', in C. Edwards, L. Gandini and G. Forman (eds), *The Hundred Languages of Children*, 49–97, Greenwich, CT: Ablex.
Marashio, P. (1982), '"Enlighten My Mind…": Examining the Learning Process through Native Americans' Ways', *Journal of American Indian Education*, 21 (2): 2–10.
Mardell, B., D. Wilson, J. Ryan, K. Ertel, M. Krechevsky and M. Baker (2016), 'Towards a Pedagogy of Play'. Available online: http://www.pz.harvard.edu/resources/towards-a-pedagogy-of-play (accessed 26 November 2018).
Marsh, J., L. Plowman, D. Yamada-Rice, J. Bishop and F. Scott (2016), 'Digital Play: A New Classification', *Early Years: An Intranational Research Journal*, 36 (3): 242–53.
Martin, C. L., and R. Fabes (2009), *Discovering Child Development*, 2nd edn, Boston: Houghton Mifflin.
Matthews, J. (2003), *Drawing and Painting: Children and Visual Representation*, 2nd edn, London: Paul Chapman.
Matusov, E., and A. Marjanovic-Shane (2017), 'Many Faces of the Concept of Culture (and Education)', *Culture and Psychology*, 23 (3): 309–36.
Matusov, E., A. Marjanovic-Shane and S. Meacham (2016), 'Pedagogical Voyeurism: Dialogic Critique of Documentation and Assessment of Learning', *International Journal of Educational Psychology*, 5 (1): 1–26.
Maurial, M. (1999), 'Indigenous Knowledge and Schooling: A Continuum between Conflict and Dialogue', in L. M. Semali and J. L. Kincheloe (eds), *What Is Indigenous Knowledge: Voices from the Academy*, 59–77, New York: Falmer.

May, H., B. Kaur and L. Prochner (2014), *Empire, Education and Indigenous Childhoods: Nineteenth-century Missionary Infant Schools in Three British Colonies*, Surrey, UK: Ashgate.

Mayall, B. (2002), *Towards a Sociology of Childhood: Thinking from Children's Lives*, Buckingham, UK: Open University Press.

McClelland, M. M., G. H. Geldhof, C. E. Cameron and S. B. Wanless (2015), 'Development and Self-regulation', in R. M. Lerner (ed), *Handbook of Child Psychology and Developmental Science*, 7th edn, New York: John Wiley and Sons.

McLoughlin, W. G. (1975), 'Evangelical Child-rearing in the Age of Jackson: Francis Wayland's View on When and How to Subdue the Willfulness of Children', *Journal of Social History*, 9 (1): Appendix 1: 35–39.

McNally, S. A., and R. Slutsky (2017), 'Key Elements of the Reggio Emilia Approach and How They Are Interconnected to Create the Highly Regarded System of Early Childhood Education', *Early Child Development and Care*, 187 (12): 1925–37.

McShane, K. (2012), 'The Environment: How to Understand It and What to Do about It', in W. P. Kabasenche, M. O'Rourke and M. H. Slater (eds), *The Environment: Philosophy, Science, and Ethics*, 1–17, Cambridge, MA: MIT Press.

Meadows, M. (1993), *The Young Child as Thinker: The Cognitive Development and Acquisition of Cognition in Childhood*, London: Routledge.

Meehan, C. L., C. Helfrecht and C. D. Malcolm (2015), 'Implications of Lengthy Development and Maternal Life History: Allomaternal Investment, Peer Relationships and Social Networks', in C. L. Meehan and A. N. Crittenden (eds), *Childhood: Origins, Evolution and Implications*, 199–220, Santa Fe, NM: School for Advanced Research Press.

Mérian, J.-B. (1984), *Mémoires sur le problème de Molyneux*, ed. Francine Markovits, Paris: Flammarion.

Midgley, N. (2008), 'The "Matchbox School" (1927–1932): Anna Freud and the Idea of a Psychoanalytically Informed Education', *Journal of Child Psychotherapy*, 34 (1): 23–42.

Miele, F. (2018), *Intelligence, Race and Genetics: Conversations with Arthur R. Jensen*. New York: Routledge. Original work published in 2002.

Miller, M. G. (2014), 'Productive and Inclusive? How Documentation Concealed Racializing Practices in a Diversity Project', *Early Years*, 34 (2): 146–60. https://doi.org/10.1080/09575146.2014.899998

Mills, G. E. (2018), *Action Research: A Guide for the Teacher Researcher*, New York: Pearson.

Milne, B. (2013), *The History and Theory of Children's Citizenship in Contemporary Societies*, Dordrecht: Springer.

Mitchell, C., and S. Weber (1998), 'The Usable Past: Teachers (re) Playing School', *Changing English*, 5 (1): 45–56.

Moffatt, S., and N. Kohler (2008), 'Conceptualizing the Built Environment as a Social-ecological System', *Building Research and Information*, 36 (3): 248–68.

Moll, L. C., C. Amanti, D. Neff and N. González (1992), 'Funds of Knowledge for Teaching: Using a Qualitative Approach to Connect Homes and Classrooms', *Theory into Practice*, 31 (2): 132–41.

Montessori, M. (1916), 'Address to the International Kindergarten Union', *Australian Kindergarten Magazine*, 6 (7): 109.

Montessori, M. (1936), *The Secret of Childhood*, London: Longmans, Green and Co.

Montessori, M. (1949), *The Absorbent Mind*, Adyar, India: Theosophical Publishing House.

Montessori, M. (2004), *The Montessori Method. The Origins of an Educational Innovation: Including an Abridged and Annotated Education of Maria Montessori's The Montessori Method*, ed. G. L. Gutek, Lanham, MD: Rowman and Littlefield. Original published in 1912.

Moore, J. (2011), 'Behaviorism', *The Psychological Record*, 61 (3): 449–64. Available online: http://opensiuc.lib.siu.edu/tpr/vol61/iss3/9 (accessed 27 November 2018).

Morris, M. (2015), 'Posthumanist Education and Animal Interiority', in N. Snaza and J. Weaver (eds), *Posthumanism and Educational Research*, 43–55, New York: Routledge.

Mosha, R. S. (1999), 'The Inseparable Link between Intellectual and Spiritual Formation in Indigenous Knowledge and Education: A Case Study in Tanzania', in L. M. Semali and J. L. Kincheloe (eds), *What Is Indigenous Knowledge: Voices from the Academy*, 209–26, New York: Falmer.

Moss, P., and P. Petrie (2002), *From Children's Services to Children's Spaces*, London: Routledge/Falmer.

Moss, P., and M. Urban (2017), 'The Organisation for Economic Co-operation and Development's International Early Learning Study: What Happened Next', *Contemporary Issues in Early Childhood*, 18 (2): 250–58.

Mott, W. T. (2010), 'Education', in J. Myerson, S. H. Petrulonis and L. D. Walls (eds), *The Oxford Handbook of Transcendentalism*, 153–171 New York: Oxford University Press.

Mtonga, M. (2012), *Children's Games and Play in Zambia*, Lusaka, Zambia: University of Zambia Press.

Mulryan, S. (2008), 'Hegel's Hold on Conceptions of Human Development', *Policy Futures in Education*, 6 (3): 312–22. Available online: http://journals.sagepub.com/doi/pdf/10.2304/pfie.2008.6.3.312 (accessed 27 November 2018).

Naito, M. (2014), 'Sociocultural Perspectives on Japanese Children's Social Understanding', in O. N. Saracho (ed) *Contemporary Perspectives on Research in Theory of Mind in Early Childhood Education*, 381–405 Charlotte, NC: Information Age.

National Association for the Education of Young Children (1986), 'Position Statement on Developmentally Appropriate Practice in Programs for 4- and 5-Year-Olds', *Young Children*, 41 (6): 20–29.

National Council for Curriculum and Assessment (Ireland) (2009), *Aistear: The Early Childhood Curriculum Framework*, Dublin: National Council for Curriculum and Assessment. Available online: http://www.ncca.ie/en/Curriculum_and_Assessment/Early_Childhood_and_Primary_Education/Early_Childhood_Education/Framework_for_early_learning/ (accessed 27 November 2018).

Nelson, K. (1995), 'From Spontaneous to Scientific Concepts: Continuities and Discontinuities from Childhood to Adulthood', in L. Martin and K. Nelson (eds), *Theory and Practice of Doing and Knowing*, 229–49, New York: Cambridge University Press.

Nelson, K. (1996), *Language in Cognitive Development: Emergence of the Mediated Mind*, Cambridge, UK: Cambridge University Press.

New, R. S. (2001), 'Early Literacy and Developmentally Appropriate Practice: Rethinking the Paradigm', in S. B. Neuman and D. K. Dickinson (eds), *Handbook of Early Literacy Research*, Volume 1, 245–62, New York: Guilford Press.

New, R. S. (2007), 'Reggio Emilia as Cultural Activity Theory in Practice', *Theory into Practice*, 46 (1): 5–13.

Newman, F., and L. Holzman (2014), *Lev Vygotsky: Revolutionary Scientist*, New York: Psychology Press.

Ngara, R. (2017), 'Multiple Voices, Multiple Paths: Towards Dialogue between Western and Indigenous Medical Knowledge Systems', in P. Ngulube (ed), *Handbook of Research on Theoretical Perspectives on Indigenous Knowledge Systems in Developing Countries*, 332–58, Hershey, PA: IGA Global.

Nicholson, T. R., S. Aybek, T. Craig, T. Harris, W. Wojcik, A. S. David and R. A. Kanaan (2016), 'Life Events and Escape in Conversion Disorder', *Psychological Medicine*, 46: 2617–26.

Nicolopoulou, A., C. B. Cates, A. de Sa and H. Ilgaz (2014), 'Narrative Performance, Peer Group Culture and Narrative Development in a Preschool Classroom', in A. Cekaite, S. Blum-Kulka, V. Grover and E. Teubal (eds), *Children's Peer Talk: Learning from Each Other*, 42–62, New York: Cambridge University Press.

Novakowski, J. (2015), *Reggio-inspired Mathematics. A Professional Inquiry Project in the Richmond School District*, Richmond, BC: Richmond School District.

Nsamenang, B. (1999), 'Eurocentric Image of Childhood in the Context of the World's Cultures: Essay Review of *Images of Childhood* edited by P. C. Hwang, M. Lamb and E. Sigel', *Human Development*, 43: 159–68.

Nsamenang, B. (2009), 'Cultures in Early Childhood Care and Education', in M. Fleer, M. Hedegaard and J. Tudge (eds), *Childhood Studies and the Impact of Globalization: Policies and Practices at Global and Local Levels*, 24–45, New York: Routledge.

Nxumalo, F. (2015), 'Forest Stories: Restoring Encounters with "Natural" Places in Early Childhood Education', in V. Pacini-Ketchabaw and A. Taylor (eds), *Unsettling the Colonial Places and Spaces of Early Childhood Education*, 21–42, New York: Routledge.

Nxumalo, F., V. Pacini-Ketchabaw and M. C. Rowan (2011), 'Lunch Time at the Child Care Centre: Neoliberal Assemblages in Early Childhood Education', *Journal of Pedagogy*, 2 (2): 195–223. Available online: https://content.sciendo.com/view/journals/jped/2/2/article-p195.xml (accessed 27 November 2018).

Oppedal, B. (2006), 'Development and Acculturation', in D. L. Sam and J. W. Berry (eds), *The Cambridge Handbook of Acculturation*, 97–112, New York: Cambridge University Press.

Organisation for Economic Co-operation and Development (2017), *Early Childhood Matters*, Paris: OECD. Available online: http://www.oecd.org/education/school/Early-Learning-Matters-Project-Brochure.pdf (accessed 27 November 2018).

Osgood, J. (2015), 'Postmodern Theorizing in ECEC: Making the Familiar Strange in Pursuit of Social Justice', in T. David, K. Goouch and S. Powell (eds), *The Routledge International Handbook of Philosophies and Theories of Early Childhood Education and Care*, London: Routledge.

Available online (subscription): https://www.routledgehandbooks.com/doi/10.4324/9781315678979.ch17
Oswell, D. (2013), *The Agency of Children: From Family to Global Human Rights*, Cambridge, UK: Cambridge University Press.
Owen, R. (1817), *A New View of Society*, 3rd edn, London: Longman, Hurst, Rees, Orme and Brown.
Owen, R. (1857), *The Life of Robert Owen*, Volume 1, London: Effingham Wilson.
Pacini-Ketchabaw, V. (2014), 'Postcolonial and Anti-racist Approaches to Understanding Play', in L. Brooker, M. Blaise and S. Edwards (eds), *The SAGE Handbook of Play and Learning in Early Childhood*, 67–78, London: SAGE.
Pacini-Ketchabaw, V., S. Kind and L. L. M. Kocher (2017), *Encounters with Materials in Early Childhood*, New York: Routledge.
Pacini-Ketchabaw, V., and A. Taylor (2015), 'Unsettling Pedagogies through Common World Encounters: Grappling with (Post-)Colonial Legacies in Canadian forests and Australian Bushlands', in V. Pacini-Ketchabaw and A. Taylor (eds), *Unsettling the Colonial Places and Spaces of Early Childhood Education*, 43–62, New York: Routledge.
Pacini-Ketchabaw, V., A. Taylor and M. Blaise (2012), 'Children's Relations to the More-than-Human World', *Contemporary Issues in Early Childhood*, 13 (2): 81–85.
Palincsar, A. S., and A. L. Brown (1984), 'Reciprocal Teaching of Comprehension-fostering and Comprehension-monitoring Activities', *Cognition and Instruction*, 2: 117–75.
Papastephanou, M. (2014), *Philosophical Perspectives on Compulsory Education*, New York: Springer.
Papert, S. (1980), *Mindstorms: Children, Computers and Powerful Ideas*, New York: Basic.
Paris, D. (2012), 'Culturally Sustaining Pedagogy: A Needed Change in Stance, Terminology and Practice', *Educational Researcher*, 41 (3): 93–97.
Paris, D., and H. S. Alim, eds (2017), *Culturally Sustaining Pedagogies: Teaching and Learning for Justice in a Changing World*, New York: Teachers College Press.
Patocka, J. (2016), *The Natural World as a Philosophical Problem*, Evanston, IL: Northwestern University Press.
Pelo, A. (2016), *The Language of Art: Inquiry-based Studio Practices in Early Childhood Settings*, 2nd edn, St. Paul, MN: Redleaf.
Penn, H. (2011), 'Traveling Policies and Global Buzzwords: How International Non-governmental Organizations and Charities Spread the Word about Education to the Global South', *Childhood*, 18 (1): 94–113.
Pente, P. (2011), 'Child Development in Art: What Do You Need to Know?' in K. Grauer, R. L. Irwin and M. J. Emme (eds), *StARTing with…*, 3rd edn, 28–37, Victoria, BC: Canadian Society for Education Through Art.
Penuel, W. R., and L. A. Shepard (2016), 'Assessment and Teaching', in D. H. Gitomer and C. A. Bell (eds), *Handbook of Research on Teaching*, 5th edn, 787–850, Washington, DC: American Educational Research Association.
Penuel, W. R., and J. V. Wertsch (1995), 'Vygotsky and Identity Formation: A Sociocultural Approach', *Educational Psychologist*, 30 (2): 83–92. https://doi.org/10.1207/s15326985ep3002_5

Percy-Smith, B., and N. Thomas (2010), *A Handbook of Children's and Young People's Participation*, London: Routledge.
Perret, P., and J. Fox (2004), *A Well-tempered Mind: Using Music to Help Children Listen and Learn*, New York: Dana Press.
Perry, R. J. (1992), 'Why Do Multiculturalists Ignore Anthropologists?' *The Chronicle of Higher Education*, 38 (26): 52.
Phares, E. J. (2001), 'Social Learning Theories', in W. E. Craighead and C. B. Nemeroff (eds), *The Corsini Encyclopedia of Psychology and Behavioral Science*, 3rd edn, Volume 4, 1564–67, New York: Wiley.
Phillips, D. C. (2016), *A Companion to John Dewey's Democracy and Education*, Chicago: University of Chicago Press.
Piaget, J. (1959), *The Language and Thought of the Child*, London: Routledge and Kegan Paul.
Piaget, J. (1962), *Play, Drama and Imitation in Childhood*, New York: Norton.
Piaget, J. (1970), *Genetic Epistemology*, New York: Columbia University Press.
Piaget, J. (1973), *To Understand Is to Invent: The Future of Education*, New York: Grossman.
Piaget, J. (1995), 'Logical Operations and Social Life', in L. Smith (ed), *Sociological Studies*, 143–71, London: Routledge.
Piaget. J., and B. Inhelder (2000), *The Psychology of the Child*, New York: Basic Books. Original work published in 1969.
Pinker, S. (1994), *The Language Instinct*, London: Penguin.
Popkewitz, T. S. (2003), 'The Production of Reason and Power: Curriculum History and Intellectual Traditions', in D. Scott (ed), *Curriculum Studies: Major Themes in Education*, Volume 1, New York: RoutledgeFalmer.
Portera, A. (2011), 'Intercultural and Multicultural Education: Epistemological and Semantic Aspects', in C. A. Grant and A. Portera (eds), *Intercultural and Multicultural Education: Enhancing Global Interconnectedness*, 12–30, New York: Routledge.
Potter, J. (2000), 'Post-Cognitive Psychology', *Theory and Psychology*, 10 (1): 31–37.
Pramling Samuelsson, I., and M. A. Carlsson (2008), 'The Playing Learning Child: Towards a Pedagogy of Early Childhood', *Scandinavian Journal of Educational Research*, 52 (6): 623–41. doi:10.1080/00313830802497265
Prochner, L. (2019), 'Placing a School at the Tail of a Plough': The European Roots of Indian Industrial Schools in Canada', in S. Carr-Stewart (ed), *From Disconnection to Reconciliation: Indigenous Education in Canada*, Vancouver: UBC Press/Purich Books.
Prochner, L., A. Cleghorn, A. Kirova and C. Massing (2016), *Teacher Education in Diverse Settings: Making Space for Intersecting Worldviews*, Rotterdam, the Netherlands: Sense.
Prochner, L., and L. Robertson (2012), 'Early Childhood Education and Care in Canada in the 1950s and 1960s: Retrenchment and Renewal', in N. Howe and L. Prochner (eds), *Recent Perspectives on Early Childhood Education in Canada*, 15–49, Toronto: University of Toronto Press.
Prodger, P. (2009), *Darwin's Camera: Art and Photography in the Theory of Evolution*, Oxford: Oxford University Press.
Purnell, C. (2017), *The Sensational Past: How the Enlightenment Changed the Way We Use Our Senses*, New York: Norton.

Ramaekers, S., and J. Suissa (2012), *The Claims of Parenting: Reasons, Responsibility and Society*, New York: Springer.

Ramirez, P. (2017), 'Preparing Pre-service Secondary Teaches in Arizona: Using Culturally Sustaining Approaches to Learn from Diverse Secondary English Learners', in C. Coulter and M. Jimenez-Silva (eds), *Culturally Sustaining and Revitalizing Pedagogies: Language, Culture and Power*, 245–68, Bingley, UK: Emerald.

Ransom, J. (1997), *Foucault's Discipline*, Durham, NC: Duke University Press.

Raver, C. C., J. S. Cater, D. C. McCoy, A. Roy, A. Ursache and A. Friedman (2012), 'Testing Models of Children's Self-regulation within Educational Contexts: Implications for Measurement', *Advances in Child Development and Behavior*, 42: 245–70.

Reagan, T., ed (2018), *Non-western Educational Traditions: Local Approaches to Thought and Practice*, 4th edn, New York: Routledge.

Reese, W. (2013), *Testing Wars in the Public Schools: A Forgotten History*, Cambridge, MA: Harvard University Press.

Reggio Children (n.d.), 'Reggio Children Exhibitions'. Available online: http://www.reggiochildren.it/activities/mostre/?lang=en (accessed 27 November 2018).

Reimann, P. (2015), 'Testing Times: Data and Their (Mis-)Use in Schools', in H. Proctor, P. Brownlee and P. Freebody (eds), *Controversies in Education: Orthodoxy and Heresy in Policy and Practice*, 39–54, New York: Springer.

Rice, B. (2005), *Seeing the World with Aboriginal Eyes: A Four Dimensional Perspective on Human and Non-human Values, Cultures and Relationships on Turtle Island*, Winnipeg: Aboriginal Issues Press.

Rinaldi, C. (1993), 'The Emergent Curriculum and Social Constructivism', in C. Edwards, L. Gandini and G. Foreman (eds), *The Hundred Languages of Children: The Reggio Emilia Approach to Early Childhood Education*, 101–11, Norwood, NJ: Ablex.

Rinaldi, C. (2005), 'Is Curriculum Necessary?' *Children in Europe*, 9: 19.

Rinaldi, C. (2006), *In dialogue with Reggio Emilia: Listening, Researching and Learning*, New York: Routledge.

Ring, E., M. Mhic Mhathúna, M. Moloney, N. Hayes, D. Breatnach, P. Stafford, D. Carswell et al. (2016), *An Examination of Concepts of School-readiness among Parents and Educators in Ireland*, Dublin: Department of Children and Youth Affairs. Available online: https://www.dcya.gov.ie/ (accessed 26 November 2018).

Ring, K. A. (2003), 'Young Children Drawing at Home, Pre-school and School: The Influence of the Socio-cultural Context', Doctoral diss., University of Leeds, United Kingdom.

Ring, K. A. (2009), 'Supporting Playful Drawing in Foundation Stage Settings', *The Psychology of Education Review*, 33 (1): 18–28.

Ripple, R. E., and V. N. Rockcastle (1964), *Piaget Rediscovered: A Report of the Conference on Cognitive Studies and Curriculum Development, March 1964*. Ithaca, NY: School of Education, Cornell University.

Ritchie, J., and C. Rau (2012), 'Early Childhood Education as a Site of Eco-centric Counter-colonial Endeavour in Aotearoa New Zealand', *Contemporary Issues in Early Childhood*, 13 (2): 86–97.

Rittel, H. W., and M. M. Webber (1973), 'Dilemmas in a General Theory of Planning', *Policy Sciences*, 4 (2): 155–69.

Roberts-Holmes, G. (2017), 'Loris Malaguzzi, Reggio Emilia and Democratic Alternatives to Early Childhood Education Assessment', *FORUM*, 59 (2): 159–67.
Roberts-Holmes, G., and A. Bradbury (2016), 'The Datafication of Early Years Education and Its Impact upon Pedagogy', *Improving Schools*, 19 (2): 119–28.
Robinson, K. H., and C. Jones-Diaz (2005), *Diversity and Difference in Early Childhood Education: Issues for Theory and Practice*, Berkshire, UK: McGraw-Hill.
Robson, S. (2006), *Developing Thinking and Understanding in Young Children: An Introduction to Students*, 2nd edn, New York: Routledge.
Rockquemore, K., D. Brunsma and D. Delgado (2009), 'Racing to Theory or Retheorizing Race? Understanding the Struggle to Build a Multiracial Identity Theory', *Journal of Social Issues*, 65 (1): 13–34. doi:10.1111/j.1540-4560.2008.01585.x
Rogers, S. (2011), 'Play and Pedagogy: A Conflict of Interest?' in S. Rogers (ed), *Rethinking Play and Pedagogy in Early Childhood Education: Concepts, Contexts and Cultures*, 5–19, London: Routledge.
Rogoff, B. (1990), *Apprenticeship in Thinking: Cognitive Development in Social Context*, New York: Oxford University Press.
Rogoff, B. (1995), 'Observing Sociocultural Activity on Three Planes: Participatory Appropriation, Guided Participation and Apprenticeship', in J. V. Wertsch, P. Del Rio and A. Alvarez (eds), *Sociocultural Studies of Mind*, 139–64, Cambridge: Cambridge University Press.
Rogoff, B. (2003), *The Cultural Basis of Human Development*, New York: Oxford University Press.
Ronda, B. A. (2017), *The Fate of Transcendentalism: Secularity, Materiality and Human Flourishing*, Athens, GA: University of Georgia Press.
Roopnarine, J. L., and J. E. Johnson (1994), 'The Need to Look at Play in Diverse Cultural Settings', in J. L. Roopnarine, J. E. Johnson and F. H. Hooper (eds), *Children's Play in Diverse Cultures*, 1–8, New York: SUNY Press.
Rossi, P. H., M. W. Lipsey and H. E. Freeman (2004), *Evaluation: A Systematic Approach*, London: SAGE.
Rousseau, J. J. (1911), *Emile, or on Education*, trans. B. Foxley, London: Dent. Original work published 1762.
Rousseau, J. J. (1964), *Jean Jacques Rousseau: His Educational Theories Selected from Emile, Julie and Other Writings*, ed. R. L. Archer, Woodbury, NY: Barron's Educational Series. Original work published 1762.
Rowan, M. C. (2017), 'Relating with Land/Engaging with Elders: Accessing Indigenous Knowledges in Early Childhood Education through Outdoor Encounters', in T. Waller et al. (eds), *The SAGE Handbook of Outdoor Play and Learning*, 395–428, London: SAGE.
Rubin, K., G. Fein and B. Vandenberg (1983), 'Play', in E. Hetherington (ed), *Manual of Child Psychology: Socialization, Personality and Social Development*, Volume 4, 693–774, New York: Wiley.
Rubio, F. D., and U. Fogué (2015), 'Unfolding the Political Capacities of Design', in A. Yaneva and A. Zaera-Polo (eds), *What Is Cosmopolitan Design? Design, Nature and the Built Environment*, 143–60, London: Ashgate.
Ruiz-Primo, M. A., and M. Li (2013), 'Examining Formative Feedback in the Classroom Context: New Research Perspectives', in J. H. McMillan (ed),

*SAGE Handbook of Research on Classroom Assessment*, 215–32, Los Angeles: SAGE.

Rushton, P. J. (1997), *Race, Evolution and Behavior: A Life History Perspective*, New Brunswick, NJ: Transaction.

Ryan, S. (2005), 'Freedom to Choose: Examining Children's Experiences in Choice Time', in N. Yelland (ed), *Critical Issues in Early Childhood Education*, 99–114, New York: Open University Press.

Sadock, B. J., and V. A. Sadock (2007), *Synopsis of Psychiatry*, 10th edn, Philadelphia: Wolters Kluwer.

Salkind, N. J. (2004), *An Introduction to Theories of Development*, Thousand Oaks, CA: SAGE.

Sam, D. L., and B. Oppedal (2003), 'Acculturation as a Developmental Pathway', *Online Readings in Psychology and Culture*, 8 (1). https://doi.org/10.9707/2307-0919.1072

Sandler, A.-M. (2012), 'Anna Freud's Influence on Contemporary Thinking about the Child', in N. T. Malberg and J. Raphael-Leff (eds), *Lines of Development: Evolution of Theory and Practice over the Decades*, 47–53, London: Karnac.

Santoro, D. A. (2017), 'Method: Intelligent Engagement with Subject Matter', in L. J. Waks and A. R. English (eds), *John Dewey's Democracy and Education: A Centennial Handbook*, 117–23, Cambridge, UK: Cambridge University Press.

Sapir, E. (1963), 'The Status of Linguistics as a Science', in D. G. Mandelbaum (ed), *The Selected Writings of Edward Sapir in Language, Culture and Personality*, 160–66, Berkeley: University of California Press. Original work published 1929.

Saracho, O. N. (2014), *Contemporary Perspectives on Research in Theory of Mind in Early Childhood Education*, Charlotte, NC: Information Age.

Schecter, B. (2011), 'Development as an Am of Education': A Reconsideration of Dewey's Vision', *Curriculum Inquiry*, 41 (2): 250–66. https://doi.org/10.1111/j.1467-873X.2011.00546.x

Scheffler, I. (1973), *Reason and Teaching*, London: Routledge/Kegan Paul.

Schick, C., and V. St. Denis (2005), 'Troubling National Discourses in Anti-racist Curricular Planning', *Canadian Journal of Education*, 28 (3): 295–319.

Schultz, B. D., and W. H. Schubert (2010), 'Cultural Epoch Theory', in C. A. Kridel (ed), *Encyclopedia of Curriculum Studies*, 164–65, Thousand Oaks, CA: SAGE.

Schwall, C. (2005), 'The *Atelier* Environment and Materials', in L. Gandini, L. Hill, L. Cadwell and C. Schwall (eds), *In the Spirit of the Studio*, 16–31, New York: Teachers College Press.

Scribner, S. (1985), 'Vygotsky's Uses of History', in J. V. Wertsch (ed), *Culture, Communication and Cognition*, 119–45, Cambridge, UK: Cambridge University Press.

Scully, V. (1980), 'Frank Lloyd Wright and the Stuff of Dreams', *Perspecta*, 16: 8–28, 31.

Seligman, L. D., and H. B. Baldacci (2005), 'Vicarious Punishment', in M. Hersen and J. Rosqvist (eds), *Encyclopedia of Behavior Modification and Cognitive Behavior Theory*, 1085–86, Thousand Oaks, CA: SAGE.

Sellers, M. (2013), *Young Children Becoming Curriculum: Deleuze, Te Whāriki and Curricular Understandings*, New York: Routledge.

Sen, A. (1999), *Inequality Reexamined*, New York: Russell Sage.

Sengupta, P. (2011), *Pedagogy for Religion: Missionary Education and the Fashioning of Hindus and Muslims in Bengal*, Berkeley: University of California Press.

Serpell, B., and A. B. Nsamenang (2014), *Locally Relevant and Quality ECCE Programmes: Implications of Research on Indigenous African Child Development and Socialization*, Paris: UNESCO.

Sharman, C., W. Cross and D. Vennis (2015), *Summative Assessment in the Early Years*, London: Bloomsbury.

Sharpe, L. (2011, May 17), 'So You Think You Know Why Animals Play…' [guest blog post], *Scientific American*. Available online: https://blogs.scientificamerican.com/guest-blog/so-you-think-you-know-why-animals-play/ (accessed 27 November 2018).

Shavelson, R. J., D. B. Young, C. C. Ayala, P. R. Brandon, E. M. Furtak, M. A. Ruiz-Primo, M. K. Tomita and Y. Yin (2008), 'On the Impact of Curriculum-Embedded Formative Assessment on Learning: A Collaboration between Curriculum and Assessment Developers', *Applied Measurement in Education*, 21 (4): 295–314.

Shields, C. M., R. Bishop and A. E. Mazawi (2005), *Pathologizing Practices: The Impact of Deficit Thinking on Education*, New York: Peter Lang.

Shweder, R. A., J. Goodnow, G. Hatano, R. A. LeVine, H. Markus and P. Miller (1998), 'The Cultural Psychology of Development: One Mind: Many Mentalities', in W. Damon and R. M. Lerner (eds), *Handbook of Child Psychology: Theoretical Models of Human Development*, 865–937, New York: Wiley.

Simpson, B. (2013), 'Challenging Childhood, Challenging Children: Children's Rights and Sexting', *Sexualities*, 16 (5–6): 690–709.

Simpson, L. (2000), 'Anishinaabe Ways of Knowing', in J. Oakes, R. Riew, S. Koolage, L. Simpson and N. Schuster (eds), *Aboriginal Health, Identity and Resources*, 165–85, Winnipeg: Native Studies Press.

Singer, E. (1996), 'Prisoners of the Method: Breaking Open the Child-centered Pedagogy in Day Care Centres', *International Journal of Early Years Education*, 42 (2): 28–40.

Siraj-Blatchford, I. (1999), 'Early Childhood Pedagogy: Practice, Principles and Research', in P. Mortimore (ed), *Understanding Pedagogy and Its Impact on Learning*, London: Paul Chapman.

Siraj-Blatchford, I. (2007), 'Creativity, Communication and Collaboration: The Identification of Pedagogic Progression in Sustained Shared Thinking', *Asia Pacific Journal of Research in Early Childhood Education*, 1 (2): 3–23.

Siraj-Blatchford, I. (2010), 'A Focus on Pedagogy: Case Studies of Effective Practice', in K. Sylva, E. Melhuish, P. Sammons, I. Siraj-Blatchford and B. Taggart (eds), *Evidence from the Effective Pre-school and Primary Education Project*, 149–65, London: Routledge.

Skinner, B. F. (1989), *Recent Issues in the Analysis of Behavior*, Columbus: Merrill.

Skutnabb-Kangas, T. (2002), *Language Policies and Education: The Role of Education in Destroying or Supporting the World's Linguistic Diversity*. Available online: http://www.linguapax.org/wp-content/uploads/2015/07/CMPL2002_Plenari_TSkutnabb-Kangas.pdf (accessed 27 November 2018).

Sleeter, C. E. (1993), 'How White Teachers Construct Race', in C. McCarthy and W. Crichlow (eds), *Race, Identity and Representation in Education*, 157–71, New York: Routledge.

Sleeter, C. E., and D. D. Bernal (2004), 'Critical Pedagogy, Critical Theory and Antiracist Education: Implications for Multicultural Education', in J. Banks and

C. A. McGee-Banks (eds), *Handbook of Research on Multicultural Education*, 240–258, San Francisco: Jossey-Bass.

Smidt, S. (2013), *Introducing Malaguzzi: Exploring the Life and Work of Reggio Emilia's Founding Father*, Milton Park, UK: Routledge.

Smuts, A. (2006), *Science in the Service of Children, 1893–1935*, New Haven: Yale University Press.

Snider, D. (1900), *The Psychology of Froebel's Play-gifts*, Chicago: Sigma.

Snow, C. E., and S. B. Van Hemel, eds. (2008), *Early Childhood Assessment: Why, What and How*, Washington, DC: National Academies Press.

Sobe, N. W. (2004), 'Challenging the Gaze: The Subject of Attention and a 1915 Montessori Demonstration Classroom', *Educational Theory*, 54 (3): 281–97.

Sobel, D. (2016), *Nature Preschools and Forest Kindergartens: The Handbook for Outdoor Learning*, St. Paul, MN: Redleaf.

Soderman, A. K. (2016), 'Authentic Assessment', in D. Couchenour and J. K. Chrisman (eds), *The SAGE Encyclopedia of Contemporary Early Childhood Education*, 119–24, Thousand Oaks, CA: SAGE.

Solórzano, D., and T. Yosso (2002), 'Critical Race Methodology: Counter-storytelling as an Analytical Framework for Education Research', *Qualitative Inquiry*, 8 (1): 23–44.

Soncini, I. (2011), 'The Inclusive Community', in C. Edwards, L. Gandini and G. Forman (eds), *The Hundred Languages of Children*, 3rd edn, 187–211, Greenwich, CT: Ablex.

Sorin, R., and G. Galloway (2006), 'Constructs of Childhood: Constructs of Self', *Children Australia*, 31 (2): 12–21.

Souto-Manning, M. (2017), 'Why Are Critical Perspectives and Ecological Approaches Needed in Early Childhood Teacher Education?: Toward a Trans/Contextual Cultural-Ecological Approach', in A. C. DaSilva Iddings (ed), *Re-designing Teacher Education for Culturally and Linguistically Diverse Children: A Critical-ecological Approach*, 13–32, New York: Routledge.

Souto-Manning, M., and A. Rabadi-Raol (2018), '(Re)Centering Quality in Early Childhood Education: Toward Intersectional Justice for Minoritized Children', *Review of Research in Education*, 42: 203–25.

Sparrman, A., and A.-L. Lindgren (2010), 'Visual Documentation as a Normalizing Practice: A New Discourse of Visibility in Preschool', *Surveillance and Society*, 7 (3–4): 248–61.

Spinka, M., R. C. Newberry and M. Bekoff (2001), 'Mammalian Play: Training for the Unexpected', *Quarterly Review of Biology*, 76: 141–68.

Spitzack, C. (1992), 'Foucault's Political Body in Medical Praxis', in D. Leder (ed), *The Body in Medical Thought and Practice*, 51–68, Dordrecht, the Netherlands: Kluwer.

Srinivasan, P. (2009), 'Languages Matter: My Subjective Postcolonial Struggle', in G. MacNaughton and K. Davis (eds), *"Race" and Early Childhood Education: An International Approach to Identity, Politics and Pedagogy*, 155–66, New York: Palgrave Macmillan.

Stacey, S. (2015), *Pedagogical Documentation in Early Childhood: Sharing Children's Learning and Teachers' Thinking*, St. Paul, MN: Redleaf.

Statistics Canada (2017), 'Immigration and Ethnocultural Diversity: Key Results from the 2016 Census'. Available online: https://www150.statcan.gc.ca/n1/daily-quotidien/171025/dq171025b-eng.htm (accessed 27 November 2018).

Steiner-Khamsi, G., M. Appleton and S. Vellani (2018), 'Understanding Business Interests in International Large-Scale Student Assessments: A Media Analysis of *The Economist, Financial Times* and *Wall Street Journal*', *Oxford Review of Education*, 44 (2): 190–203.

Stitzlein, S. M. (2017), 'Growth, Habits and Plasticity in Education', in L. J. Waks and A. R. English (eds), *John Dewey's Democracy and Education: A Centennial Handbook*, 38–45, Cambridge, UK: Cambridge University Press.

Stone, J. E. (2012), 'A Vygotskian Commentary on the Reggio Emilia Approach', *Contemporary Issues in Early Childhood*, 13 (4): 276–89. http://dx.doi.org/10.2304/ciec.2012.13.4.276

Stringer, P. (2018), 'Dynamic Assessment in Educational Settings: Is Potential Ever Realized?' *Educational Review*, 70: 18–30.

Strong, T. (2002), *Jean-Jacque Rousseau: The Politics of the Ordinary*, Lanham, MD: Rowman and Littlefield.

Sullivan, J. (2017), 'Teaching as Contemplative', in P. M. Bamber and J. C. Moore (eds), *Teacher Education in Challenging Times: Lessons for Professionalism, Partnership and Practice*, New York: Routledge.

Super, C. M., and S. Harkness (1994), 'The Developmental Niche', in S. W. J. Lonner and R. Malpass (eds), *Psychology and Culture*, 95–99, Boston: Allyn and Bacon.

Super, C. M., and S. Harkness (2002), 'Culture Structures the Environment for Development', *Human Development*, 45 (4): 270–74. doi:10.1159/000064988

Sutton, P. W. (2007), *The Environment: A Sociological Introduction*, Cambridge, UK: Polity Press.

Sutton-Smith, B. (1997), *The Ambiguity of Play*, Cambridge, MA: Harvard University Press.

Sutton-Smith, B. (2008), 'Play Theory: A Personal Journey and New Thoughts', *American Journal of Play*, 1 (1) Summer: 80–123.

Swadener, B. B., and S. Lubeck, eds (1995), *Children and Families 'At Promise': Deconstructing the Discourse of Risk*, Albany: SUNY Press.

Talalay, K. (1995), *Composition in Black and White: The Life of Philippa Schuyler*, New York: Oxford University Press.

Tarr, P. (2011), 'Reflections and Shadows: Ethical Issues in Pedagogical Documentation', *Canadian Children*, 36 (2): 11–16.

Taylor, A. (2007), 'Playing with Difference: The Cultural Politics of Childhood Belonging', *International Journal of Diversity in Organisations, Communities and Nations*, 7 (3): 143–49.

Taylor, A. (2013), *Reconfiguring the Natures of Childhood*, New York: Routledge.

Taylor, A., and V. Pacini-Ketchabaw (2015), *Unsettling the Colonial Places and Spaces of Early Childhood Education*, New York: Routledge.

Taylor, A., and V. Pacini-Ketchabaw (2017), 'Kids, Raccoons and Roos: Awkward Encounters and Mixed Affects', *Journal of Children's Geographies*, 15 (2): 131–45.

Taylor, A., and V. Pacini-Ketchabaw (2019), *The Common Worlds of Children and Animals: Relational Ethics for Entangled Lives*, New York: Routledge.

Teaching Strategies (2018), *GOLD*©. Available online: https://teachingstrategies.com/solutions/assess/gold/ (accessed 27 November 2018).

Thomas, Chief J. (1994), *Teachings from the Longhouse*, Toronto: Stoddart.

Thompson, C. (2010), 'Teachers as Intellectuals', in C. Kridel (ed), *Encyclopedia of Curriculum Studies*, 869–70, Thousand Oaks, CA: SAGE.

Thompson, C. (2015), 'The Authority of Bildung: Educational Practices in Early Childhood Education', *Ethics and Education*, 10 (1): 3–16.

Thompson, W. I. (1989), *Imaginary Landscapes: Making Worlds of Myth and Science*, New York: St. Martin's Press.

Tolisano, S. R., and J. A. Hale (2018), *A Guide to Documenting Learning: Making Thinking Visible, Meaningful, Shareable and Amplified*, Thousand Oaks, CA: Corwin.

Toulouse, P. R. (2011), *Achieving Aboriginal Student Success: A Guide for K to 8 Classrooms*, 9–10, Winnipeg: Portage and Main Press.

Tracy, F. (1909), *The Psychology of Childhood*, Boston: D. C. Heath. Available online: https://archive.org/details/psychologyofchil00ta (accessed 27 November 2018).

Trevathan, W. R., and K. R. Rosenberg (2016), 'Human Evolution and the Helpless Infant' in W. R. Trevathan and K. R. Rosenberg (eds), *Costly and Cute: Helpless Infants and Human Evolution*, 1–28, Albuquerque: University of New Mexico Press.

Tudge, J. (2008), *The Everyday Lives of Young Children: Culture, Class and Child Rearing in Diverse Societies*, New York: Cambridge University Press.

Tunison, S. (2007), *Aboriginal Learning: A Review of Current Metrics of Success*, Saskatoon: Aboriginal Learning Knowledge Centre. Available online: http://en.copian.ca/library/research/ccl/aboriginal_learning_review/aboriginal_learning_review.pdf (accessed 27 November 2018).

Ukrainetz, T., S. Harpell, C. Walsh and C. Coyle (2000), 'A Preliminary Investigation of Dynamic Assessment with Native American Kindergartners', *Language, Speech and Hearing Services in Schools*, 31: 142–54.

Ullrich, H. (2014), *Rudolph Steiner*, trans. J. Duke and D. Balestrini, London: Bloomsbury.

UNESCO (2015), *Incheon Declaration – Education 2030: Towards Inclusive and Equitable Quality Education and Lifelong Learning for All*, World Education Forum. Available online: http://unesdoc.unesco.org/images/0023/002331/233137E.pdf (accessed 27 November 2018).

UNESCO Ad Hoc Expert Group on Endangered Languages (2003), 'Language Vitality and Endangerment'. Available online: http://www.unesco.org/new/fileadmin/MULTIMEDIA/HQ/CLT/pdf/Language_vitality_and_endangerment_EN.pdf (accessed 25 November 2018).

United Nations (1989), *Convention on the Rights of the Child*, Geneva: United Nations. Available online: http://www.ohchr.org/EN/ProfessionalInterest/Pages/CRC.aspx (accessed 26 November 2018).

United Nations (2005), 'General Comment No. 7, Implementing Child Rights in Early Childhood'. Available online: http://www2.ohchr.org/ (accessed 26 November 2018).

United Nations (2009), *General Comment no. 12, The Right of the Child to Be Heard*, Retrieved from http://www2.ohchr.org/english/bodies/crc/docs/AdvanceVersions/CRC-C-GC-12.pdf

United Nations Population Fund (UNFPA) (2005), 'Human Rights Principles'. Available online: https://www.unfpa.org/resources/human-rights-principles (accessed 25 November 2018).

Urbistat (2017), 'Municipality of Reggio Nell'emilia'. Available online: https://ugeo.urbistat.com/AdminStat/en/it/demografia/stranieri/reggio-nell-emilia/35033/4 (accessed 26 November 2018).

Valk, U., and D. Savbörg (2018), *Storied and Supernatural Places: Studies in Spatial and Social Dimensions of Folklore and Sagas*, Helsinki: Finnish Literature Society.

Valkanova, Y. (2016), 'The Psychoanalytic Kindergarten Project in Soviet Russia, 1921–1930', *The Society for Co-operation in Russian and Soviet Studies Digest*, 13 (2): 12–15.

Van Ausdale, D., and J. R. Feagin (2001), *The First R: How Children Learn Race and Racism*, Lanham, MD: Rowman and Littlefield.

Van Den Berghe, P. L. (1967), *Race and Racism: A Contemporary Perspective*, New York: Wiley.

Van Oers, B. (2014), 'Cultural-Historical Perspectives on Play: Central Ideas', in L. Brooker, M. Blaise and S. Edwards (eds), *The SAGE Handbook of Play and Learning in Early Childhood*, 56–66, London: SAGE.

Vandervert, L. (2017), 'Vygotsky Meets Neuroscience: The Cerebellum and the Rise of Culture through Play', *American Journal of Play*, 9 (2): 202–27.

Vaughn, M. S. (2002), 'A Delicate Balance: The Praxis of Empowerment at a Midwestern Montessori School', *Communication Education*, 51 (2): 183–201.

Vianna, E., and A. Stetsenko (2006), 'Embracing History through Transforming It: Contrasting Piagetian versus Vygotskian (Activity) Theories of Learning and Development to Expand Constructivism within a Dialectical View of History', *Theory and Psychology*, 16 (1): 81–108.

Vissing, Y. (2016), 'Child Rights in the United States: 25 Years Later and Counting', in T. Liefaard and J. Sloth-Nielsen (eds), *The United Nations Convention on the Rights of the Child: Taking Stock after 25 Years and Looking Ahead*, 73–100, Leiden, the Netherlands: Brill Nijhoff.

Vittrup, B. (2016), 'Ethnic and Racial Identity Development', in D. Couchenour and J. K. Chrisman (eds), *The SAGE Encyclopedia of Contemporary Early Childhood Education*, 549–50, Thousand Oaks, CA: SAGE.

Voneche, J., and M. Bovet (1982), 'Training Research and Cognitive Development: What Do Piagetians Want to Accomplish?' in S. Modgil, C. Modgil and B. Inhelder (eds), *Jean Piaget: Consensus and Controversy*, 83–94, New York: Praeger.

Vygotsky, L. S. (1967), 'Play and Its Role in the Mental Development of the Child', *Soviet Psychology*, 5 (3): 6–18.

Vygotsky, L. S. (1978), *Mind in Society: The Development of Higher Psychological Processes*, Cambridge, MA: Harvard University Press.

Vygotsky, L. S. (1981), 'The Genesis of Higher Mental Functions', in J. V. Wertsch (ed), *The Concept of Activity in Soviet Psychology*, 144–88. Armonk, NY: M. E. Sharpe.

Vygotsky, L. S. (1986), *Thought and Language*, trans. A. Kozulin, Cambridge, MA: MIT Press.

Vygotsky, L. S. (1987), *The Collected Works of L. S. Vygotsky*, ed. R. W. Rieber and A. S. Carton, trans. N. Minick, New York and London: Plenum. Original work published 1934.

Vygotsky, L. S. (1994), 'The Problem of the Environment', in R. van der Veer and J. Vlasiner (eds), *The Vygotsky Reader*, 338–54, Cambridge, MA: Blackwell.

Vygotsky, L. S. (1997a), *The Collected Works of L. S. Vygotsky. Volume 4, The History of the Development of Higher Mental Functions*, ed. R. W. Rieber, trans. M. J. Hall, New York: Plenum.

Vygotsky, L. S. (1997b), 'The Problem of Consciousness', in R. W. Rieber (ed), *The Collected Works of L. S. Vygotsky, Volume 3, The Problems of the Theory and History of Psychology*, 147–61, New York: Plenum.

Vygotsky, L. S. (1998), 'Child Psychology', in R. W. Rieber (ed), *The Collected Works of L. S. Vygotsky, Volume 5, Child Psychology*, New York: Plenum.

Vygotsky, L. S. (2004), 'Imagination and Creativity in Childhood', *Journal of Russian and East European Psychology*, 42 (1): 7–97.

Ulich, M., and T. Mayr (1999), 'Observing Children in German Daycare Centres: Practitioners' Attitudes and Practice', *International Journal of Early Years Education*, 7: 25–37.

Waddington, D. I. (2010), 'Uncovering Hegelian Connections: A New Look at Dewey's Early Educational Ideas', *Education and Culture*, 26 (1): 67–81.

Wajcman, J., M. Bittman and J. E. Brown (2008), 'Families without Borders: Mobile Phones, Connectedness and Work-Home Divisions', *Sociology*, 42 (4): 635–52.

Walker, P. O. (2004), 'Decolonizing Conflict Resolution: Addressing the Ontological Violence of Westernization', *American Indian Quarterly*, 28 (3/4): 527–49.

Walkerdine, V. (1990), *School Fictions*, London: Verso.

Waller, T., and A. Bitou (2011), 'Research with Children: Three Challenges for Participatory Research in Early Childhood', *European Early Childhood Education Research*, 19 (1): 5–20.

Wallerstedt, C., and N. Pramling (2012), 'Learning to Play in a Goal-directed Practice', *Early Years* 32 (1):1–11. doi:10.1080/09575146.2011.593028

Warner, M. (1993), *Fear of a Queer Planet: Queer Politics and Social Theory*, Minneapolis: University of Minnesota Press.

Wartofsky, M. (1979), *Models, Representation and the Scientific Understanding*, Boston: Reidel.

Watson, J. B. (1930), *Behaviorism*, revised edn, New York: Norton.

Watson, J. B., and R. A. R. Watson (1928), *Psychological Care of Infant and Child*, New York: Norton and Co.

Watson, K. (2018), 'We Are All Friends: Disrupting Friendship Play Discourse in Inclusive Early Childhood Education', *Contemporary Issues in Early Childhood*, 1–12. doi:10.1177/1463949118772575

Wells, G. (1987), *The Meaning Makers*, Sevenoaks, UK: Hodder and Stoughton.

Wenger, E. (1998), *Communities of Practice: Learning, Meaning and Identity*, Cambridge, UK: Cambridge University Press.

Wentzel, K. R. (2002), 'Are Effective Teachers like Good Parents? Teaching Styles and Student Adjustment in Early Adolescence', *Child Development*, 73 (1): 287–301.

Wertsch, J. (2007), 'Mediation', in M. Daniels, M. Cole and J. V. Wertsch (eds), *The Cambridge Companion to Vygotsky*, 178–92. Cambridge, UK: Cambridge University Press.

West, M. I. (2006), 'Censorship', in J. Zibes (ed), *The Oxford Encyclopedia of Children's Literature*, Oxford: Oxford University Press.

Whitfield, P. (2009), 'The Heart of the Arts: Fostering Young Children's Ways of Knowing', in M. Narey (ed), *Meaning Making: Constructing Multimodal*

*Perspectives of Language, Literacy and Learning through Arts-based Early Childhood Education*, 153–65, Pittsburgh: Springer.
Wiberg, M., and A. Qvortrup (2017), 'Prerequisites of Learning from Various Means and Aim Perspectives', in A. Qvortrup and M. Wiberg (eds), *Dealing with Conceptualizations of Learning: Learning between Means and Aims in Theory and Practice*, 13–23, Rotterdam: The Netherlands: Springer.
Wien, C. A., V. Guyevskey and N. Berdoussis (2011), 'Learning to Document in Reggio-inspired Education', *Early Childhood Research and Practice*, 13 (2). Available online: http://ecrp.uiuc.edu/v13n2/wien.html (accessed 27 November 2018).
Wien, C. A., B. Jacobs and E. Brown (2015), 'Emergent Curriculum and the Tension between Relationship and Assessment', in O. N. Saracho (ed), *Contemporary Perspectives on Research in Assessment and Evaluation in Early Childhood Education*, 93–114 Charlotte, NC: Information Age.
Wilderspin, S. (1835), in 'Report on the Select Committee on Education in England and Wales,' Parliamentary Papers, Volume 7.
Wilderspin, S. (1852), *The Infant System for Developing the Intellectual and Moral Powers of All Children, from One to Seven Years of Age*, London: Hodson.
Wiliam, D. (2018), *Embedded Formative Assessment*, 2nd edn, Bloomington, IN: Solution Tree.
Willan, J. (2009), 'Revisiting Susan Isaacs: A Modern Educator for the Twenty-first Century', *International Journal of Early Years Education*, 17 (2): 151–65.
Williams-Siegfredsen, J. (2017), *Understanding the Danish Forest School Approach*, 2nd edn, London: Routledge.
Williams, A. (2004), '"Right, Get Your Book Bags!": Siblings Playing School in Multiethnic London', in E. Gregory, S. Long and D. Volk (eds), *Many Pathways to Literacy: Young Children Learning with Siblings, Peers, Grandparents and in Communities*, 52–65, New York: RoutledgeFalmer.
Williams, K. (2014), 'Compulsion and the Educational Conversation', in M. Papastephanou (ed), *Philosophical Perspectives on Compulsory Education*, 49–60, New York: Springer.
Willinsky, J. (1999), 'Curriculum after Culture, Race, Nation', *Studies in the Cultural Politics of Education*, 20 (1): 89–103.
Wonderwood, K., A. Valeo and R. Wood (2012), 'Understanding Inclusive Early Childhood Education: A Capability Approach', *Contemporary Issues in Early Childhood*, 13 (4): 290–99.
Wood, D. (1998), *How Children Think and Learn*, 2nd edn, Oxford: Blackwell.
Wood, D., J. Bruner and G. Ross (1976), 'The Role of Tutoring in Problem Solving', *Journal of Child Psychology and Psychiatry*, 17: 89–100.
Wood, E. (2007), 'New Directions in Play: Consensus or Collision?' *Education*, 35 (4): 309–20.
Woodhead, M. (2005), 'Early Childhood Development: A Question of Rights', *International Journal of Early Childhood*, 37 (3): 79–98.
Woods, A. (2015), 'Child-centred', in S. Wallace (ed), *A Dictionary of Education*, 2nd edn, Oxford: Oxford University Press.
Woods, M. Z., and I.-M. Pretorius (2016), 'Observing, Playing and Supporting Development: Anna Freud's Toddler Groups Past and Present', *Journal of Child Psychotherapy*, 42 (2): 135–51.

World Health Organisation (WHO) (2005), 'Report of a WHO Technical Consultation on Birth Spacing, Geneva, Switzerland, 13–15 June 2005', Geneva: WHO. Available online: http://apps.who.int/iris/bitstream/handle/10665/69855/WHO_RHR_07.1_eng.pdf?sequence=1 (accessed 27 November 2018).

World Health Organisation (WHO) (2011), 'World Report on Disability'. Available online: http://www.who.int/disabilities/world_report/2011/report.pdf (accessed 27 November 2018).

Wulf, A. (2015), *The Invention of Nature: Alexander von Humboldt's New World*, New York: Knopf.

Zavershneva, E., and R. van der Veer, eds. (2018), *Vygotsky's Notebooks: A Selection*, Singapore: Springer.

Zhang, Q. (2017), 'Do Learning Stories Tell the Whole Story of Children's Learning? A Phenomenographic Enquiry', *Early Years*, 37 (3): 255–67.

Zimba, R. F. (2002), 'Indigenous Conceptions of Childhood Development and Social Realities in Southern Africa', in H. Keller, Y. H. Poortinga and A. Schömerich (eds), *Between Culture and Biology: Perspectives on Ontogenetic Development*, 89–115, Cambridge, UK: Cambridge University Press.

# INDEX

Abdallah-Pretceille, M. 147
Abdi, A. 151
abnormal development 14
Aboriginal (Indigenous) identity 56
accommodation process, schema 15
acculturation development model 51–2
action research 170
*Acts of Meaning* (Bruner) 108
Adams, M. 54
adaptive variability, play as 137
adult–child relationships 2, 95–6, 100, 140
agentic child perspective (agency) 18–21
agentic materials 66–7
ages of man perspective 14–17
*Aistear* framework in Ireland 27
Akerman, J. 22
Alberta Education (2008) x
Amanti, C. 48
animal play 137
*anthroparchal* 79
anthroposophy 67
antiracist education 163–4
Aristotle 84
Arndt, S. 195
art/art making, children's 118–22
    multimodalities 119–21
    in Reggio Emilia approach 122
artefacts 52, 172, 178
    cultural 60, 89
    levels of 181
    material 42
artistic development 120
assessment 185–93
    authentic 187
    for learning 192–3
    of learning 189–92
    school readiness 188–9
    support learners 193–5

assimilation process, schema 15
*An Atlas of Infant Behaviour* (photographic frames by Gesell) 177
attachment theory 13, 70
attention, subjects of 75–6
audit-style approach to testing 195
authentic learning 186–8
authoritarian/authoritative parenting style 33
auto-education 193

'Baby PISA' study 190–2
Baker, L. S. 189
Bandura, A. 10, 36, 38, 173–4
Baumrind, D. 33–4
Beatty, B. 17
Beckstead, Z. 50
Becoming ontology of the East 54
behaviourism 8
    behaviour analysis 10
    behavioural regulation 77
    behavioural science 84
    behaviourally based teaching technique 191
*Behaviourism* (Watson) 10
Bekhterev, V. 8
Bennett, N. 141
Berdoussis, N. 172
Bhabha, H. K. 60
biogenetic approach 12
biological organism 64, 68, 74
biology-based theories of development 70–1
birth/child spacing 29
*The Birth of the Clinic: An Archaeology of Medical Perception* (Foucault) 174
Bitou, A. 196
Blair, C. 16

Blaise, M. 157, 159
Boddice, R. 64
Bodrova, E. 96, 133, 135
Bowlby, J. 70
Bradbury, A. 190
Bronfenbrenner, U. 194
    ecological system framework (child development) 28–32, 40
    framework criticisms of 32
    model of development 30
Brooks, M. 120–1
Browne, N. 160
Bruner, J. 105, 107–8, 110, 112–13
Buchignani, N. 146
built environment 64
Burman, E. 71

Cannella, G. S. 51, 125
capability approach in education 160
Carlsson, M. A. 143
Carr, M. 190, 195
*Casa dei Bambini* (preschool) 12
Castellano, M. B. 83
Chaiklin, S. 94, 96
Chen, R. 159
child and species perspective 10–13
child-centred education 17, 27–8, 38, 40, 88, 194
child development 12, 29, 32, 67–70
    biology-based theories of 70–1
    contextual theories of 71–3
    knowledge 2
    psychoanalytic theory of Freud 13
    relationship with human world 74–7
    relationship with nonhuman world 77–9
child education, challenges for UN Convention 35–6
child observation 167, 174, 183, 186
    educational research 179
    recording and reporting 175, 177
child-rearing ideologies 34, 72
child socialization 4, 21–2, 33–4, 68, 72, 151
child–animal relations 79
childhood, images of 1–22
    conventional images (*see* conventional images of childhood)
    as frames for practice 22–3

    worldviews 21–2
children's rights
    citizenship rights 34–5
    parenting practices 32–4
    teacher's role 36–9
chronosystem 29
cinemanalysis 178
Cleverley, J. F. 3
co-construct knowledge 90, 100
cognitive constructivism 85–8
    meaning-making of world 102–3
cognitive development 77, 89, 94, 111–12, 130, 154, 156
Cole, M. 79
collectivism 46
collectivistic (C) culture 46, 52, 61
Comenius, J. A. 147
Committee on the Rights of the Child 26, 124
communities (and children) 104, 115
    citizenship rights of children 34–6
    cultural 41–6, 48, 50
    family and 73, 93–4
    identity development (*see* identity development of children)
    Indigenous 88, 138
    Inuit community 79
    socialization agents 57–8
Comrie, B. 111
concrete operational stage of development 15–16
conditioned child perspective 8–10
conflict of interest 140
connected/interdependent selves 55
Connolly, P. 88
constructivism
    cognitive 85–8, 102–3
    constructivist (theory) teaching practices 74, 128, 130
    dialectical/social 89, 91
    on Reggio Emilia philosophy 97–9
contextual theories of development 71–3
Convention on Human Rights 26
conventional images of childhood 2
    agentic child view 18–21
    ages of man view 14–17
    child and species view 10–13
    conditioned child view 8–10
    environmentalist view 6–8

free and constrained child view 4–6, 13
loss of innocence view 13–14
upbringing fit for society view 17–18
cooperative breeding activity 64
Cöté, J. 56
Cowie, B. 195
creativity (play and learning) 143
critical race theory (CRT) 60–1, 153
cultural and linguistic genocide 115
cultural deprivation 71, 189
cultural development 89
cultural difference 150, 163
cultural diversity in symbols 118
cultural-ecological approach 32
cultural-historical theory 57, 136, 151
cultural identity 52–5, 152
cultural mediation tools 47
cultural psychology 72
cultural recapitulation 12
cultural scripts, children playing 109–10
culturally recognized encounter 50
culture-as-pattern approach 47–8
culture, children and 41–6, 150–1
  aspects of 42
  as authorship 60
  as boundary 49–51, 59, 61
  as close/open socialization 48, 50
  developmental niche theory 45–6
  experiences 53
  I–C perspective 46–7
  identity of 52–5, 152
  paediatric *vs.* pedagogical model 44–5
  as pattern 43–4, 47–8, 59, 61
culture-epoch theory 12–13, 16
culture-free approach 137
curriculum 13, 16, 18, 38, 124, 140–4, 163, 186, 190. *See also* school(s)
  formal formative assessment 193
  integrating play into 141–3
  international framework 27
  Irish framework 28
  kindergarten 23
  playing-learning child 143–4
  *Te Whāriki* 190, 195–6
Curtis, S. 178

Dahlberg, G. 39, 171, 178
Darras, B. 120
Darwin, C. 84–5, 175, 177
Davin, N. F. 148
Davis, B. 82
Davis, R. 105, 107
decentring process 128
Declaration of Human Rights (1948) 26
Dei, G. S. 150
*Democracy and Education* (Dewey) 28
Development as the Aim of Education (Kohlberg and Mayer) 73
development, children. *See* child development
developmental discourse on play 127
developmental niche theory 45–6
developmental stage theories 14–15
developmentalism 67–8, 74, 137, 157
developmentally appropriate practice (DAP) 23, 61, 68, 74, 127, 137, 151, 153
deviation-free society 47
Dewey, J. 12, 17–18, 28, 35, 38, 63, 74, 88, 169, 186–7, 198
dialectical constructivism 89, 91, 100
difference, social 145–6
  children's right to be different 162–4
  as deficiency 147–9, 162
  and diversity 146–7
  markers of (*see* markers of difference)
disability (social difference) 160–2
discourse of play characteristics 125
diversity 146–7
  cultural 59–61, 118, 163–4
  difference and 146–7
  gender 156–60
  linguistic 115
  of play 125, 140
documentation 170, 172, 181–3, 195. *See also* pedagogical documentation
  and democratic participation 171
  dilemma 180
  as display 176
double move in teaching 96

# INDEX

Dubiel, J. 195
dynamic assessment 196–9

early childhood care 58
early childhood education (ECE)
22–3, 38, 58, 67, 74, 79, 85, 88,
124–5, 137, 140, 151, 157, 164,
171
   aim of 73
   assessment in 191
   child observations in 175
   children's agency 18
   DAP in 23
   developmentalism 67–8
   inclusive 162
   intervention programs 149
   nature-based 77–8
   pedagogical documentation 168, 173
   and pedagogy 141
   play and development in 127–8
   play-based learning in 97
   policies 1
   positioning children in 2
   principles of 61
   programs 3, 67
   quality in 149
   Western practices 88
ecological systems framework (child development)
   Bronfenbrenner 28–32, 40, 45, 194
   Souto-Manning 32
ecological theories of development 72
ecology 29
economy of representation 107
ecosystem 29
education 4, 16, 47, 87–8, 95
   antiracist 163–4
   auto-education 193
   capability approach in 160
   challenges for UN Convention in child 35–6
   child-centred 17, 27–8, 38, 40, 194
   for cultural diversity 163
   Dewey concept of 74
   and difference 148
   goals of 47
   guiding principles for x
   intercultural 59–60, 163–4
   kindergarten (*see* kindergarten system of education)
   linguistic genocide in 115–18
   literacy 118–19
   Montessori idea of 67
   multicultural 59, 151, 163–4
   nature 77–8
   negative 4, 6
   objective of (Malaguzzi) 98
   philosophy of (*see* philosophy of education)
   public 116, 149, 192
   rights-based 26–8, 35–6
   self-regulation 77
   Waldorf schools 67
educational assessment 185, 192
educators 12, 16, 39, 58. *See also* teacher(s)
   early childhood 159, 161–3
   in Reggio Emilia schools 4, 162, 170
   role of 103–4
   social difference and 146
   taken-for-granted (play) 138–9
ego psychology 13
egocentric speech 113–14
egocentricity 16, 154
Elkonin, D. 130, 133, 135
*Emile, or On Education* (Rousseau) 173
emotional interdependence model 33
enactive mode of representation 105
environment 63–7, 89, 111–12
   children's interactions with different 86
   factors and development 69
   formal learning 65
   human-centred 64
   human-made 64
   influencing learning and development 73–9
   microsettings 65
   stable cultural 45
environmentalist perspective 6–8
epigenetic theory (Piaget) 14–16, 67
Epstein, J. L. 58
Erikson, E. 52
   identity formation theory 56
Esteban-Guitart, M. 50, 52, 57

ethological theory 70
eugenics ideology 71
Eurocentrism 59, 152
evaluation in social research 186
everyday concept development 47–8, 93–4, 96
evolutionary theory 70–1, 137
exosystem 29
explicit mediator 93

facilitate-play approach 143
faculty psychology 8
Fallace, T. 18
false uniformity/uniqueness (cultural difference) 150
Feagin, J. R. 154
Feuerstein, R. 198
fixation 14
Fleer, M. 54, 97
flexible intellectual interest 169
Flynn, J. R. 16
forest preschool 78
formal learning environment 65
formal operational stage of development 15–16
formative assessment 185–6, 192–6
 example of 196
 principles for children 194–5
 teaching strategies for 193
Foucauldian analysis 4, 65, 190–1
Foucault, M. 138, 174
Fox, J. 121
free and constrained child perspective 4–6, 13
free play 10, 140
Freud, A. 13, 177
Freud, S. 13, 173
Frideres, J. 56
Froebel, F. 11–12, 20, 65, 67–8, 88
Fromberg, D. P. 125
Frost, J. L. 141
funds of identity 57, 61
funds of knowledge 50, 57, 148

gallery teaching 191
games (with rules) 133. *See also* play
Gardner, H. 8
Garrison, J. W. S. 74
Gaskins, S. 136, 144

gender identity/diversity 156–60
genetic epistemology 15
genetic theory 16
genuine behaviourism 8
Gesell, A. 15, 84, 177–8, 182
Gesell school readiness tests 188
Ghosh, R. 151
Gidley, J. 13
Giordano, P. 54
González, N. 48
Graue, E. 188–9
Gredler, M. 77
Greenwood, M. 83
Grunditz, S. 177
Gutek, G. 83–4
Guyevskey, V. 172

Hall, G. S. 12, 71
Hall, S. 54–5
Hallpike, C. R. 16
Handsome Lake 116
Harkness, S. 45
Hart, M. 54
Hawkins, C. 78
Hedegaard, M. 96
Hennig, K. 60
Herbart, J. F. 12
Herodotus 147
heteronormativity 159
higher-order symbolic mediators 91
HighScope approach 16
*Histories* (Herodotus) 147
Hoffman, D. M. 150, 152
Hofstede, G. 46
Holzman, L. 112
human-centred environment 64
human cognitive development 89
human development 68
human-made environment 64
human mediators 91–3
human rights 26, 46, 50, 116, 147, 163
*The Hundred Languages of Children* exhibition 170

iconic mode of representation 105–6
identity development of children 52–4, 61
 personality and ego 56–7
identity formation theory (Erikson) 56

ideologies
    child-rearing 34, 72
    childhood 67–8, 79
    developmentalism as 68
    eugenics 71
    heterosexual 159
Ignelzi, M. 103
imaginary situation in play 131–4
immature play 135
immigrant children 51
*Implementing Child Rights in Early Childhood* 38
implicit mediator 93
inborn faculties 8
*Incheon Declaration–Education* 2030 147
independence model 33
Indigenous identity 55
Indigenous images of childhood 21–2
Indigenous knowledge 65, 83, 100
Indigenous language revitalization programs 118
Indigenous worldview, principles of 82
individualism 46
individualistic (I) culture 46–7, 61
infant curiosity 44–5
infant schools 4, 6, 191
innocence perspective, loss of 13–14
integrated theory of overlapping spheres 58
intelligence testing 192
intelligent reasoning 105
interactionist theory 112
intercultural education 59–60, 163–4
interculturalism 164
interdependence model 33
International Early Learning Study (IELS), OECD's 190, 192, 194
International Kindergarten Union (1915) 12
intersectionality 61, 146, 148–9, 163
intervention programs 71, 149, 161–2, 171
Isaacs, S. 13–14, 175

James, A. 21
Jarvis, P. 102
Jenkins, H. 8
Jerome, L. 35
Jewitt, C. 119
Jones-Diaz, C. 147, 163

Kaestle, C. F. 191
Kağitçibaşi, Ç. 33, 40, 46, 150–1, 194
Kamii-Devries approach 16
Kegan, R. 102–3, 107
Keller, E. F. 68
kindergarten movement 12
kindergarten system of education 65, 67–8, 130, 133, 189. *See also* preschool(s)
    American 67
    curriculum 23
    Germany 11–12, 65
    psychoanalytic laboratory 13
Kindler, A. 120
Kirova, A. 60
knowledge representation 101, 104–7
    as communication 107–8
knowledge, traditional sources of 83
Kobayashi, A. 147
Kocher, L. M. 171
Kohlberg, L. 73, 154, 157
Kohler, N. 64
Kuschner, D. 124

laboratory preschools 13, 169, 178
Ladson-Billing, G. 164
Lambert, W. E. 116
Langer, E. J. 143
language 82, 152, 156
    children's linguistic rights 115–18
    role of 110
    and thought 111–13, 115
language-based mediation 199
Lather, P. 46
leading activity (play) 130, 132–3, 144
learn-and-teach-through-play approach 143
learning 81–6, 104, 112, 186
    assessment for 192–3
    assessment of 185, 189–92
    to document 171–3, 183
    European philosophical thought 83–6
    language 82
    in maturationist theory 188
    mediated 198–9

Piaget theory of 85–7
  to play 135
  spontaneous 136
  technologies for making visible 177–8, 181
  traditional sources of knowledge 83
  sociocultural theory of (Vygotsky) 89, 91
learning stories approach 170, 195–6
Lee, I.-F. 190
Lenz Taguchi, H. 50, 181
Leonard, M. 21
Leong, D. J. 96, 133, 135
Levenson, E. A. 173
LeVine, R. A. 44–5, 47, 54
Levinson, S. 111
Lewit, E. M. 189
Lillard, A. S. 136
Lindgren, A.-L. 177, 182
linguicism 148
linguistic colonialism/lingoracism 116
linguistic genocide in education 115–18
Lipponen, L. 178
literacy education 118–19
lived experience 48, 52, 54
Locke, J. 8
loss of innocence perspective 13–14
Luria, A. 12

MacBlain, S. 88
macrosystem 29
majority-world 23, 44, 85
  children's play and games in 136
  cultures 121, 138, 144
  education system 47
  and Indigenous images 21–2
Malaguzzi, L. 22–3, 38–9, 85, 97–8, 162, 168, 190
Malting House School, sexual expression at 14
Marjanovic-Shane, A. 50, 59, 182
markers of difference 150
  (dis)ability 160–2
  culture/cultural differences 150–2
  gender identity/diversity 156–60
  race and ethnicity (*see* racial identity/ethnicity)
Matthews, J. 120–1

maturationist theory 14–15, 188
mature play 135
Matusov, E. 50, 59, 182
Maurial, M. 83
Mayer, R. 73
Mayr, T. 175
Meacham, S. 182
meaning-making theory 101, 122
  of world, children 102–4
mediation, theory of 91–2
  human mediators 91, 93
  language-based 199
  learning 198–9
  symbolic mediators 91
Meehan, C. L. 64
memorization learning strategy 191–2
Mérian, J.-B. 174
mesosystem 29
microsettings, environment 65
microsystem 29, 31
Miller, M. G. 182
miniature students 190
minority-worldview 21, 33, 44, 60, 85, 135–8
modal affordances 119
modern theories of play 127
modes 119
Moffatt, S. 64
Moll, L. 48, 52, 57
Montessori, M. 8, 12–13, 75, 88, 174, 193
morality, teaching of 44
Mtonga, M. 136, 141
multicultural education 59, 151, 163–4
multiliteracies 119, 122
multimodality 119–21
multiply minoritized backgrounds, children from 149

narratives of self 54–6
National Association for the Education of Young Children (NAEYC) 23
natural cognition 67
nature education 77–8
Neff, D. 48
negative education 4, 6
Nelson, K. 110
new literacies 119, 122
Newman, F. 112

nonhuman agency 20
normative collectivism 46
normative model of behaviour 14
Novakowski, J. 98
Nsamenang, A. B. 136
Nsamenang, B. 21
Nxumalo, F. 78

object-centred play 133
observation-based assessment 186
observational learning 10, 174–5
official language 115
oneness cultural identity 55
Ontario First Nations community 22
ontology of Being 54
open-mindedness 168–9
open-style classrooms 6
Oppedal, B. 51
*Orbis Sensualium Pictus* (Comenius) 147
Organisation for Economic Cooperation and Development (OECD) 190
'origin of species' 84–5
Osgood, J. 85
Oswell, D. 18–19
Owen, R. 4, 6

Pacini-Ketchabaw, V. 79
paediatric *vs.* pedagogical model (child care) 44–5
Papert, S. 16
paranormal cognition 67
parental behaviour 44
parental ethnotheories 45
parenting styles 32–4
Parker, F. W. 4
participatory pedagogy in Finland 77
Pavlov, I. 8
pedagogical documentation 167, 185, 195–6. *See also* documentation
 challenge dominant discourse 173–82
 in classrooms 171–3
 criticism of 181–2
 learning process 168–71
pedagogical narration 170
Penn, H. 36
Penuel, W. R. 56, 194, 198
*perezhivanie* 47–8, 54, 89

permissive parenting style 33
 permissive indifferent parenting style 33
 permissive indulgent parenting style 33
Perret, P. 121
Pestalozzi, J. H. 12, 174
Phillips, D. C. 3
philosophy of education
 European 83–6
 Froebel 12
 intercultural 59–60
 negative education 6
 Reggio Emilia 97–9
 teacher's 2
photographic technology 177–8, 181–2
phrenology 8
Piaget-Dewey concept 73
Piaget, J. 14–15, 58, 65, 71, 85–7, 97–8, 102–3, 107, 111, 113, 125, 128, 130, 137, 154, 160, 196
 cognitive theory 112
 readiness concept 87
 constructivist theory on practice 128, 130
 stage theory of development 58
 theories criticism 87–8, 130
 theory of learning 85–7
picture lessons 174
Pinker, S. 111
Plains Cree children, study of 22
Plato 84, 104
play 123–7
 as adaptive variability 137
 challenge of defining 124–7
 characteristics of 125
 controlling children through 139
 and development in ECE 127–8
 developmental theories of 138
 free 10
 gendered activity 159
 imaginary situation in 131–4
 immature 135
 key dimension of education 124
 mature 135
 modern theories of 127
 Native American conceptions of 22
 object-centred 133
 period 17
 play-gifts 12, 20

postdevelopmental perspectives on 137–8
in psychological development 17
reflection of child's current level of development 128
related to learning (*see* curriculum)
relationship-centred 133
risky 78
romantic/nostalgic discourse of 125
as source of development 130–3
structural elements of (Elkonin) 133
symbolic 137
and work 17
play-based learning 29–30, 97
playful pedagogy 140–2
playing-learning child 143–4
playing school 3
Popkewitz, T. S. 36
positioning children as learners 2
post-Vygotskian theory
on classroom practice 135–6
of play 133, 136
postdevelopmental theories
on classroom practice 138, 140
on play 137–8
posthuman theory 20
power of representation 107
Pramling Samuelsson, I. 143
preoperational stage of development 15–16
preschool(s) 191. *See also* kindergarten system of education
-aged children 77
forest 78
laboratory 13, 169, 178
nature 78
play in 131–2
programs 70, 188–9
teachers 181
pretend play 97, 133, 136–7, 141, 143–4
primary artefacts 181
principle of variation 137
private speech 114
provocations 98–9
psychoanalytic laboratory kindergarten (Soviet Russia) 13
psychoanalytic theory (Freud) 13–14
psychodynamic theory 13
psychological theory, developmental stage 14

psychosexual stages of development 13
public education 116, 149, 192
push-down effect 190

queer theory 159

Rabadi-Raol, A. 61, 149, 152–3, 164
race theory 71
racial identity/ethnicity
children's development of 154–6
markers of difference 152–4
radical behaviourism 8
Ransom, J. 95
Ray, B. 147
readiness, Piaget concept of 87
realism-centred stage theories 120
recapitulation theory 10, 12, 71
recitation 192
reconceptualist ECE movement (1980s) 23
refugee children 51
Reggio Emilia approach 27, 38–40, 74, 168–9, 172, 183, 190
and children's artistic representations 122
constructivist theories on 97–9
Reggio Emilia schools 4, 22–3, 38, 85, 162, 170, 195
reification process 178
relationship-centred play 133
residential school system 148
respect-obedience model 45
rights-based education 26–8, 35–6, 171
rights-based legislation 26
Ring, E. 189
risky play 78
Roberts-Holmes, G. 190
Robinson, K. H. 147, 163
Robson, S. 110
Rogers, S. 140
Rogoff, B. 73, 91, 93, 132
romantic/nostalgic discourse of play 125
Rousseau, J. J. 4, 6, 27, 65, 173
advice to tutor 6
Émile (fictional student) 6, 11
negative education 4
on reading 6
Rowan, M. C. 229

Sam, D. 51
Santoro, D. A. 169
Sapir, E. 111
Saracho, O. N. 108
Savbörg, D. 67
scaffolding method 91, 93–4, 96, 198
Schecter, B. 74
Schmidt, V. 13
school(s) 93–4, 151, 174. *See also* curriculum
   boarding 71–3
   culture as pattern in 47–8
   environment 60, 65, 79
   experiences 53
   infant 4, 6, 191
   kindergarten (*see* kindergarten system of education)
   playing 3
   preschool (*see* preschool(s))
   readiness 149, 188–9, 199
   residential 116, 148
   urban-based 78
   Waldorf 13, 67
scientific concept development 48, 94
secondary artefacts 181
self-awareness 75–6
self-efficacy 36, 38
self-regulation 76–7
Sellers, M. 21
Sen, A. 160
sensorimotor stage of development 15
Serpell, B. 136
shared activity 96
Shepard, L. A. 194, 198
Shields, C. M. 148
Shrobe, H. 105
Simpson, L. 82
Singer, E. 88
Skinner, B. F. 8
Skutnabb-Kangas, T. 115
Snider, D. 20
Sobe, N. W. 75
social constructivism 89, 91, 100, 146
   meaning-making of world 103–4
*Social Development* (Isaacs) 14
social difference. *See* difference, social
social ecologies 28–9
social identity 146, 153
social interactionist theory 112

social learning theory 10, 157, 173–4
social research, evaluation in 186
socialization
   and acculturation of newcomer children 51–2
   child 4, 21–2, 33–4, 68, 72, 151
   culture 42–4, 48, 50
   and education 47
sociocultural based assessment 196
sociocultural-historical theory 154
sociocultural theory 73, 135
Soncini, I. 162
Souto-Manning, M. 32, 61, 149, 152–3, 164
Sparrman, A. 182
spiritual recapitulation 12
spontaneous learning 136
Srinivasan, P. 148
stable cultural environment 45
Stacey, S. 173
standardized testing 190, 194
Steiner-Khamsi, G. 192
Steiner, R. 13
Stewart, K. 79
Stone, J. E. 98, 168
summative assessment 173, 186, 189, 192–4
Super, C. M. 45
supernatural cognition 67
Sutton-Smith, B. 130, 137
symbolic mediators 91, 93
symbolic mode of representation 105–7
symbolic play 137
Szolovits, P. 105

'taken-for-granted' play 45, 60, 88, 138, 140
Taylor, A. 23, 78–9, 159
*Te Whāriki* curriculum 190, 195–6
teachable moments 193
teacher(s) x, 2–3, 12–13, 16–17, 35, 57–9, 167–71, 178, 188, 195, 199. *See also* educators
   assessments of learning 192, 194
   to co-construct knowledge with children 95–7
   feedback from 193
   learn to document 171–3

in Reggio Emilia schools 195
responsibilities 167
role in children rights 36–9
role of (Piaget) 88
surveillance of students 6
teacher-guided environment 17–18
tertiary/imaginary artefacts 181
Tesar, M. 195
testing movement 190
theory of empirical evolutionism 15
theory of mind (ToM) 108, 110, 122
theory of multiple intelligences 8
theory of play 127
    adaptive variability 137
    critique of Piaget 130
    developmental 138
    post-Vygotskian 133
theosophy 67
*Thinking and Speech* (Vygotsky) 113
'third space,' culture 60
Thompson, C. 177
travelling policy tool 192
Trends in International Mathematics and Science Study (TIMSS) 191
trust-in-play approach 142

Ulich, M. 175
un-built environment 64
UN Committee on the Rights of the Child 124
UN International Convention on the Prevention and Punishment of the Crime of Genocide 115
UNESCO Ad Hoc Expert Group on Endangered Languages 115
unfoldment theory 10, 12
The United Nations Convention on the Rights of the Child (UNCRC) 26–7, 29, 34–6, 39, 116, 124, 144, 146–7, 182
upbringing fit for society view 17
urban-based schools 78

Valk, U. 67
Van Ausdale, D. 154
Vandervert, L. 137
Vaughn, M. S. 8
vertical collectivism 46
Vico, G. 84–5

Vittrup, B. 152–3, 156
volition 77
voluntary attention 75
von Humboldt, A. 64
Vygotskian theory 137, 168
    on classroom practice 135–6
    of play 136
Vygotsky, L. 15, 47, 56, 73, 77, 97, 107, 113, 118, 120, 125, 130–1, 140, 151, 156, 178, 188, 196, 198
    children's drawings 120–1
    on creativity (imagination) 144
    everyday concept 93–4
    on play 132–3
    scientific concept development 94
    sociocultural theory of learning 89, 91
    theories criticism 94–5
    theory of mediation (*see* mediation, theory of)
    theory of speech and thinking 113

*waldkindergarten* (forest preschools), German 78
Waldorf schools 13, 67
Walkerdine, V. 88
Waller, T. 196
Wartofsky, M. 181
Watson, J. B. 8, 10
Watson, K. 140
Wenger, E. 178
Wertsch, J. 56
Whitfield, P. 121
Whorf, B. L. 111
Wien, C. A. 172, 195
Wilderspin, W. 174
Wiliam, D. 193
Williams, A. 3
*The Wonder of Learning* exhibition 170
Wonderwood, K. 160
Wood, D. 73, 93
worldviews
    Indigenous 55, 65, 82
    majority-world (*see* majority-world)
    minority-world 21, 33, 44, 60, 85, 135–8
    and narratives of self 54–6

Yelland, N. J. 190

Zhang, Q. 196
Zimba, R. F. 21

zone of mediation 102
zone of proximal development (ZPD) 94–6, 98, 113, 137, 143, 198